ON YOUR WALLS, O JERUSALEM

Meir Lamberski

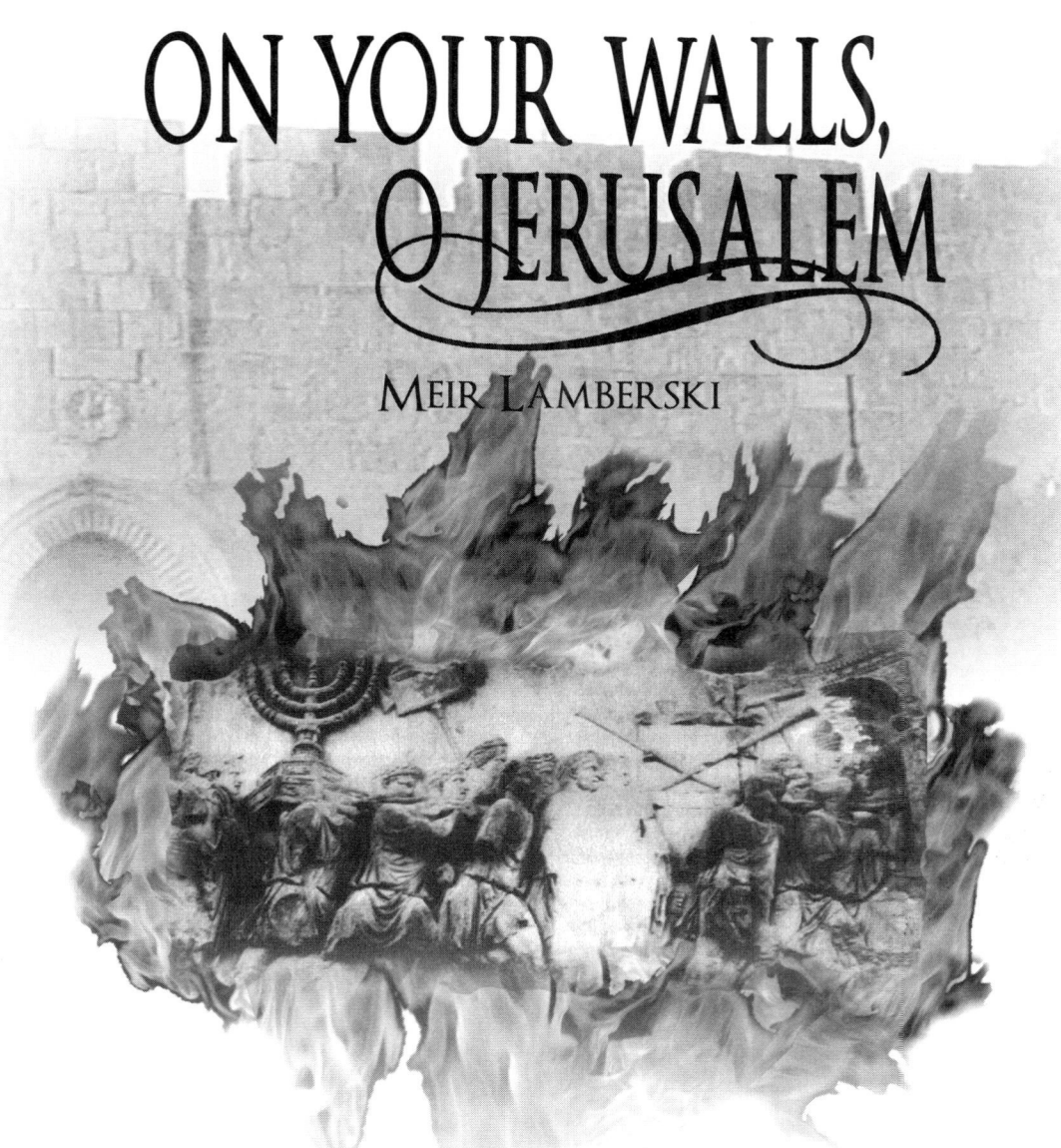

The Complete Story of the Churban

Translated from the Hebrew Al Chomosayich
by Rabbi Meir Lamberski

ISBN: 978-1-60091-024-1

Copyright 2007 : Meir Lamberski

All rights reserved. No part of this book may be reproduced or transmitted in any form or by any means (electronic, photocopying, recording or otherwise) without prior written permission of the copyright holder.

Please send questions or comments to the author at 02-5003353

....
Published and distributed by:
Shanky's Judaica, Jerusalem
0525-341-852   02-538-6936
Fax: 02-538-6921
sales@shankysjudaica.com

Printed in Israel

מכתב ברכה ממו"ר המשגיח הגה"צ ר' דב יפה שליט"א*

אשר זכיתי להסתופף בצל קורתו, ואשר העמידני על דרך הישר וקירבני מעודי

(המכתב ניתן לספר הראשון מסדרת 'על הניסים' - ונדפס כאן שנית ברשות)

בס"ד, י"ח שבט תשס"ו

לידידי היקר, רב הכשרון, הרב מאיר למברסקי שליט"א

אחרי שכבר זכית להיות שותף בעריכת כמה ספרים חשובים, הינך מתכונן להוציא לאור חיבור חשוב על מגילת אסתר, אשר יחדש הרבה דברים לרוב בני אדם, מחז"ל ומהמפרשים.

ויהי רצון שיביא החיבור רוב ברכה, ויהי רצון שתזכה לחבר עוד חיבורים חשובים, ומעלים בקודש.

ברכת אוהבך מכבדך

דב יפה

*סדר הדפסת ההסכמות - לפי סדר נתינתן

מכתב ברכה ממו"ר ראש ישיבת חברון כנסת-ישראל הגאון ר' דוד כהן שליט"א

(המכתב ניתן לספר הראשון מסדרת 'על הניסים' - ונדפס כאן שנית ברשות)

בס"ד

י"ח שבט תשס"ו

מכתב ידידות

הנני הראני ידידי וחביבי הרב מאיר למברסקי שליט"א חיבור שלם על מגילת אסתר, שכולו מיוסד על דברי חז"ל ופירושי גדולי המפרשים על המגילה, ומאיר באור יקרות את כל מהלך התגלות והשתלשלות נס הפורים. והספר שוה לכל נפש, נכתב בשפה ברורה ובהירה, דברים ערבים ושמחים המיוסדים על מקורות נאמנים, וכבר זכה והסכים על ידו מורנו ורבינו מרן המשגיח שליט"א, שהרהמ"ח קיבל הרבה מתורתו ומדרכי הנהגותיו, והנני להצטרף אליו כיהודה ועוד לקרא, לברך את הרהמ"ח שליט"א שימשיך בדרך עליה לזכות את הרבים בתורתו ובכשרונותיו המבורכים, ובשאיפותיו הגדולים. יזכה לעלות ולהתעלות, ויהנו ממנו ומתורתו.

בברכת כהנים באהבה

דוד כהן

Table of Contents

Introduction 1
Historical Background to the Destruction 5
The Glory of Yerushalayim 11
The Beginning of the End 34
Under Siege 45
The Period of the Three Weeks 58
On the Shores of Bavel 78
Rachel Cries over her Children 94
Gedalia ben Achikam 106
What We Lost When We Lost Yerushalayim 113
The End of the Second Temple 119
Political Turmoil 126
On the Verge of War 136
Under Siege Again 152
The City is Conquered 169
The Spiritual Strength of the Children 196
The Fall of Beitar 204
The Ten Martyrs 218
The Light in the Darkness 248

Introduction

Every year during the period of national mourning over the Holy Temple, we find ourselves wondering how we will be able to fulfill our obligation to grieve over the destruction of a city that we've never even seen! We have to cry over the loss of the *Bais Hamikdash*, whose glory we've never experienced! Unfamiliar with the great blessing that they brought upon us, we wonder how we are supposed to bring our hearts to feel the loss.

We can use the tools that *Chazal* gave us and focus on the descriptions of Yerushalayim in its glory, on the grandeur of the Temple when it was still standing, on the closeness of God to His people when the Jews were settled in their land. By doing so, we can acquire for ourselves and pass on to our children the feelings of loss and longing, the pain and mourning emanating from a broken heart over what we've lost.

Each one of us is so preoccupied with the difficulties of our daily lives and our individual set of problems that it's sometimes hard to clear our minds to focus on the *Bais Hamikdash* and Yerushalayim.

If we manage, though, to take a small break in our daily marathon for real introspection, we can focus on how, actually, all these problems we are dealing with stem from the fact that we no longer have a *Bais Hamikdash* or enjoy Hashem's closeness, that channel that directly connected us to our Father in heaven.

Even those tribulations that are so much a part of our daily existence that we don't even pay attention to them come from our lowly spiritual level, from God hiding His face and the loss of His closeness.

2 | On Your Walls, O Jerusalem

When the Temple was destroyed, the gates of prayer were locked. When they were open the world was a different place. Every Jew knew that he could pour out his heart to Hashem and know that his prayers went straight to Hashem's throne, not needing to contend with locked gates or twisted paths.

So many troubles and tragedies, so much pain and suffering, could have been avoided had we had access to the tremendous power of prayer when the gates of heaven are open.

Since the *Mikdash* was destroyed, we no longer have the gift of prophecy. A person used to be able to tell his troubles, express his doubts and difficulties to the prophet, who could provide him with a direct communication from the Master of the World.

So many mistakes, so many arguments could have been avoided had we had someone who could direct our paths and show us what to do.

When the Temple was destroyed, the glory of the Torah disappeared with it. The sweetness of learning and depth and clarity of understanding are gone and no more. We are left with just the smallest bit of that spiritual abundance that our fathers had when they lived in their own land and the glory of Hashem rested with them constantly.

So many broken hearts, so many lost souls would have found their path lit up were this magnificent light still shining for the Jewish people.

Every person sins. But when the *Mikdash* was in existence and the *lashon shel zoharis,* the red string hanging in the Temple, would turn white, each person experienced the incredible happiness of knowing that his sins were atoned for. The divine pleasure of knowing that one is at peace with his Maker and with himself is no more.

Chazal have told us that no one slept in Yerushalayim with a sin on his hands. The daily offering of the morning would atone for sins committed at night; the afternoon daily sacrifice would atone for sins committed during the day. So much despair, so many broken hearts, so much suffering was avoided when they lived lives free of sin. Our rabbis have taught, "There is no death without sin, no suffering without wrongdoing."[1] Our sins are what cause our suffering, and we no longer have access to that which erased them.

But we have not merited those things… we have not merited the gates of prayer remaining open to all, nor forgiveness for our sins, nor experiencing the Torah in all its glory. We have to contend with the stresses and troubles of daily life. We can't feel Hashem's closeness, but rather are stuck in the mire of our suffering with our hearts blocked.

The rivers of tears that the Jewish people cry over their afflictions when they plead with God to save them from the problems of their daily lives would be better spent entreating God to bring His presence back to His home so that we can finally be truly at peace!

If we focus on what we are missing due to our sins, if we look at what happened to our ancestors when they didn't walk in Hashem's ways and didn't appreciate the bliss they experienced when God was in their midst, we will reach a turning point. We can begin to tread on the path where all of our desire is to do God's will, leading to the final redemption. We will come to a time when Hashem's presence will rest on us. We will be close to Him, and our city and Temple will be rebuilt. Amen V'Amen.

---

1. Shabbos 55.

1

Historical Background to the Destruction of the First Temple

In order to fully understand the events that led up to the destruction of the First *Bais Hamikdash*, we have to delve into, at least superficially, the situation the Jews were in during the period that preceded the *churban*. We have to describe the kingdom of Israel and the exile of the Ten Tribes,[1] and the *galus* of Yechanya eighteen years before the destruction of the Temple.[2] We must also mention the role of the prophets that Hashem sent every day and every night for ninety years before the destruction took place,

---

1. Melachim II through chapter 17
2. Melachim II 24

warning the Jewish people to repent from their evil ways before Hashem was forced to bring retribution.[3]

Many years before the destruction of the First Temple, the Ten Tribes were exiled in three stages:

The first stage was in the days of Pekach the son of Remliyahu. Taglis Plaser, the king of Ashur (Assyria), exiled a number of towns, namely, Iyun, Avel Bais Maacha, Yanuch, Kadesh and Chatzor, along with the Gilad, the Glila, and the whole land of Naftali.[4]

The second stage of exile occurred when *Bnai Yisrael* refused to heed what had happened to part of their people who were exiled and didn't do *teshuva* so they shouldn't suffer the same fate. Hashem put it in the king of Ashur's heart to come back and exile another part of the Land of Israel. This time, the tribes of Reuvain, Gad and half of the tribe of Menashe were brought to Chalach, Chabor, Hara and Nahar Gozen.[5]

The third stage of the exile of the Ten Tribes took place in the days of Hoshea ben Aleh. *Bnai Yisrael* continued to sin, as the Navi describes, and the rest of the Ten Tribes were sent into exile.

Only Binyamin and Yehuda were left in the Land of Israel under King Chizkiyahu, a righteous king who brought the Jewish people close to Hashem.

The king of Ashur, through his general Sancheriv, also tried to conquer the kingdom of Yehuda. Yet, since the people under King Chizkiyahu were righteous, Hashem decreed that they be saved miraculously from the attack. The mighty Sancheriv's army was wiped out in one night by an angel, leaving behind only a few survivors.

---

3. Yalkut Melachim 247:234
4. Melachim II 15:29
5. Divrei Hayamim I 5:26

Historical Background to the Destruction | 7

The people under Chizkiyahu flourished spiritually until Menashe, Chizkiyahu's son, took the throne upon his father's death. Menashe turned away and forgot Hashem.[6] Menashe actually did *teshuva* at the end of his lifetime, but before that managed to do much evil in Hashem's eyes. Menashe's son Amon became king after him, also not following in Hashem's ways. His servants deposed him from the throne and Yoshiyahu, his son, took his place as king.[7]

Yoshiyahu was a virtuous king, but he didn't understand that the people were still loyal to the idols they had served in the generations before he took the throne. This mistake led him to make the faulty decision to go to war against Pharaoh Necho, the king of Egypt, disregarding the words of the *navi*, by not letting him pass through his land. Yoshiyahu died during this war.

After Yoshiyahu came his son, King Yehoyakim. Yehoyakim was not like his father and returned to the wicked ways of the kings that had preceded him.

During the third year of his reign, Nevuchadnezar came to power. Until Nevuchadnezar's rise to power, Bavel was a small kingdom under Ashur's rule. However, in the first year of his sovereignty, the young ruler conquered Ninvei, Ashur's largest city,[8] and destroyed the kingdom of Ashur completely.

Nevuchadnezar merited ruling over Bavel, a mighty kingdom that eventually ruled over the whole world, due to the following story:[9]

In his youth, Nevuchadnezar served as the chief scribe of the king Merodach Beladan. Part of his responsibility was to oversee the

---

6. Sanhedrin 102:
7. Divrei Hayamim II 33:24-25
8. Erchin 12:
9. Sanhedrin 96.

8 | On Your Walls, O Jerusalem

handling of the letters that the king wrote. One day, Merodach Beladan heard that King Chizkiyahu was ill. Merodach Beladan decided to send the Jewish king a letter wishing him well. The job of writing the correspondence fell on his scribes.

Nevuchadnezar wasn't on duty at the time and another scribe wrote the following letter: "Peace unto you, King Chizkiya! Peace unto the city of Yerushalayim! Peace unto the great God!"

When Nevuchadnezar heard about the letter that had been written in his absence, he asked to see what was written. He became upset at the contents, saying, "You called God 'the Great God,' yet you put His name last? You should have written the following: 'Peace unto the Great God! Peace unto the city of Yerushalayim! Peace unto you, King Chizkiya!'" He even ran four steps after the messengers in order to stop them on their way to leave to deliver the letter so that the letter could be revised to read more respectfully.

In the merit of those four steps, Nevuchadnezar merited greatness. Even more, if the angel Gavriel wouldn't have stopped Nevuchadnezar from running further, the *rasha* Nevuchadnezar would have been given permission to destroy the Jews completely![10]

Consequently, in the second year of Nevuchadnezar's reign, which was Yehoyakim's fifth year, Nevuchadnezar started a war against the

---

10. See Shir Hashirim Rabba (3:3). There the story is told with some small changes. According to the *Midrash*, Nevuchadnezar was Merodach's son (and it is possible he was also his scribe) and Merodach was the one who rose from his throne and walked **three** steps to stop the messengers. It was Merodach who put "Peace unto the Great God" last and realized he made a mistake and tried to fix it. According to the *Midrash*, Merodach's merit is what helped Nevuchadnezar rise to power and rule over the whole world, along with his sons Evil Merodach and Belshazar.

Historical Background to the Destruction | 9

kingdom of Yehuda. If Yehoyakim would have returned to serving the true God, as the prophets urged him to, Yehuda could have been saved. But Yehoyakim stubbornly stuck to his ways.

Yirmiyahu advised Yehoyakim to act subservient to the king of Bavel. Against the word of Hashem, Yehoyakim decided to rebel in his ninth year as king. Nevuchadnezar came to Yehuda to quell the rebellion in the third year of the uprising, which was the eleventh year of Yehoyakim's rule. Nevuchadnezar took Yehoyakim in copper chains[11] to jail in Bavel, where the pampered king met his death. He didn't even merit a respectable burial, but was buried like a donkey, as is described in *Chazal*.[12]

After Yehoyakim's death, Nevuchadnezar appointed Yehoyachin, Yehoyakim's son, also called Yechanya, to rule. His reign didn't last very long, just three months and ten days, when Nevuchadnezar exiled him to Bavel, regretting that he had appointed him in the first place.

Yechanya wasn't exiled alone. Nevuchadnezar took with him all the officers and strong men of Yehuda. He took 3,023 men from Yehuda and 7,000 from Binyamin. Besides that, he took the "*choresh v'masger*," the *talmidei chachamim* and great Torah scholars. They numbered an additional 1,000. Only the simple people[13] were left in Yehuda.

To rule over those left in Yehuda, Nevuchadnezar appointed Yoshiyahu's son Masania, who changed his name to Tzidkiyahu. Nevuchadnezar forced Tzidkiyahu to swear on a *sefer Torah*[14] that he

---

11. Divrei Hayamim II 36:6
12. Yalkut Melachim II 247:249
13. Melachim II 24:16
14. Yalkut Yirmiyahu 247:326

wouldn't rebel against him. Tzidkiyahu was also appointed to rule over Edom, Moav, Amon, Tzur and Tzidon.[15]

Tzidkiyahu was a truly righteous man. He had only one fault and that was that he rebelled against Nevuchadnezar even before Nevuchadnezar managed to return to his country. In addition, Tzidkiyahu was held responsible for the sins of his generation. Because he didn't reprimand the sinners, it was as if he had committed those same sins. The people of his generation were very immoral, committing even the three cardinal sins – idol worship, immorality and murder.

The generation was also plagued by false prophets, who led the nation astray with deceitful promises that everything would be okay. Yirmiyahu prophesized that the people must repent or their end would be bitter, and that they must subjugate themselves to Bavel. But false prophets, like Chananya ben Azor, declared in God's name that the yoke of Bavel had been broken.[16]

The people flocked to the false prophets, stubbornly refusing to bow to God's will. Hashem waited and waited, hoping that His children would return to Him and not have to endure the terrible punishments that their sins mandated. The disastrous consequences of their behavior will be discussed in the following chapters.

---

15. Yirmiyahu 27:3
16. Yirmiyahu 28

2

The Glory of Yerushalayim

When we come to the period of *Bain Hametzarim*, the time period between the seventeenth of Tammuz and Tisha B'Av, our thoughts automatically turn to Yerushalayim. Indeed, we pray every day for the city of Yerushalayim to be rebuilt.

The basic question that begs to be asked is: what are we mourning for? We know that Yerushalayim is central to the identity of the Jewish people and that it is the holiest city in the world. We know that it symbolizes the eternity of the eternal people. Still, much more than that, we don't really know.

We all pray for the rebuilding of the *Bais Hamikdash*, which we are all truly pining to see, but it is still hard for us to understand just how central the *Bais Hamikdash* was to the life of *Klal Yisrael* and how wonderful and uplifted the lives of the Jews were during the period it stood.

That is what we are going to describe according to *Chazal* in this chapter – what Yerushalayim was like and the glory of the *Bais Hamikdash*. Through these descriptions, we'll be better able to understand what we had… and, therefore, what we are missing.

Because every Jew was obligated to go up to Yerushalayim three times a year and the *maasros* and different *kadshim* could only be eaten in Yerushalayim, many people chose to make their homes within its borders from the start.

Indeed, besides the *Bais Hamikdash*, the sages tell us that there were 480 *shuls* in Yerushalayim before the *churban*. Each *shul* was a community in its own right, complete with its own educational institutions. That is to say, that in Yerushalayim alone there were 480 *shuls* with 480 schools for studying the *Mikrah*, 480 schools for studying the *Mishna* and 480 houses of learning for studying the Talmud![1] All of those were destroyed when Yerushalayim was destroyed.

Yerushalayim, that is to say, was an empire! It contained 480 *kehillos*, each of which was large enough to support a separate school for *Mikrah, Mishna* and *Gemara*.

Chazal also further detail the number of people that lived in Yerushalayim.[2] Even if we are to say that the numbers are exaggerated to paint a picture of what life was like in Yerushalayim,[3] we are still left with a fantastically large populace.

---

1. Eitz Yosef quoting the Yalkut Yeshaya
2. Eichah Rabba 1:2
3. This is how the Yifei Ainaim says the numbers should be understood. He explains that the number twenty four that the calculations are based on is hinting to the twenty four books of the Tanach that the Jews of Yerushalayim were always busy learning. There are, though, many *mefarshim* who explain that the numbers are meant literally. These *mefarshim* agree that the number twenty four relates to the books of

In *Chazal*'s description, in Yerushalayim there were twenty four main squares. Each square had twenty four main thoroughfares leading to it. Every main thoroughfare had twenty four smaller streets. From every one of these smaller streets, you could reach twenty four smaller pathways. Every one of these smaller pathways had twenty four courtyards. Every courtyard had twenty four homes.[4] Passing through each of these courtyards every day were double the amount of people that left Egypt![5]

Those are the words of the Midrash. Let's do some calculations:

Every one of the twenty four squares had twenty four main thoroughfares. That means that Yerushalayim had 576 main roads. Every one of these roads had twenty four side roads. That means that there were 18,824 side roads!

Every one of these roads had twenty four smaller passageways, or up to 331,776 smaller passageways. The twenty four courtyards that came out of each of these leaves us with 7,962,624 courtyards! If each of these had twenty four homes, there were 191,102,976 homes in Yerushalayim!![6] An empire!

Tanach (as the Eitz Yosef describes), but that this is the number of people that lived in Yerushalayim.

4. Eitz Yosef
5. Radal
6. Even though this would seem to be impossible, as all of *Eretz Yisrael* couldn't contain this many people, *Chazal* say (Gittin 57.) that *Eretz Yisrael* is compared to a deer. Once the skin of the deer is removed it can't cover the deer's whole body, so to *Eretz Yisrael* seems too small to contain all the inhabitants it does, but like the deer's skin, it stretches to contain them. When *Bnai Yisrael* are not in their land, the land shrinks and can't contain that much.

14 | On Your Walls, O Jerusalem

Besides being home to almost 200,000,000 people, Yerushalayim had an incredible flow of visitors coming and going every day. Double the amount of people that went out of Egypt went in and out of each of these courtyards every day. If 600,000 people went out of Egypt, then 1,200,000 went in and out of each courtyard each day. That means 9,555,148,800,000 people were traveling back and forth.

Now, even if we say that these numbers aren't literal and are just meant to paint a picture, *Chazal* here are telling us that we can't fathom the sheer magnitude of the size of Yerushalayim before it was destroyed. We can't imagine what was lost.

The following story, brought in the Midrash,[7] also describes how large Yerushalayim was:

A man traveled to Yerushalayim with 200 camels laden with the type of peppers that were used only for spicing food. The average camel can carry a load of thirty *seah*, about 200 liters. That is to say, his camels were carrying about 40,000 liters of peppers for spicing food. That's an incredible amount!

On his way to Yerushalayim, the spice merchant passed the gates of the city Tzur, where he met a tailor.[8] The tailor saw the camels and their load and asked the spice merchant to sell him a certain amount of the peppers. The merchant refused, saying that he wanted to sell the whole amount to one person. The tailor told him to look elsewhere for a buyer because there was no one in Tzur to buy such a large amount at once.

The merchant left with his load. When he reached the gates of Yerushalayim, he met another tailor, who also inquired about the

---

7. Eichah Rabba 1:2

8. The Radal comments on the significance of the fact that he met a tailor, saying that there are very deep principles being hinted at.

merchandise. Having lost his faith in tailors, the spice merchant mockingly told him, "Honored tailor, continue cutting your material and do your work and don't get involved in what has nothing to do with you!"

The merchant continued on his way, where he met another tailor. The spice seller answered in the same mocking way when the tailor inquired about his wares. This tailor, though, stubbornly insisted that the merchant tell him what he was selling, promising that if he wouldn't buy his wares, he would find someone who would. The spice merchant told him that he had 200 camels worth of peppers for spice.

The tailor took him to a storehouse full of golden coins and asked the merchant if these coins were usable in his country. When he was answered that they were, he told the spice seller to take what was due to him for all the merchandise.

Having completed the business deal to his satisfaction, the spice seller decided to stay in Yerushalayim for a spell. The next morning he met an old friend who asked him what brought him to Yerushalayim. When he heard that the man had come to sell peppers, he became excited and asked his friend to sell him the small amount of peppers that he needed for his morning meal.

The spice merchant said that, unfortunately, he was unable to fulfill his friend's request as he had sold the whole quantity to a tailor, suggesting afterwards that he take his friend to the tailor who would certainly agree to sell him some peppers.

The two friends went to the tailor who said that he had already sold the peppers to another tailor and offered to take them to him.

But when they got there, the group of three found that, since there was a pepper shortage in Yerushalayim, news had spread very quickly that there was someone who had peppers to sell and everyone had come to buy....

16 | On Your Walls, O Jerusalem

Now there were no peppers left! Not only that, but each of the purchasers was only allowed to buy a small amount. The first group that came was allowed to buy an *oonka*,[9] a small weight's worth of peppers. The second group was only allowed to buy half that amount. The third group found that there weren't any peppers left at all![10] From that massive amount, there wasn't even enough to give each customer the smallest amount!

We don't know how many *oonka* were in that huge load of peppers, but we do know that enormous amounts of *oonka* were sold that day. As we said, there were 200 camels carrying about forty liters each. If we say that each liter had in it at least ten *oonka*, then at least one million people[11] passed through that tailor's courtyard[12] in one day!

Another way we can get a picture of how many people lived in Yerushalayim is from figuring out how many *Kohanim* served in the *Bais Hamikdash* at the time. We can assume that the *Kohanim* didn't make up more than five percent of the population.[13] Therefore,

---

9. Some of the commentaries say that an *oonka* is a coin, not a measurement of weight.

10. Some say that the third group was able to buy a small amount of peppers, but the amount was so small that you wouldn't notice it because it was so lightweight.

11. Half the buyers bought an *oonka* and half bought half an *oonka* and the third group didn't buy any at all (or just a tiny amount).

12. The amount of people that could fit into his courtyard at one time shows how incredibly large each courtyard was. It was able to hold hundreds of thousands of people at once. Again, even if these numbers are exaggerations, they still describe an amazingly large city.

13. The *Kohanim* were only a small part of the Tribe of Levi, who was only one of the twelve tribes.

The Glory of Yerushalayim | 17

we can multiply the number of *Kohanim* that worked in the *Mikdash* to get an idea about the population in general.

Our sages make a similar type of calculation when trying to figure out how many people lived in Yerushalayim during the reign of Shlomo Hamelech.[14] This is what they say:

On the day the *Bais Hamikdash* was dedicated, we find[15] that King Shlomo brought 22,000 *olah* sacrifices and 120 sheep. In the *Mishna* in Yuma we find further[16] that bringing an *olah* sacrifice required twenty four *Kohanim*. To bring the sheep, the *eilim*, required eleven *Kohanim*.

Having said that, let's calculate how many *Kohanim* were in the *Mikdash* that day.

22,000 cattle were sacrificed, each one using twenty four *Kohanim*. That means, for these sacrifices, there were 528,000 *Kohanim* serving in the *Mikdash*. They also brought 120,000 sheep, each using 11 *Kohanim*. That means there were 1,320,000 *Kohanim* taking care of those sacrifices. If we add those two numbers together, we are talking about 1,848,000 *Kohanim*!

---

14. Eichah Rabba 1:2

15. Melachim I 8:3. Those *pesukim* relate to the *shelamim* sacrifices. These calculations don't apply to those sacrifices. One cow that was brought as an *olah* needed twenty four *Kohanim* to bring it as a sacrifice, because the whole animal was burnt on the altar. The cows that were brought for *shelamim* didn't require as many *Kohanim*, because only the *emurim* (parts of the animal burnt on the altar) were burnt on the altar. Either way, those *pesukim* discuss the *shelamim* but say that King Shlomo brought many other *olah* sacrifices that day. Since the *pasuk* doesn't give a number, the sages deduce that it was the same number as the *shelamim* mentioned there.

16. Yuma 26:

18 | On Your Walls, O Jerusalem

Even if we say that each of the *Kohanim* was involved in a number of the sacrifices, something that would drastically lower the final number, there were still an amazingly large amount of *Kohanim* serving that day,[17] especially considering that there were more *Kohanim* needed to take care of the other services not directly related to the large amount of sacrifices.[18]

Even if we say that there were "only" one million *Kohanim* working in the *Mikdash* that day, the number does not include the many *Kohanim* who weren't fit to serve in the *Bais Hamikdash* and the women. So we see that in Yerushalayim at the time there were millions of *Kohanim*. How many people lived there besides the *Kohanim*? It's unfathomable!

Besides, these numbers relate to Yerushalayim at the time of King Shlomo, which was just at the beginning of the blossoming of the city. There is no question that natural growth doubled the population a number of times throughout the period of the First Temple.

Yet another way to calculate the population during the holidays is also brought in *Chazal*,[19] this time referring to the period of the Second Temple. King Agrippas wanted an estimate of how many people were in Yerushalayim for the Pesach holiday, so he told the *Kohanim* to put aside the kidneys of every *Korban Pesach* so that they could be counted.

---

17. Eitz Yosef

18. We also have to consider the shelamim that were brought. Even though they didn't use as many Kohanim as the olah, they still needed scores of Kohanim for that many. There were also more Kohanim needed to process the meat of the shelamim.

19. Eichah Rabba 1:2

The *Kohanim* followed his request and had 1,000,200 kidneys from the Pesach sacrifice!

Chazal say that every *Korban* Pesach was brought by at least ten people, as one was allowed to include as many people in each sacrifice as could receive a *kzayis* of meat. Therefore, we see that at that time there were at least twelve million people in Yerushalayim who brought the *Korban Pesach* – and that is not including those who weren't able to bring the sacrifice, for whatever reasons, such as being impure or unable to come. Those people brought their Pesach offering on Pesach Sheini, the fourteenth of Iyar.

Actually, *Chazal* said that many of the Pesach sacrifices were brought by tens or hundreds of people. That would bring the amount of people bringing the sacrifices in Yerushalayim to tens or hundreds of millions!

Perhaps you are wondering how there could have been such a large population explosion in such a short time. Our sages tell us that in those days the boys would be married off at twelve. By the time they were thirteen, they already had children. In other words, at the age of twenty six they were already grandparents!

No matter how the calculations work out exactly, we certainly get the picture of Yerushalayim as being a large, bustling empire, not just a regular city! And this is what we lost, due to our sinful ways.

Yerushalayim wasn't just a large city; it was also the center of wisdom for the whole world.

The wise men of every country in the world would come to bask in the wisdom of the people of Yerushalayim and learn from them. Any time someone traveled from Yerushalayim elsewhere, everyone would listen carefully to what he had to say. This wisdom was also lost during the *churban*, along with prophecy.

20 | On Your Walls, O Jerusalem

Let's look into some stories from the sages that describe the wisdom of Yerushalayim.

Here is the first account:[20]

There was a man from Yerushalayim who traveled to a distant land on the other side of the sea for his business. Unfortunately, when he got there he felt that his end was near. Besides the distress of his imminent demise, he was worried about what would happen to his property and how he could ensure that it would reach the hands of its rightful heir and not a charlatan.

He went to the innkeeper where he was staying, convinced that he was an upright man, and told him, "I know that after I pass away, my son will come here. I told him where I was staying, and he will surely come to ask for my possessions. I trust you to give him all of my things.

"I was worried, however, that if I passed away someone might pretend to be my son to claim the inheritance. Therefore, before I left, I made up with my son[21] that if for any reason I don't come home, he should go to where I stayed and present three[22] signs that he is wise. When someone comes claiming that he is my son, check that he proves his wisdom in three ways and then give him the entire inheritance. If he can't show you three times that he is wise, he is an imposter!"

The innkeeper agreed to the deal. Soon after, the businessman from Yerushalayim died. After a time, the son did come to try and find the inheritance.

The first obstacle that he faced in trying to find where his father stayed was overcoming a city ordinance that it was forbidden to give

---

20. Eichah Rabba 1:4
21. Eitz Yosef
22. One or two acts of wisdom, you can find with anyone. Three, therefore, was the minimum to properly identify him as his son (Eitz Yosef).

The Glory of Yerushalayim | 21

directions to a stranger saying where someone lived. Apparently, they were worried about uninvited guests. When the son came to find where his father had stayed, he had to figure out where the inn was on his own, using the intelligence of someone from Yerushalayim.

He went to the gates of the city where he saw a porter carrying a load of wood. He asked him if the load was for sale. When the porter answered that it was, he bought it and told him to take it to the inn he was looking for. The unsuspecting porter went there, with the son following right behind.

The porter called to the innkeeper that the wood had arrived. Seeing how surprised the innkeeper was, since he hadn't ordered any wood, he pointed to the man next to him, saying that he was the one who had ordered the wood. The innkeeper immediately understood that this was the son of the man from Yerushalayim who had died and that he had indeed just displayed the first sign of wisdom, having found his way to the right place.

After greeting the man warmly, the innkeeper invited him to lunch. The invitation was accepted and the innkeeper asked his guest to serve the hens. The problem was that there were five hens and seven people eating – the innkeeper and his wife, his two sons and two daughters and the guest.

The visitor tried to get out of the job, but the innkeeper insisted that he take care of dividing the portions. Since he knew the *Chazal*[23] that one must do as his host bids him to do, the Yerushalmi had no choice but to accede to his request.

He now faced a complicated task.[24] He couldn't give the man and his wife each one hen, one for the boys to split, one for the girls to split

---

23. Pesachim 86:
24. Eitz Yosef

and one for himself. It wouldn't be good manners to take a whole one for himself and leave the man's children with only a half each. If he gave the boys one whole one each and had the girls split one, he would have none left for himself and the girls would be jealous.

He found a solution. He put one in front of the couple, one in front of the boys and one in front of the girls, keeping two for himself.

Obviously, the innkeeper did not appreciate what the guest had done. It seemed gluttonous, not in keeping with the refined character he expected of a person from Yerushalayim. Still, the owner of the inn decided to remain silent.

When it came time for the evening meal, the guest was asked to divide the food again. This time, it was a whole roasted chicken. The host again was witness to what he considered strange behavior. After the man tried his best to get out of the job, he divided it as follows: the head of the bird was given to the innkeeper, the innards to his wife. The legs went to the sons and the wings to the daughters. The body of the bird he took for himself.aH

This time, the innkeeper couldn't hold himself back. Complaining, he asked the Yerushalmi man, "This morning, when you divided the meal in such an odd fashion, I didn't say a word. But now you again acted with a great lack of manners, taking the bulk of the food for yourself! How do you explain what you did?"

He answered him, "I explained to you that I shouldn't be the one dividing the food, but I couldn't refuse your insistence that I do so.[25]

"You served five hens. I made a simple calculation. If I give you and your wife one, then together you are three. The same with your

---

25. It's obvious that this wasn't the normal way to divide the hens, but the Yerushalmi son understood that the head of the house was checking his ability to use his wisdom to solve the problem, and not in the typical way.

sons. The same with your daughters. Now, since we know that there is danger in pairs, I didn't want to leave even one pair on the table, so I divided it as I did,[26] making the last two hens plus me equal to three!

"I also divided the later meal properly! You are the head of the house, so you got the head. It is my blessing to you that you should lead your household for many years! Your wife, who bears the children, got the innards, with its blessings that she should have many more children. Your sons keep the house standing on its feet, and may they continue to do so. They were given the feet. Your daughters are only here until they marry and then they will build their own nests with their husbands. They got the wings, with my blessing that they will never return to your home after they marry, but will live happily with their spouses!

"The body of the bird – without its head, innards, legs and wings looks like a boat. I came in a boat and want to return in a boat in the near future when you give me what I deserve since I showed you three acts of wisdom: that I found your house, how I divided the hens and how I divided the chicken."

When he finished his explanation, the innkeeper gave him his father's full inheritance, and they parted as friends.

Another story that shows how the Jews from Yerushalayim were blessed with more than just a natural, logical understanding, but also a supernatural insight, is as follows:

Four people from Yerushalayim went to Athens and stayed by one of the locals who ran a hostel. Towards evening, the host prepared a

---

26. Yefeh Anaf. There is another reason brought in the commentaries why he insisted on threes, as the number three hints to a lasting connection. By insisting on threes, he was blessing his host that there should be total harmony between him and his wife, as well as between his two sons and two daughters.

meal for them and then offered them four beds to sleep in. He really had only three functional beds and one with a broken leg. Not wanting to lose the income of four guests staying at his home for an extended period, he put out the broken bed leaning on the others.

When the four went to sleep, the host eavesdropped on their discussion. Having heard of the wisdom of the people of Yerushalayim, he wanted to experience it firsthand.

The host was sure that his guests wouldn't notice the broken leg. He heard, though, the man who was sleeping on the broken bed say, "You think I am sleeping on a bed? I'm sleeping on the ground, but I am suspended in air."

The guest spoke against the innkeeper to warn his friends not to trust the man, as he had tried to trick them. His friends continued to describe other ways the man had shown that he wasn't straight.[27]

The second guest said, "You think only the beds are bad? The food we ate tonight tasted like dogs!"

The third man said, "You think only the beds and the food are bad? The wine had the taste of a grave!"

The fourth man added his opinion, "It's no surprise, the man who is hosting us is not his father's son at all. Obviously, a man who is born out of impurity can't do anything perfectly."

The owner of the inn, who had been listening, noted to himself that the only true thing they had said was that the bed was broken.

Still, once he had heard what they said, he decided to check if what they said had any truth to it. He approached the butcher that sold him the meat, asking him to sell him more of the meat he had purchased for that meal.

---

27. Eitz Yosef

"I'm sorry," the butcher answered him, "that meat is gone."

The host asked the butcher, "Can you tell me what made the meat so delicious?"

The butcher answered honestly, "We had a lamb who was still nursing whose mother died. I had no choice but to let her nurse from our dog, who was feeding her pups at the time."[28]

Seeing that the Yerushalmi men were able to discern such an infinitesimal taste, he went on to the wine seller to check their next claim.

The same scenario repeated itself. The host asked for more of the wine he had purchased the day before, but the wine seller said it was finished. When he asked about the wine in more detail, the seller told him that the grapes that the wine was made out of were from a vine that grew over his father's grave.

Now the host had no choice but to check if their fourth claim about him was true as well. He went to his mother's home to try and ascertain the facts. "Mother," he asked, "tell me truthfully, whose son am I?" The bewildered mother told him the facts as they were, verifying that the Yerushalmi men had been correct.

The man now became worried that his secret should be kept. He was worried that others would find out about his lineage. He therefore worked to have a law instated that it was forbidden in all of Athens to host people from Yerushalayim. This way, this foul secret, as well as any other information the people from Yerushalayim might discern, would not become known.

---

28. Only one of the guests noticed the taste difference. Apparently, the dog's milk was more in his portion than the others. That must also be what happened with the wine and the grave (Eitz Yosef).

26 | On Your Walls, O Jerusalem

The Jews of Yerushalayim, though, outwitted this new law and continued to visit Athens, as we'll see in the following story.

It came to pass,[29] that a Jew from Yerushalayim came to Athens. He couldn't find a place to stay because of the law that had been enacted, forbidding anyone from hosting people from Yerushalayim.

The Jew, left with no choice, decided to go to a store that sold wine, a pub of sorts, and act as if he was there to buy a drink. In reality, though, he had no intention of leaving until the morning.

After a while, the store owner saw that there was no way to get the man from Yerushalayim to leave. He came up with a plan to trick him to get out.

"It is the custom here," he began, "that no one can sleep over until he takes three large jumps. I don't know why this tradition exists, but I am not interested in veering from the way things are done. If you will be so kind as to jump three large jumps, I will show you to a bed for the evening."

His real plan was to have the man take three large jumps which would lead him close to the door. He would then push the Jew out and lock the door before he could get back in.

"I certainly agree," said the Jew, "but I don't understand exactly what you mean. Show me what to do and I'll follow."

The storekeeper took three big jumps, landing near the door. The man from Yerushalayim quickly went and shut the door on him. "I just did to you what you planned on doing to me," he explained to the angry wine merchant before he went to bed, leaving the owner to look for a different place to spend the night.

---

29. Eichah Rabba 1:5

The Glory of Yerushalayim | 27

Even the children of Yerushalayim were blessed with a great degree of understanding. There is a story[30] told of a man from Athens who met a child near the gates of Yerushalayim during his travels. "Child," he asked him, "could you please do me a favor and go buy me some food that I may eat until satisfaction, but still have some left over for the road?"

The boy agreed, and the man handed him a handful of small coins. The boy hurried away and soon returned with salt.

"Did I ask you for salt?!" the man from Athens asked, surprised.

"You asked me for some food that you could eat, be satisfied with and have left over. With the small amount of money you gave me, did you think I could get you any real food?[31] Salt was the only option that fit the bill!"

There is yet another story about a man from Athens who came to Yerushalayim and met a child. "Take some money and buy me eggs and cheese."

The boy happily agreed and soon returned with the items. The man decided to try and confuse the child by asking him, "Can you tell me, please, which cheese comes from a white goat and which from a black goat?"

Instead of being stumped, the boy answered him right away, "Sure I can tell you, but first answer me how you can tell which egg came from a black hen and which from a white one. Then I'll answer you."[32]

---

30. Eichah Rabba 1:7
31. Eitz Yosef
32. The Radal explains the depth of the question and the sharpness of the child's answer. The man from Athens was referring to the Jews who are far removed from the Torah and don't keep mitzvos. He was saying that just like you can't tell the difference between cheeses that come

28 | On Your Walls, O Jerusalem

Even the servants of the people of Yerushalayim were wise.[33] *Chazal* tell the following story:[34]

There was a man from Athens who came to find wisdom in Yerushalayim. He stayed there for three and a half years, but, frustrated by his lack of accomplishment, he decided to go home. Before he left he purchased a slave.

Shortly after, though, he realized he had been taken advantage of. The slave was blind in one eye. Bitterly, he complained to his friends, "For three and a half years I tried to learn the wisdom of Yerushalayim, and I still couldn't even tell that this slave had such a severe defect!" He went to the slave trader to return the slave.

The man convinced him to keep the slave, saying that although he is partially blind, he is extremely wise and can see many things that others cannot. The man from Athens decided to keep him.

Soon after, when he was making his way home with his slave, the slave said to his new owner, "It would be a good idea for us to quicken

---

from a black or white goat, you can't tell the difference between Jews and the other nations. Even though the parents may have been different, the cheeses — their descendants — are the same.

The boy answered that the parable is not to the cheese, but to the eggs. You can't tell the difference between eggs that came from a black hen and those that came from a white one, but when they hatch the difference is obvious. The black hen's chick is black and the white hen's chick is white. So too it is with the Jews. They may seem for a period in history no different than the nations of the world, but in the end the difference between them will be obvious, because they carry the genes of their forefathers.

33. Some of the commentators (Eitz Yosef) explain that the servant in the story is a Jew, saying that even the simplest people, who would sell themselves as slaves, were clever.

34. Eichah Rabba 1:12

our pace so we can join the gentile who is four miles ahead of us. He has a female camel that is blind in one eye. The camel is pregnant with twins. She has two flasks on her back, one filled with wine and one filled with oil."

"How do you know?" the man from Athens asked, surprised. He was sure that the servant was mocking him, as he had no way to know such specific details about a camel he had never seen.

"I know she is blind," answered the slave, "because I see that the grass is only eaten on one side of the road. From here I deduce that she can only see with one eye.

"I know she is carrying twins, because I see that where she crouched when she rested there are two indentations in the ground.

"I know she is burdened with two flasks, one of oil and one of wine, because I see drops that have dripped on the two sides of the path. One set of drips was absorbed by the ground and the other wasn't. Therefore, I know one is wine, that is absorbed quickly, and the other is oil that is thick and not easily absorbed.

"I know the camel is led by a gentile and not a Jew, because I saw that the camel owner relieved himself in the middle of the road. Jews are modest and would never relieve themselves except on the side of the road.

"I can also say with certainty that they are four miles[35] ahead of us because camel prints are only visible for the amount of time it would take the camel to walk four miles.

---

35. What the slave said doesn't seem to explain how he knew that the camel was exactly four miles ahead. Maybe he saw that the footprints were about to disappear so he knew, or perhaps he looked behind him and saw that the footprints had already disappeared, leading him to conclude that they were exactly four miles behind the camel.

"Since we can still see her footprints, she must not be more than four miles ahead of us." The servant concluded his words, which were soon proven correct when they met up with the camel driver.

From the above story we see the greatness of the servants of Yerushalayim and just how much wisdom the inhabitants had… and what was lost.

One of the signs of how respected a person was in those days was how much of a dowry the person would be given upon his marriage.[36]

When a person from out of Yerushalayim wanted to marry a woman from Yerushalayim he would pay her weight in gold as a dowry! A man from Yerushalayim who deigned to marry a woman from another city was given his weight in gold as a dowry! That shows us how well respected the people of Yerushalayim were.

The people of Yerushalayim were very conscious of their reputation. A resident of Yerushalayim would never go to a banquet his friend was hosting without being invited twice. The first invitation, he felt, might have been given out of social sensibilities and not because the host really wanted the guest to participate. Only the second invitation showed that the guest's presence was really appreciated.

They would also inquire as to who the other guests at the banquet would be.[37] They were careful not to attend a meal attended by the uneducated or frivolous whose conversations would revolve around trivialities.

They would also make sure to roll up their sleeves when attending a meal at someone else's house to keep themselves above suspicion,

---

36. Eichah Rabba 4:2
37. Eichah Rabba 4:4

making it clear that they hadn't pilfered any of the eating utensils by hiding them in their sleeves. They were very careful to keep their reputations clean, even in a situation where they could assume no one would accuse them of wrongdoing.

The hosts were also very aware of social mores and honorable activity. When making a banquet, they would hang a kerchief in the window to let passerby know that there was a banquet and all were invited. When there wasn't enough room to invite everyone, they would remove the kerchief, saying there was no sitting room. The people were invited a few steps in to offer the host their good wishes, leaving it to the host's discretion if he wanted to invite them to stay.

Interestingly, not only was the chef in charge of preparing the meal and the quality of the food, he was in charge of making sure that the meal would be befitting the host.

If the meal came out to be of poor quality, the chef lost his pay and was required to pay a fine. This fine was calculated according to the standing of the host and the guests that had attended. The more important the host and the more important the guests, the greater the fine.

In order to further assure the satisfaction of the guests, samples of the menu were sent to their homes before the affair so the guests could choose wisely what they wanted to eat at the party, waiting for their favorite foods.

Another tradition that the people of Yerushalayim had was that if they found out that someone on their guest list already had previous obligations to attend a different party, they would not invite that person. This was done in order to save the guest the need to show his appreciation for the invitation to an affair he certainly wouldn't attend.[38]

---

38. According to Matnos Kehuna

32 | On Your Walls, O Jerusalem

The joyous atmosphere in Yerushalayim was so great that there was even an ordinance that it was forbidden to be sad! There was a special building outside of the city limits specifically for anyone who wanted to think about something that might depress him. There was no place for melancholy in Yerushalayim.[39]

And there was great reason to rejoice in Yerushalayim. No one ever went to bed guilty of sin. The daily sacrifice of the morning atoned for sins committed at night, while the daily afternoon sacrifice atoned for sins committed during the day.[40] The joy of knowing that one was living free of sin is unfathomable.

Further, if anyone ever sinned accidentally, he could buy an animal in the marketplace and bring it as the appropriate sacrifice and know for certain that he had achieved atonement.

Our rabbis tell us in the Midrash[41] that Yerushalayim was called *mesos kol haaretz*,[42] the joy of all lands. They explain that joy spread from the *Bais Hamikdash* to the whole land. This is how they described it:[43]

When a man realized he had sinned, he would become worried, but he had a way to solve his problem. The man would go and take an animal and slowly make his way to Yerushalayim, crying in pain over the mistake that he had made. Along the way, he would meet people who would ask him why he was so pained. Bitterly, he would tell them that he had accidentally sinned.

---

39. Eichah Rabba 2:19
40. Bamidbar Rabba 21:21
41. Yalkut Tehillim 755
42. Tehillim 48:3
43. According to the description of the Maggid of Yerushalayim, R' Shabsai Yudelevitch zt"l.

He would finally reach the *Bais Hamikdash* and approach the *Kohein* to bring his sacrifice. He would hear the *Leviim* sing and see the *Kohanim* prepare themselves to slaughter the animal.

The man would rest his hands on the animal and declare, "This is what should have been done to me. I should have been killed to atone for my sin!"

He would repeat these sentiments as he saw the sacrifice being skinned. "That should have happened to me!" He would feel as if it was, in fact, happening to him. The same was true for the burning of the sacrifice. He felt himself being sacrificed.

Then a heavenly voice would declare, "Your sin is gone! You have atonement!"

The joy was incredible. Yerushalayim would bring an amazing happiness to the people of the Land of Israel. But, alas, that joy is no more.

3

The Beginning of the End

Nevuchadnezar didn't wake up one morning and decide to do battle against Yerushalayim and destroy the *Bais Hamikdash*. It was something that he had considered for quite some time.

He was actually very nervous about going to fight against the Jews and pushed off the plan for eighteen years.[1] Throughout those eighteen years,[2] a heavenly voice[3] would announce to Nevuchadnezar,

---

1. Pesichta 23

2. Those eighteen years begin with his rise to power, which was in the fourth year of Yehoyachin's rule. Yehoyachin ruled for eleven years, as did Tzidkiyahu after him. That means twenty two years passed from the beginning of Yehoyachin's rule until the end of Tzidkiyahu's rule, when Yerushalayim was captured. If we subtract the first three years of Yehoyachin's rule (as Nevuchadnezar came to power in his fourth year), we are left with eighteen years from the beginning of his reign until he fought against Yerushalayim (Maharzav).

3. The Maharzav brings two explanations for what the heavenly voice was. Either it was actually a heavenly voice that sounded like the purring of a dove in his courtyard that called on him to fight against Yerushalayim or, according to another explanation, Nevuchadnezar heard the prophecies

"Wicked servant,[4] go destroy your Master's house, for His children don't listen to Him!"

Nevuchadnezar was hesitant to listen to the voice; he feared it was giving him bad advice[5]. He remembered what had happened to his grandfather Sancheriv, who had waged a war against the Jews during the days of King Chizkiyahu. An angel had killed out his entire mighty army in one night, leaving only ten survivors[6], one of whom was Nevuchadnezar.

During his eighteenth year, when Nevuchadnezar decided that he actually would fight against Yerushalayim, he did so with great trepidation. On his way to the city, he came to a fork in the road. The right path led to Yerushalayim and the left one to Amon[7]. He stopped there to check with his magical powers if he was making the right decision.

First he shot an arrow, proclaiming that it was against Rome. In other words, asking if he should fight Rome. The shooting of the arrow

---

of Yirmiyahu. From there he understood that Hashem wanted to destroy the Bais Hamikdash. It says in the Gemara (Sanhedrin 96) that we find that the people of Amon and Moav, the Jews' two evil neighbors, told Nevuchadnezar that the prophets of the Jewish people were saying that he would win in his fight against them.

4. He was called a wicked servant because he was doing a wicked thing. However, if he would have been doing what Hashem called for out of a desire to follow Hashem's command, it would have been a merit for him (Anaf Yosef).

5. Pesichta 30

6. There are a number of different opinions in the Midrash. Some say there were ten people left; some say nine; some say five; some say fourteen. All agree, though, that Nevuchadnezar was one of the survivors of Sancheriv's army.

7. Maharzav

was ineffective, symbolizing that he would not be successful in fighting against Rome. He then shot an arrow, stating it was against Alexandria. Again, the shooting was ineffective, indicating he wouldn't win in a war against Alexandria. When he shot a third arrow against Yerushalayim, the shooting went well, hinting that in his fight against Yerushalayim he would win.[8]

After, Nevuchadnezar planted seeds and plants in the name of Rome, but the plants didn't take well. He did the same for Alexandria with the same results. Only when he planted in the name of Yerushalayim did the plants grow well. This symbolized that he would be able to rule over the city.

His third magical test was done with candles and torches – first for Rome, then Alexandria, and finally for Yerushalayim. The first two sets of candles didn't give off light, telling him that his path to fight those cities would not be lit. The candles for Yerushalayim shone brightly.

A fourth and similar test involved boats that Nevuchadnezar floated on the Peras River. The boats that were sailed for Rome and Alexandria didn't move. Those for Yerushalayim immediately began to sail, showing Nevuchadnezar that the path to conquer Yerushalayim was open to him.[9]

---

8. The Eitz Yosef brings a different understanding of this, saying there was a way to read the arrows, similar to how people nowadays "read coffee" and the like. They would sharpen and polish the arrow until it shined like a mirror. Then the magicians would be able to look into it and see answers to their questions. Rashi in Yechezkel (21:26) explains the test differently. He says that Nevuchadnezar shot the arrow straight up, wanting to see in which direction it would fly. It went to the right, in the direction of Yerushalayim.

9. Koheles Rabba 12:7

After these tests were done, Nevuchadnezar used a different black magic tool called *Terafim*. These *Terafim* were images that would speak at a certain time known to the sorcerers. They also guaranteed that the king of Bavel would have a clear victory against Yerushalayim.

Nevuchadnezar also used a liver of an animal, which, when removed from the carcass, was able to hint at answers to various questions. This method also encouraged Nevuchadnezar to fight Yerushalayim, declaring that Hashem had decided to destroy it due to *Bnai Yisrael*'s sins.

In all, Nevuchadnezar employed supernatural tests forty nine times! Every one of them told him to go to war. That was enough to convince him to go up against Yerushalayim.

The nations of Amon and Moav also worked to convince the king of Bavel to fight the Jews.[10] They told him that the Jews' prophets were prophesizing about their own destruction.

Nevuchadnezar shared his fears. "Perhaps God will do to me what He did to previous generations who tried to fight the Jewish people."

They answered him that "The Man is not in His house." In other words, God has already abandoned His people and doesn't pay attention to what is happening to them anymore.

Nevuchadnezar said, "But He can come back any minute!"

They assured him that He was far away.

"But what of the righteous people of the city?"

They told him that God already took them with Him. That is to say, they had died.

---

10. Sanhedrin 96:

38 | On Your Walls, O Jerusalem

"And what if the wicked repent and beg God for mercy?" the king asked further, as even a wicked king like Nevuchadnezar understood the power of *teshuva*.

The other sinful kings had an answer. "Their God already promised that He won't bring them back until seventy years have passed."

They were wrong, though. Had the Jews cried just once, regretting how they had acted and wanting to become closer to Hashem, the *churban* wouldn't have happened! Hashem gave them many, many chances, hoping they would turn to Him. Again and again, He pushed off the imminent *churban*.

Nevuchadnezar was still nervous and tried to get out of fighting the Jewish people with different excuses. "It's Teves, the middle of winter. I am afraid of the rain and snow that will delay me." The kings of Amon and Moav suggested that he travel by a path close to the bottom of the mountains, in order to protect him.

"And where will I set up camp in the Land of Israel? I'm used to a life of comfort in my own country."

The kings answered him that even the graves of *Eretz Yisrael* are more glorious than his castles. "You don't have to worry about anything! Just leave your country and go conquer Yerushalayim!"

Finally they convinced him. Deep down, despite all his worries, the evil Nevuchadnezar wanted to destroy Yerushalayim and the Holy Temple.

Still, Nevuchadnezar wasn't brave enough to go out at the head of his army against Yerushalayim.[11] He camped in the city of Dafne in Antiochia, between Bavel and Yerushalayim. He sent the head of his army, Nevuzaradan, to do the actual conquering.

---

11. Pesichta 30

The Beginning of the End

Nevuchadnezar was to take great pride in the war he waged against the Jews, but actually he wasn't the one who fought at all. In his fear of divine retribution, he stayed behind and sent others in his place.

Still, it was his war and he was held responsible. It was as if Nevuchadnezar was standing over Nevuzaradan as he fought. Some of the rabbis say[12] that Nevuchadnezar's image was engraved on Nevuzaradan's chariot, in order that Nevuzaradan should remain in constant trepidation of his master. Others say that was unnecessary, as Nevuzaradan was petrified of Nevuchadnezar and no reminders were necessary.

When the punishment came, it was Nevuchadnezar who suffered, even though the war was carried out by his general.

There were three instructions that Nevuchadnezar gave Nevuzaradan before sending him to war:[13]

1: Have mercy on the prophet Yirmiyahu. Meaning, have mercy on him, but on him alone. Have no mercy on the rest of the nation, even if Yirmiyahu requests that you do.[14]

2: Do no evil to Yirmiyahu. Do no evil to him, but be as wicked as you want to his nation.

3: Do to Yirmiyahu whatever he asks of you for himself. Only for himself. Don't listen to anything he asks for his nation.

As an aside, before we continue, we want to mention that Nevuchadnezar also used his magic to decide on strategy in the war. For example, his enchanted experiments told him that it would be effective to: use trumpets to scare the people, make a siege on the city,

---

12. Sanhedrin 96:
13. Pesichta 34
14. Eitz Yosef

build embankments to stand on while aiming their slingshots, build ramps from the ground to the walls to climb on to enter the city, and build battering rams to smash the walls. Nevuzaradan also used these tactics to destroy the city.

One of the other main factors that encouraged Nevuchadnezar to fight against the Jews was King Tzidkiyahu's rebellion. As we mentioned previously, Nevuchadnezar appointed the Jewish king Tzidkiyahu to rule over the people in the Land of Israel as well as over the surrounding nations. He made Tzidkiyahu swear on a *Sefer Torah* that he wouldn't rebel.

Under normal circumstances, Tzidkiyahu would never have considered rebelling. The Jews, though, had sinned, and Hashem had decreed that the *Bais Hamikdash* was to be destroyed.[15] Tzidkiyahu, therefore, did break his promise to remain loyal to Nevuchadnezar. To aid his rebellion, he sent messengers to Egypt, asking them for help with horses and soldiers so that he could throw off the yoke of Bavel.[16]

Actually, Pharaoh Necho, the ruler of Egypt, decided to respond positively to Tzidkiyahu's request. He sailed with many military men and horses to help Tzidkiyahu's rebellion against Bavel.

When the Babylonians heard, they made the decision to retreat.[17] Although they had been prepared to fight Yehuda, they weren't prepared to fight on two different fronts. Their withdrawal caused great rejoicing amongst the Jews.

---

15. Nedarim 65.
16. Yechezkel 17:15
17. Yirmiyahu 37:5

The Beginning of the End | 41

Their joy was premature, as Yirmiyahu prophesized at the time:[18] "So says Hashem the God of Israel: So you should say to the king of Yehuda that sent you to ask for me. The army of Pharaoh that is coming to help you has returned to its land, Egypt. The Kasdim will return and fight this city. They will conquer it and burn it down. So says Hashem, don't convince yourself saying, 'The Kasdim have gone away from us.' They won't go. Even if you smite the whole army of the Kasdim that are fighting you and there are only wounded men left, they will get up and burn this city!"

Yirmiyahu's prophecy came true. While the Egyptian ships were on the way to the Land of Israel, Hashem sent swollen water skins that looked like human insides.[19] Wondering what they were, they were told that they were the skeletons of their ancestors that the Jewish people had drowned while leaving Mitzrayim.[20]

It seems to be that they immediately returned to Egypt, saying to themselves that they were not interested in helping a nation that

---

18. Yirmiyahu 37:7-10

19. Radal and Eitz Yosef in the name of Rashi

20. The Eitz Yosef says that the Egyptians honestly thought that they were Egyptian skeletons that had miraculously lasted until then. It seems, though, from the Radal that they didn't think they were actual skeletons, but rather that they were a sign to remind them what the Jews had done to their people, in order to stop them from helping them. It is obvious that these weren't really the skeletons of the Egyptians that drowned, for they merited burial. Also, they didn't drown in the Yam Hagadol, the Mediterranean, but rather in the Yam Suf.

Another opinion is brought by the Yifei Ainaim that it is possible to say they didn't really see anything. Rather, Hashem made them remember what had happened in the past to make sure they didn't go help. It is allegorical to say that they saw the skeletons of their ancestors in the water.

drowned their predecessors in the sea. This left the Jews with no hope for help from the surrounding nations, not even the "broken reed staff," as the Egyptians are described.

Tzidkiyahu was breaking his vow to the king by rebelling and seeking Egyptian help in his fight. The promise not to rebel was not the only promise to Nevuchadnezar that Tzidkiyahu broke, as we see in the Midrash:[21]

Since Nevuchadnezar appointed Tzidkiyahu as king over the Land of Israel and the five other kings,[22] he became very important and was allowed free access to all the rooms of the king's palace. One day, he entered a room where he saw Nevuchadnezar pulling the limbs off a live rabbit and eating them raw.

Nevuchadnezar was not eating the live rabbit in this manner out of hunger. As king, he had the most delectable dishes available at whim. Nevuchadnezar was trying to develop the character trait of cruelty by performing acts of brutality, assuming it would help him in battle.

No matter what his reasoning, we can understand that Nevuchadnezar was certainly not interested in the incident becoming public. He made Tzidkiyahu swear seriously on the altar in the *Kodesh* that he would never tell anyone about what he had seen.

Tzidkiyahu had no reason to break his promise and share the story about the rabbit, especially since he had sworn that he wouldn't. However, the other five kings he ruled over were not pleased about being ruled by a Jew, and decided that they would set a trap to cause his downfall.

Once, when Tzidkiyahu was with the gentile kings he ruled over, they began speaking derogatorily about the king, each mentioning what

---

21. Eichah Rabba 2:14; also Nedarim there, briefly
22. See introduction.

he perceived as the Babylonian king's faults. They concluded by saying that, in their opinion, Nevuchadnezar wasn't fit to rule, and Tzidkiyahu would be the preferred replacement as king. They flattered Tzidkiyahu until his tongue loosened and he told them that he had seen Nevuchadnezar eating the limbs off a live rabbit.

The kings jumped at the opportunity that they had been waiting for. That very day, they sent messengers to Nevuchadnezar accusing Tzidkiyahu of bad-mouthing him, saying that Tzidkiyahu had even said he had seen Nevuchadnezar eat the limbs off a live animal. They feigned innocence, acting as if they were simply worried about the king's honor.

Their trick worked. Nevuchadnezar became furious – furious that the promise had been broken and furious that his honor was being trampled. He immediately decided to wage war against the Jews and left Bavel for Dafne in Antiochia.[23]

He ordered the Sanhedrin to come to him, assuming that they must have annulled the vows that Tzidkiyahu had made to him.

When the members of the Sanhedrin arrived, Nevuchadnezar asked them to tell him what is in the Torah. They began reading the

---

23. It sounds from the Midrash that this incident happened before the churban, when Nevuchadnezar called the members of the Sanhedrin to Antiochia and they came on their own. In Yirmiyahu (52:10) it is brought that when Tzidkiyahu was captured, Nevuchadnezar killed his sons before his eyes and also killed the officers of Yehuda. The commentaries explain that these officers were the members of the Sanhedrin. It seems that both are referring to the same incident.

It is possible that he didn't kill them right away, but first dragged them through the streets with horses as is mentioned henceforth. After the churban, when Tzidkiyahu was captured, Nevuchadnezar also killed the Sanhedrin. The Targum there says, though, that the officers of Yehuda that are referred to are not the Sanhedrin, but other important people from Yehuda.

44 | On Your Walls, O Jerusalem

Torah, translating into Babylonian as they read. When they got to the section about vows, Nevuchadnezar asked them, "Tell me, please, if someone makes a vow, may he go back on it?"

The wise men answered that there was a way that that could be done.

"So that explains it!" Nevuchadnezar exclaimed. "You were obviously the ones that annulled Tzidkiyahu's vows to me not to rebel and not to reveal my secret! You can't claim that you didn't know which vows of his you were annulling, as you are not allowed to annul a vow before knowing what it is about. You must have known that you were annulling the vows that he made to me! You, therefore, are guilty of rebelling against the king!"

He first humiliated them by making them sit on the floor. He later brought them back to Yerushalayim. From there, he dragged them to Lod with their hair tied to horses' tails.

After that, Nevuzaradan, at Nevuchadnezar's command, laid siege on Yerushalayim on the tenth of Teves in the ninth year of Tzidkiyahu's reign for three and a half years. The city contained not only the people native to Yerushalayim, but also all the people that lived in Yehuda and Binyamin at the time.[24] When they had heard that Nevuchadnezar was coming to wage war against the Land of Israel, they ran to take refuge within the city's walls.

During the siege, large piles of dirt were placed around the city in order to aid in conquering it. The piles made it impossible for anyone to sneak out of the walls unnoticed and bring bread into the city. A terrible famine, causing many casualties, ensued.

---

24. Yirmiyahu 8:14

4

Under Siege

Nevuzaradan came up against Yerushalayim with a massive army of soldiers, chariots and cavalry. His army was so vast that it is described as being as "deep as the ocean."[1] Still, his army stood no chance against the fortified walls and brave people that lived there.

Chazal describe[2] the incredible strength and bravery of the inhabitants of Yerushalayim. As one example, a man named Avika ben Gevatria was able to catch the enormous rocks the Babylonians would send in catapults against the Jews and throw them back against the Babylonians, causing them many casualties. Later, he would even kick the stones back with his feet, acting as a human shield to protect the people of the besieged city.

At one point,[3] the Babylonians came up with a plan to rid themselves of this man who had caused them so many casualties. They decided that they would send a lighter stone than usual. When Avika would try to stop it using the full force he used with the heavier rocks, he would lose his balance due to its lighter weight and fall off the wall.

---

1. Pesichta 23
2. Yalkut Eichah Remez 1109
3. Pesichta 29

The plan worked, but only partially. Avika did lose his balance and fall... but the fall left him unharmed! After taking a few seconds to reacclimatize himself, he climbed back up the wall to continue fighting. While the story was taking place, his people used the time to prepare him a special meal – a whole roasted cow.

The natural strength of these great men of Yerushalayim was enough to protect the Jews against their enemies, but since they had sinned, Hashem removed His protection. This was obvious from the unexpected way that Avika met his end. A strong wind blew him off the wall to his death. The message to the Babylonians was clear: Your plans to conquer My children are futile, unless I decide that they should fall.

Nevuzaradan, seeing the incredible strength of the people he was fighting against, decided that his best recourse was to starve them to death by besieging the city for an extended period of time, not allowing any water or food to enter.

The Jews managed to survive for a while, using up their stored resources. Soon, though, the famine became unbearable. In Eichah,[4] the starvation is described vividly as follows: "The children and babies swoon in the broad places of the city. They say to their mothers, 'Where is the corn and wine?' When they swoon like wounded men in the broad places of the city, when their soul is poured out into their mother's bosom...."

The women of Yerushalayim gave their husbands their expensive elegant jewelry to barter in the marketplace for some food for their famished families. But there was no food to be bought for all the gold and silver in the world. The husbands would search and search,

---

4. Eichah 2:11-12

wandering the marketplace in search of food, until their strength gave out and they died right there in the streets.

When the women saw that their husbands were late in returning, they sent their children to find out what happened. The weakened, starved children found their fathers' corpses lying in the street, but the sight was too overwhelming and they, too, died.

The fate of the children who remained at home was no better. The nursing babies would cry to be fed as always. The mothers who had not tasted food in so long were not able to provide nourishment. The frustrated babies tried and tried unsuccessfully to nurse, until they also perished in their mothers' arms.

The women,[5] who had never stepped foot in the marketplaces and streets before, were left to go search for food. A woman would meet her friend in the street. Surprised, she would ask her what she was doing out in the public street. "You have never gone out to the marketplace before!"

Her friend would answer, "I cannot hide the fact from you that the famine is intolerable!" Together, they would search for food... but none was to be found. Women's corpses were seen in every corner of the city.

Some of the people tried to satisfy their hunger by eating different wild grasses and roots. The plants did fill them up, but they pierced their stomachs, leaving them to die feeling as if they had been stabbed by swords.

Another heart wrenching tale[6] is told of a family who had four sons and one spoonful of flour to cook. While the woman of the house

---

5. Pesichta Rabasi 26
6. Midrash Zuta Eichah 1

was stirring the pot she was cooking the flour in, a drop fell out. Starved, one of the children stuck out his finger to lick it. The father, though, pushed his hand away, admonishing him not to steal from his brothers. He then left the house.

However, before the family was able to taste the dish, the Babylonians came and killed the entire family. The father, who had left in the meantime, came back and saw his entire family murdered and the food still cooking on the fire. He was so overwhelmed that he took the finger of his son that had wanted to lick the food and poked his own eyes out with it, declaring, "The finger that I wouldn't let lick the food that dropped from the pot should be the one to poke out my eyes!"

A story is brought by *Chazal*[7] of another woman whose two older sons had gone out to war. While they were away, crazed with hunger, she took her baby and cooked him. When her sons returned from battle, they sat down to eat, not wondering where the food had come from. In the middle of the meal, though, they saw their small brother's hand in the pot. Horrified by the thought that they had eaten their sibling, they went up to the roof and jumped to their deaths.

It is further told about one of the distinguished inhabitants[8] of Yerushalayim who sent his son with a pottery jug to bring some water to quench his thirst. The father was so thirsty that he waited on the roof, watching for his son's return. He saw him returning, the jug empty, as there was no water at all to be found!

Despairing, the father told his son to throw the jug to the ground, after which the father jumped to his death on top of the broken shards. His broken limbs intermingled with the broken pieces.

---

7. Midrash Zuta Eichah 1
8. Eichah Rabba 4:5

One of the horrible stories that really show how desperate the situation was is the story of the wife of Doeg ben Yosef. Doeg had died, leaving behind one son. This son was the light of Doeg's widow's life. She loved her son so much that every year she would weigh him and send his weight in solid gold to the *Bais Hamikdash*.[9]

During the siege, the woman became so dreadfully hungry that she took this child that she loved more than anything and killed him to eat him.

Yirmiyahu lamented[10] this horrible incident: "Hashem, look and see who You have done this to! Should the women eat their fruit, their babies?!"

The voice of *ruach hakodesh* answered him, "It was that a *Kohein* and prophet were killed in My *Mikdash*!" Hashem was saying that all the tremendous suffering was coming as a punishment for the murder of Zecharia the prophet, which will be discussed at length later.

The Babylonians weren't satisfied with the hunger they had inflicted. In addition, they made fires near the walls where they would cook a vegetable called Ochvinin. The smell of this vegetable was known to stimulate the appetite. When the smell reached the poor, starving Jews, their hunger would be so overwhelming that their stomachs would burst, causing their death.

---

9. Eichah Rabba 1:51. This story is also brought in Yuma 38:, but there it states that she would weigh him every day and send his weight in gold to the Mikdash. Rashi explains that she would send the difference in his weight from the day before. It wouldn't be possible to say that she sent such an enormous amount of gold every day. Another difference between the Gemara and the Midrash is that it seems according to the Gemara that the son's name was Doeg and the father's name was Yosef.

10. Eichah 2:20

50 | On Your Walls, O Jerusalem

Besides the hunger, disease was rampant in the besieged city and also left behind many dead. An enormous amount of people were killed by the sword, but that number only accounts for a third of the deaths!

Nevuzaradan besieged the city for three and a half years but was unable to conquer it.[11] Hashem was waiting and hoping that the Jewish people would repent and return to Him so that He could save them.[12]

The Babylonian army brought 300 mules loaded with iron sledgehammers that could break through iron. They were totally ineffective, though. The assault on just one of the gates of Yerushalayim used up the whole supply.[13]

After three and a half years, Nevuzaradan decided it was time to concede defeat. He decided that if three and a half years didn't lead to the capture of Yehuda, then the city would never be his. He also began to worry that Hashem would vent His wrath on him for fighting against His people, just as He had done to Sancheriv.

Still, Hashem had decided that Yerushalayim should be destroyed, and so it was to be. A heavenly voice said to Nevuzaradan, "Go conquer Yerushalayim! The time has come for it to be destroyed!"[14] Hashem waited for the enemy to despair of conquering the Jews and only then allowed them. He wanted the Babylonians to know that it was His decision alone that allowed the city to be conquered.

Hashem then put a strange idea into Nevuzaradan's head so that he would stay and conquer the city – to measure the height of the walls

---

11. Pesichta 30
12. Yalkut Eichah 1109
13. Sanhedrin 96:
14. Sanhedrin 96:

of Yerushalayim each day.[15] Nevuzaradan found that the walls were actually sinking two and a half *tefachim* each day. After he saw that, he decided against retreating, waiting to see how events would unfold.

Slowly the wall sank into the earth until there was none left at its lowest point. Nevuzaradan walked straight into the city, destroying what was left of the higher parts.[16]

The day that Nevuzaradan broke through the walls and gates of Yerushalayim was the ninth of Tammuz. At that point, Nevuzaradan only penetrated the first of the three walls and did not enter the city. After they broke through the first wall, the officers of Bavel proudly set up camp within the gates of the middle wall.[17] From there they began to plan the rest of the capture.[18]

---

15. Pesichta 30

16. The story is told a bit differently in Sanhedrin 96:. After Nevuzaradan despaired of capturing Yerushalayim, he hit one of the gates of Yerushalayim with his last ax, sort of as an afterthought. He was very surprised to find that the gate that had swallowed the load of 300 donkeys filled with axes opened now with one hit that he had just tried as an afterthought. The conclusion was again obvious – Yerushalayim was never captured, she turned herself over to the hands of Bavel.

17. Yirmiyahu 39:3. Look carefully at the Radak there.

18. On this topic, there is a strong point of disagreement between the Talmud Bavli and the Talmud Yerushalmi. In Yirmiyahu (39:2) it says that the ninth of Tammuz was the day the wall was broken. But the Talmud Bavli (Taanis 28:) says that even though the wall was broken during the destruction of the First Temple on the ninth of Tammuz, the seventeenth of Tammuz was the day that the wall was broken during the destruction of the Second Temple. The Yerushalmi disagrees (Taanis 4). The Yerushalmi says that the walls were broken on the seventeenth of Tammuz during the destruction of the First Temple also. The date that is written in Yirmiyahu, according to the Yerushalmi, is "kilkul chesbonos," i.e., a wrong calculation. The Radak gives a third opinion,

52 | On Your Walls, O Jerusalem

It must be stressed again that Bavel never conquered Yerushalayim, but rather it was given to them on a silver platter. Hashem opened the gates of Yerushalayim to its enemies, inviting them in to come and conquer.

We can assume that the Jews also noticed at some point that the walls were sinking. They must have felt a tremendous sense of grief and despair, understanding that the end was near. They should have concluded that they certainly could no longer rely on their own strength to withstand the enemy. They should have turned to Hashem and begged him to forgive them in His infinite mercy. They didn't, though. Had they done so, the destruction would never have come, for the sole purpose in the travails was to cause the Jews to repent.

But, unfortunately, that's not how the Jews responded. They didn't change their actions at all. They didn't focus on how helpless they were against what Hashem wanted to happen. They didn't pay attention to

---

it seems. He says that the outer wall was broken on the ninth of Tammuz, but the internal wall that let the Babylonian soldiers into the city was not broken until the seventeenth of Tammuz, eight days later. It is easy to accept his position, as it fits in well with both the simple reading of the text and the comments of Chazal.
According to the Radak, the Babylonians set up their camp in the gates of the upper wall, which was the middle wall. The Bavli says the walls were broken on the ninth of Tammuz. The Yerushalmi feels that the events described here happened after the seventeenth of Tammuz, when the walls were penetrated completely. According to the Yerushalmi, the Babylonians set up their officers' quarters in the courtyard of the Bais Hamikdash, in the gates that are between the courtyard of Israel and the courtyard of the Kohanim. In the Gemara (Sanhedrin 103.) it describes the audacity of the Babylonians to use a place that was so holy and meant to be used in the service of the King of all kings and to use it for their own common purposes.

the fact that they were about to succumb to the enemy. Instead, they trusted in their own strength to save themselves.

Even though the outer wall had been broken, many of the inhabitants of the city still believed that their own strength and bravery would save them.[19] They took pride in their abilities rather than falling in supplication to God.

As an example, they destroyed most of the homes of the city and used the rocks from those homes to strengthen the walls around the city and fill the cracks that had appeared. The last water that was left in the city was used to make cement to fix the cracks, as well.

There was really nothing wrong with what they did. Chizkiyahu had acted similarly in his days. However, Chizkiyahu trusted completely in God and knew that the actions he was taking were merely to fulfill the Torah's obligations to work within the framework of natural law. Here, the people were actually sure that their abilities would save them. The actions were similar, but there was a vast difference.

According to the natural ways of war, it should have taken about forty or fifty days to conquer the houses,[20] where the Jewish warriors gathered to fight on the rooftops. If we use the calculations that we made earlier[21] and assume that there were millions of homes in Yerushalayim, it would be impossible to conquer all of them had Hashem not given them over.

It says in the Midrash that Chanamel, Yirmiyahu's uncle, also bid the angels to fight for them. He made them swear loyalty and then

---

19. Pesichta 24
20. Eichah Rabba 2:5
21. First chapter

lowered them to the walls in full armor.[22] When the Babylonians saw the angels were coming to fight them, they panicked and began to run away.

Hashem, though, decided that the angels should not help the Jews. He changed the angels' names so that Chanamel would no longer be able to control them and then brought them back to heaven.

Chanamel found another idea. He called the angel of the world to his service and lifted Yerushalayim into the air, where the Babylonians wouldn't be able to conquer it. Hashem, though, kicked Yerushalayim back down to the world. It was time for Yerushalayim to fall. Nothing could help. It was a decree from heaven; the Babylonians were just called in to fulfill the decree.

Before we go on to discuss how events unfolded, we need to discuss a parallel episode. Tzidkiyahu the Jewish king ran away, with tragic results.

---

22. In the Midrash Rabba (Eichah Rabba 2:5) it is brought that Bnai Yisrael said that the enemy would never be able to rule over them since they even had the heavenly army to fight for them. One said he could call angels that would build a wall of water around Yerushalayim. Another said that through the angels he could build a wall of fire. A third said he would stop the enemies with a wall of iron that the angels would build. Hashem answered them, "You want to use My angels to stop Me from doing what I want in order to allow yourselves to continue and sin against Me? It shall not be!" Hashem then mixed up the jobs of the angels. The angel that was in charge of fire became in charge of water, etc. When the inhabitants called the angels to do the job they thought they were able to, they found them unable to fulfill their requests.

When we think about the fact that the "terrible sinners" of those days had so much control over the heavenly spheres that the only way to stop them was to change the jobs of the angels, we get a picture of just how different the "sinners" of those days compare to the sinners of our generation.

When Tzidkiyahu saw that the city was about to fall, he understood that he was in grave danger, as he had rebelled against the king and revealed his secret. He decided to escape while he still could. He fled through a passageway that he entered through a cave that had been prepared in case of necessity. It was eighteen *mil* long[23] and stretched from his castle within the middle wall of the city to the plains of Yericho. He didn't travel alone, but rather traveled slowly behind his ten sons.[24] He was sure that he would find refuge out of the city.

He should have escaped successfully, but Hashem decided otherwise. The prophet had already warned him that if he wouldn't subjugate himself to the yoke of Bavel, his end would be bitter and he would die in Bavel.[25]

Hashem made a beautiful deer[26] run along the path of the escape route. The Babylonian soldiers, intent on catching the deer, followed its path. The deer led them to the exit of the pathway just as Tzidkiyahu and his sons were emerging. They were caught.

The soldiers brought Tzidkiyahu and his sons to Nevuchadnezar. Nevuchadnezar was determined to bring him to judgment. "Why did you rebel against me?" he asked Tzidkiyahu. Tzidkiyahu remained silent. He had no answer.[27]

"What should be your judgment?" he then asked Tzidkiyahu. "According to the laws of your Torah you deserve death for breaking

---

23. Bamidbar Rabba 2:9
24. Pesikta Rabasi 26
25. Yechezkel 12:13
26. Rashi on Yechezkel 12:13
27. Pesikta 26

56 | On Your Walls, O Jerusalem

an oath you took with God's name.[28] According to civil law you deserve death for rebelling against the king."

Tzidkiyahu again remained silent. He realized that Nevuchadnezar had decided to put him to death and nothing would change that.

He did request that he be put to death before his sons, so as not to have to suffer seeing their death. His sons made the same request, that they be put to death before their father. Nevuchadnezar, wanting Tzidkiyahu to suffer as much as possible, decided to kill the sons first.

Tzidkiyahu saw all ten of his sons executed before his eyes. It was the last thing he saw, as right after they were slain Nevuchadnezar poked out Tzidkiyahu's eyes and threw them in the oven.[29] He then put Tzidkiyahu in jail, where he remained until the day he died.[30]

Tzidkiyahu was a righteous man, perfect in his ways.[31] He was, though, held responsible for the sins of his generation. He did do the wrong thing by breaking his oaths to the king. Tzidkiyahu justified the punishments he received, saying,[32] "Everyone come and see!

---

28. Even though Nevuchadnezar knew that the oath had been annulled (as he punished the members of the Sanhedrin for annulling the oath), it is possible that since the annulment wasn't done in Nevuchadnezar's presence, the oath was still in force.

29. It's possible that there was another wicked purpose in blinding Tzidkiyahu, besides to inflict the suffering of blindness. It was a terribly horrible thing for Tzidkiyahu to see all ten of his sons killed before him. It was something that would not be easily forgotten. However, it was possible that the other things he would see would dull his memory a bit. Nevuchadnezar, therefore, blinded him. The final thing he saw was the slaughter of his sons. There were no other scenes to later dull the memory.

30. Yirmiyahu 52:11

31. Kerisos 5:

32. Pesikta 26

Yirmiyahu[33] prophesized about me that I would go to Bavel and die in Bavel but wouldn't see Bavel with my eyes. I didn't listen to him and here I am in Bavel without seeing it."

---

33. Yechezkel 12:13

The Period of the Three Weeks

In the last chapter we mentioned that the Babylonians broke through the outer city walls on the ninth of Tammuz and camped in the gates of the middle wall.[1] At that time the Jews undertook to protect themselves, falling into the trap of believing in their own strength rather than trusting Hashem.

Only eight days passed between when the Babylonians broke through the outer wall and when they broke the middle wall and took over the city. These eight days were their last chance to do *teshuva*. The eighth day was the seventeenth of Tammuz. It was on this day that there were no sheep left to bring as the daily sacrifice. When they lost the merit of the daily sacrifices, the Babylonians overtook the city.

The period that begins from that point, the seventeenth of Tammuz, until the day theBais HaMikdash *Mikdash* was burned on the ninth of Av, are days that are prone to

---

1. See note 18 in previous chapter. The Radak explains the development of the events as we do here.

tragedy. During this period, there is a *mazik*, a dangerous spirit, called Ketev Meriri[2] who is able to destroy and damage in a horrible way.

We find a frightening description of this spirit in *Chazal*. Rabbi Yochanan describes him as full of eyes, scales and hair. Rabbi Shimon bar Yochai describes him as having only one eye, on his heart, and that anyone who looks at him dies on the spot, except for the greatest of men like Shmuel. Shmuel saw this evil spirit, but didn't get excited. He said that the spirit is like a house snake that doesn't know how to do harm.

We can learn the powers of destruction that this harmful spirit has from the story that happened with Rabbi Avahu.

One day, Rabbi Avahu noticed a person holding a wooden stick, about to hit his friend. The blow from the stick itself wasn't dangerous, but the evil spirit Ketev Meriri was standing behind his friend. He was waiting for the light blow from the wooden stick to allow him to beat the friend to death with a metal bar.

Rabbi Avahu noticed the spirit. He said to the man, "Do you want to kill your friend?"

The man didn't understand why Rabbi Avahu said that. "A strike from a wooden stick like this can't kill someone."

Rabbi Avahu agreed. "The blow from a wooden stick like this can't kill, but there is an evil spirit waiting for the opportunity to kill your friend with an iron bar. He will find the chance when you hit your friend."[3]

---

2. Eichah Rabba 1:29

3. It is explained in the Midrash that because he was worried about the power of Ketev Meriri, Rabbi Yochanan forbade the teachers of young

60 | On Your Walls, O Jerusalem

That's the nature of the spirit Ketev Meriri, its power of destruction. He finds a situation where he can get involved and cause greater harm. This power is potent during the period between the seventeenth of Tammuz and the ninth of Av, from the period between the capture of Yerushalayim and the burning of the Temple.

After they captured the city, Nevuzaradan commanded his troops to exit and then reenter the city, giving the impression that there were many more troops than there actually were, thereby scaring the Jews into giving up without a fight.[4]

After that, the Babylonians went on an immensely cruel killing rampage, which included pillaging the city and other abominable acts they committed against the people.

They pitied no one. They killed the young men and women along with the old people. The honored people with the regular ones. Even the small babies were brutally murdered. They took the babies and smashed their heads against the rocks to kill them. Our sages witnessed nine *kav* of children's brains on one rock.[5] Others saw 300 babies hanged on one branch.[6]

They didn't only kill; they destroyed the city. They completely razed the houses and palaces, the walls and streets, and also burned

---

children from hitting their pupils, even lightly, during this time period. Even a light rap could have disastrous results if this evil power got involved. Rabbi Shmuel bar Nachmani went even further. He called to end the day's lessons during the fourth hour of the day that this period begins. He was worried that one of the teachers might hit one of his students out of habit, and that could be dangerous.

4. Pesichta 23
5. Gittin 58.
6. Eichah Rabba 5:13

them.[7] The Jews' Edomite neighbors stood on the side and encouraged them, "Raze it to the foundations!"[8] They burned Tzidkiyahu's palace and the 480 *shuls*.

Some of the people managed to escape to the mountains and deserts, but not many. The people were not strong, healthy people, but rather walking skeletons starved by the years of siege, and, therefore, couldn't escape easily. Most of the people were mercilessly slaughtered.

Of the people that escaped, many were caught. The Babylonians didn't give up on their prey easily and chased after the people in the deserts and valleys, the hills and forests, anywhere they could. Whoever was found was killed. The Babylonians were so intent on catching everyone that when they heard that many people had escaped to the forest, they burned down all the trees in order to "smoke out" the survivors and kill them.[9]

Even those who actually managed to flee didn't fare much better. As an example, there were 80,000 *Pirchei Kehuna*, young *Kohanim*, who managed to escape the enemy soldiers and run to the people of Yishmael,[10] carrying golden shields from the treasuries of the *Bais Hamikdash*Bais HaMikdash.

The Yishmaelim acted as if the Jews were their beloved relatives, offering them food and drink. They served them salty foods in order to increase their thirst and then gave them flasks that looked as if they were full of water but were actually full of air.

---

7. Melachim II 25:9
8. Tehillim 137:7
9. Eichah Rabba 4:22
10. Eichah Rabba 2:4

The *Kohanim* had just left the severe lack of food and drink in Yerushalayim and asked to drink first. The Yishmaelim told them it was better for them to eat first and then drink as much as they wanted. The *Pirchei Kohanim* listened and ate the salty food until they were desperately thirsty. When they tried to drink, they drank the air instead. They died immediately, as the air burst their stomachs.

The people of Edom also caused the Jews suffering. A *mil* away from where the Babylonian soldiers fought, they waited to kill anyone who managed to escape. It wasn't their war, but they grabbed the opportunity to kill Jews and happily helped the Babylonians.[11]

The murder and plunder went on for three weeks. Had the Jews done *teshuva* even at this point, theyBais HaMikdash would still have been saved. But they didn't....

On the seventh of Av,[12] an angel came down from heaven[13] and put his feet on the walls of the Temple and broke them, crying, "Let the enemies come into the house of the Master who isn't inside and pillage it and destroy it. Let them come into the vineyard and harvest its grapes; the Watchman has abandoned it. They should not praise themselves saying they captured it.... A captured city they have captured, a killed nation they have killed."

The enemies came into theBais HaMikdash *Mikdash* and set up their command in the gates of that hallowed building. They gathered on the *bima*, the platform where King Shlomo would sit and ask the advice of the elders. They sat in the same place and took advice and planned... but how horrible their plans were! They were planning how to burn the Holy Temple!

---

11. Yalkut Ovadia 549
12. Taanis 29.
13. Pesikta 26

It may seem like it was a simple thing to destroy the Bais HaMikdash after the city had been captured. *Chazal* tell us, though, that it was actually impossible, had Hashem not chosen to look the other way and allow the *goyim* to destroy it, promising not to take revenge on them right then.[14]

Just as Yerushalayim was never captured, but was **given** over to the Babylonians, so too was the Bais HaMikdash. *Chazal* tell us[15] that when Nevuzaradan was about to burn the *Mikdash*, an angel came before Hashem, saying, "Master of the World, are You going to allow this wicked man to boast that he destroyed God's house? If You've decreed that Your house should be destroyed, then it is better if You send down a fire from heaven and don't let someone else do it!"

Hashem accepted the argument of the angel and sent a fire from heaven to destroy the Bais HaMikdash. The Bais HaMikdash tried to go up in one piece to the heavens, but it was thrown back down.

Nevuzaradan never burned the Bais HaMikdash. Hashem Himself did. Nevuzaradan was nothing but a puppet. By the way of a parable, he ground flour that was already ground… killed a dead lion… burned a burnt city.

Truthfully, it was to *Bnai Yisrael*'s benefit that God chose to allow the *Mikdash* to be destroyed.

We find that when the Bais Hamikdash was destroyed, Assaf the poet sang,[16] "A song unto Assaf. God, the gentiles have come into Your inheritance!" *Chazal*, in the Midrash,[17] question

---

14. Pesichta 24
15. Eichah Rabba 1:41
16. Tehillim 79:1
17. Eichah Rabba 4:14

the wording – a song unto Assaf? It should say a lamentation! He should be mourning the entrance of the gentiles into the Holy Temple, not singing!

The rabbis give a parable to the situation about a king who prepared an elaborate wedding for his son. He built a special hall and decorated it elegantly. He prepared a special feast in honor of the occasion on decorative tables that were built especially for the occasion.

Moments before the ceremony was supposed to take place, the king found out that his son had become delinquent. In his rage, the king went to the hall, tore the tablecloths, broke the tables, threw the golden vessels with the food on them to the floor and even ordered that the wedding hall he had so carefully built be destroyed.

When the prince's confidante saw what the king was doing, he took a flute and began to play and sing. The people who were present thought he was mad. "This is the time you pick to sing? You should be bemoaning the situation!" they said.

The man answered them, "You are mistaken. If the king wouldn't have diffused his anger on the wedding hall, he would have vented his fury on his son! Now that the king is destroying wood and stones, I am sure his son will not have to feel the full brunt of the king's wrath."

That's the parable. The parallel is exact. If Hashem wouldn't have destroyed the Temple, that is to say, if Hashem hadn't vented His anger on wood and stones, the Jews would have been deserving of total annihilation! Now that the *Mikdash* was destroyed, the judgment against them was less severe and they weren't totally destroyed.

Therefore, when Assaf saw that theBais HaMikdash *Bais Hamikdash* was destroyed, that the gentiles had entered the sanctuary, he hurried and sang a song of gratitude and praise to God. He thanked Him for taking revenge on sticks and stones and not destroying the

The Period of the Three Weeks | 65

Jewish people. The destruction of the Temple was actually for the Jews' benefit.

The *Mikdash* was only able to be destroyed after the *Shechina* had left. The *Shechina* leaving was a slow process that took place over years. Hashem slowly went farther and farther away from the *Mikdash*, hoping that *Bnai Yisrael* would do *teshuva* and He could return. Hashem left in ten steps.[18]

The first step[19] already took place in the sixth year of Yechanya's exile.[20] Hashem moved His place from the right *keruv*, one of the two images that were on the *aron hakodesh*, to the left *keruv*.[21] There He waited for *Bnai Yisrael* to repent.

The second stage was when the *Shechina* moved from the left *keruv* to the threshold of the *Kodesh Kedoshim*, on the wall that separates the *heichal* and the inner *Kodesh*. *Bnai Yisrael* still stuck to their evil ways.

The third stage[22] was when Hashem went from the entrance of the *heichal* back to the *keruvim* that were in the *Kodesh Kedoshim*. It was as if Hashem returned to His home to say goodbye. As a king who left his temple in anger, but returns to bid it a tearful goodbye, Hashem went back to the *Kodesh Kedoshim* and cried[23] goodbye.

---

18. Pesichta 25; Rosh Hashana 31.
19. This is how the steps are described in the Midrash. In the **Gemara**, the first stage is described as the Shechina leaving the kapores, the covering of the aron, to one of the keruvim.
20. Yechezkel 9:3
21. Maharzav. The Eitz Yosef explains that the Shechina was originally on both keruvim, not just one.
22. This stage isn't mentioned in the Gemara.
23. Obviously, when we speak of Hashem crying, we can't literally apply a physical concept to Him. It is only to help us understand the ideas we are speaking about (see Anaf Yosef).

66 | On Your Walls, O Jerusalem

Bnai Yisrael didn't change, so Hashem had to go to the fourth stage.[24] The *Shechina* exiled itself to the entrance of the *heichal*. At the fifth stage He left to the courtyard of the *azara*.

From there, in the sixth step, Hashem left to the roof of the *Bais Hamikdash*Bais HaMikdash. After each step, He waited, hoping that the Jews would return to Him.

Hashem then went to the altar that was in the courtyard of the *azara*, thus completing the seventh stage.[25] From there, Hashem went to the walls of the *azara*. The ninth step was from the walls to the city of Yerushalayim. And from Yerushalayim to outside the city to Har Hazeisim[26] was the tenth and final step. There, Hashem stayed for three and a half years, waiting for the Jews' repentance. During those years,

---

24. This stage isn't mentioned in the Gemara.

25. The order is reversed in the Gemara. There it is explained that the Shechina first went to the mizbeiach and then to the roof. The mefarshim (Anaf Yosef) explain that it is more likely that since the threshold of the heichal faced the courtyard that the Shechina would move to the mizbeiach that was in the courtyard and only after go up to the roof, rather than the Shechina first going up and then coming back down to the chatzer and the mizbeiach. According to the Midrash, it makes sense to say that the Shechina first went up to the roof, meaning the roof of the heichal, and then went to the middle of the courtyard. That is more logical than saying that the Shechina went to the chatzer and then went back to the roof of the heichal.

26. The Gemara says that after going to Har Hazeisim, the Shechina went to the desert. The Yefeh Anaf explains that the Midrash disagrees, seeing no reason for the Shechina to go to the desert, a place where there were no Jews. Still, once we see that two of the stages mentioned above were not mentioned in the Gemara, and that there are two stops added in the Gemara that are not in the Midrash, both of the sources come to a total of ten stops.

The Period of the Three Weeks | 67

a heavenly voice[27] would announce, "Return, sinful children! Return to Me and I will return to you!"

When there was still no repentance, Hashem had no choice but to leave to the heavens until it was time for the final redemption,[28] in order to save the Jews from destruction. Out of His great love for the Jews He waited and waited, but to no avail.

After weeks of the cruelest of murders, the Babylonians turned to pillage. They took all the vessels of the Holy Temple to Bavel.[29] They left nothing. Even the copper pillars of the *Mikdash* were broken and taken to Bavel![30]

When the Babylonians went in to the *heichal*, the Amonim and Moavim[31] went with them. They harbored a tremendous hatred for the Jews whose laws didn't allow them to become part of the Jewish people.[32]

---

27. The Maharzav explains that this was not literally a voice from heaven, but rather that the fact that the Shechina left Klal Yisrael was enough of a cry for them to realize that they had to repent.
28. In Alon Bachut, it is brought in the Eitz Yosef that the Shechina left the Land of Israel until the days of the final redemption. During the period of the Second Temple there was no hashra'as hashechina. Hashem's presence did not rest in the Temple. There was no aron kodesh, keruvim, urim v'tumim or heavenly fire. The Alshich, though, says the Shechina has only left until Bnai Yisrael does teshuva and asks for Hashem to come back.
29. There is a difference of opinion amongst the sages about what happened to the aron. Some say that even the aron was taken to Bavel. Others say that the aron was hidden by Yoshiyahu the king well before the destruction of the Temple.
30. Divrei Hayamim II 25
31. Pesichta 9
32. Eichah Rabba 1:38

Therefore, while the Jews' other enemies were ransacking the *Mikdash*, trying to grab as many worldly goods as possible, the Amonim and Moavim concentrated on desecrating and destroying the holy Torah, wherein is written the commandment not to allow them to convert.

The Midrash brings a parable to explain what they were doing. Imagine a fire ravaging the king's castle. Most people would use the time to grab as much as possible from the king's treasure houses. The king's servant, though, would rather spend his time searching for the document that states he is a slave and destroy it, thus bringing about his freedom and restoring his honor.

Besides wanting to erase the *mitzvos* that were negative about them, they decided that they would disgrace the Torah and the Jews' religion at all costs. Their opportunity came soon enough. When they came in to the *heichal* and saw the golden *keruvim* that were on the *aron ha'eidus*,[33] they took them and put them in a cage with holes that allowed viewing from all sides.[34]

They took this and paraded all around Yerushalayim announcing, "Here is the answer to all those who claim that the Jews don't worship idols! We found these golden images in the Holy of Holies – the direction to which the Jews perform their holy service and bring their

---

33. The Maharzav explains that this Midrash fits in only with the opinion that the aron was exiled to Bavel. It doesn't fit with the opinion that King Yoshiyahu hid the aron. The Yefeh Anaf (brought in the Eitz Yosef) explains that these weren't the keruvim that Moshe Rabbainu made, but the image of the keruvim that Shlomo Hamelech drew on the walls of the heichal. According to the Yefeh Anaf, the gentiles peeled the pictures off the wall and took those around the city.

34. Matnos kehuna.

sacrifices! These are the idols that the Jews worship. All people are the same — they all serve idols!"

One of the most horrific and repulsive stories of the *churban* is the story of the avenging of the blood of Zecharia Hanavi.[35]

In Yerushalayim, there was a true prophet whose spiritual perfection was so great that we have no way of fathoming who he was. His name was Zecharia ben Yehoyada. He was a very great man, in all senses of the word. Firstly, he was the son of Yehoyada who was a *Kohein Gadol*.[36]

Secondly, his father was King Yehoram's father-in-law. King Yehoram was the grandfather of Yoash who ruled in the days of Zecharia. So we see that Zecharia himself was the grandson of a king as well as the second cousin of the king who was ruling at the time. Zecharia was also a *navi*. *Chazal* also say that he was a judge for his generation.[37] To summarize, Zecharia had *yichus*. He also personally reached incredible spiritual heights.

We have absolutely no concept of what he did wrong, but *Chazal* do fault Zecharia for talking down to the people just the very smallest bit. He rebuked the people in a way that implied that the situation was hopeless and that the chance of their ever returning to their previous level was next to nil.[38] He implied that Hashem had left them because they had left Him.

---

35. Pesichta 23; Gittin 57:
36. The Maharzav explains that it doesn't mean that Zecharia himself was a Kohein Gadol, but rather that he was the son of Yehoyada the Kohein Gadol.
37. The Maharzav says that it requires further investigation where Chazal learn this from.
38. Eitz Yosef in the name of Yifei Ainaim

70 | On Your Walls, O Jerusalem

Zecharia wasn't afraid of rebuking the people in public, since he knew he was a very respectable man and the date he picked for his rebuke was Yom Kippur that fell on Shabbos. He was certain that no one would harm the leader of the generation, a prophet of illustrious lineage, on such a holy day.[39]

None of this helped, though. Not his standing, his prophetic level, his greatness, not even the tremendous sanctity of the day. Yoash, the ruling king, ordered the people to stone him in the holy *azara* of the *Kohanim* in the *Mikdash*, where entrance is permitted to *Kohanim* only.

Before his soul departed, Zecharia uttered one last sentence. "Hashem will see and judge!"[40] It was as if he was saying, "Master of the World, You know that I was only killed after prophesizing in Your name, fulfilling Your command. It is only right that You avenge my blood!"[41] The revenge came during the destruction of the Temple and was dreadful, as we will soon see.

When the Jews killed Zecharia, they sinned in seven severe ways. They killed a *Kohein* – disgracing the *Kehuna*. They killed a prophet – disgracing his prophecy. They killed a judge – disgracing his Torah. They shed innocent blood. They caused a *chilul Hashem* – the gentiles saw that the Jews killed their leader who rebuked them on the holiest of days. They made the *azara* impure with *tumas meis*. If someone is not allowed into the *azara* when he is *tamei meis*, ritually impure from contact with a dead person, of course you can't allow a corpse itself in. And all of this was done on Yom Kippur that falls on a Shabbos, the most holy of days.[42]

---

39. Rashi on Divrei Hayamim II 24:20
40. Divrei Hayamim II 24:20
41. Rashi on Divrei Hayamim II 24:20
42. There are eight sins listed here. The commentators disagree which of these sins is not counted amongst the seven. The Yerushalmi in Taanis

The Period of the Three Weeks | 71

Hashem couldn't overlook such a heinous crime. Zecharia's death had to be avenged. In order that the deed shouldn't be forgotten, He made the people feel an inappropriate pride[43] in what they had done which made them refuse to cover the *navi*'s blood. Jewish law requires that the blood of the animals that were sacrificed be covered with dirt above and below, but the blood of the prophet they left on a hard rock in the *azara* and didn't even cover it with dirt!

The time for vengeance came a few generations later, during the destruction of the Temple. When Nevuzaradan entered the *heichal*, Hashem hinted to the blood that the time had come for revenge.[44] The blood began to boil and bubble.[45]

Nevuzaradan saw the strange sight of the boiling blood and asked the *Kohanim* present what the blood was.

The *Kohanim* were afraid to answer truthfully, worried that Nevuzaradan would use it as an excuse for bloodshed. They told him

---

(perek 4 end) doesn't count the sin of desecrating God's name. The Eitz Yosef says that the desecration of God's name and the desecration of Yom Kippur were counted as one sin. The punishment for the desecration of Shabbos is stoning. The punishment for the desecration of Yom Kippur is kareis. The harsher punishment includes the lighter one. The Radal, though, explains that the sin of "innocent blood" isn't part of the list. If he was a prophet they would be deserving of the death penalty and it wouldn't matter if he was a Kohein, prophet or judge. It comes out that the fact that there was "innocent blood" was what caused the first three sins – that they killed a Kohein, navi, and judge.

43. According to the commentary Eitz Yosef and others
44. Koheles Rabba 10:4
45. According to the Gemara it seems that the blood was boiling continuously from the day he was killed until the above incident with Nevuzaradan.

it was the blood of the cows, goats, rams and sheep that were brought as sacrifices.

Nevuzaradan didn't believe them. The sight of the boiling blood made him realize that something else was happening. He killed cows, goats, rams and sheep to compare their blood to the blood that was bubbling. He soon concluded that the boiling blood was not the blood of animals that had been sacrificed.

Nevuzaradan was now intent on discovering the history of the blood. He threatened the *Kohanim* that if they didn't tell him the honest truth about the source of the blood, he would comb their flesh with iron combs!

The threat worked. They answered, "What should we say? We had a prophet that rebuked us for our sins. Not only did we not listen to him and not improve our ways, but we even killed him! Since then, for many years,[46] the blood has not been swallowed up by the ground, and now it has even begun to boil!"[47]

The evil Nevuzaradan decided that, as a supposed act of goodwill, he was going to pacify the prophet's blood, whatever the cost....

The cost was very great, indeed.

Nevuzaradan brought the Great Sanhedrin and the Lesser Sanhedrin, who were the wise men of the generation, and slaughtered

---

46. According to the calculations of the years the kings ruled, it was over 250 years.

47. From the Midrash here it seems like the blood boiled continuously from the day Zecharia was killed. This is what the Kohanim said that it's been many years and the blood hasn't rested. In the Midrash Koheles that we mentioned previously it seems that Hashem only hinted to the blood to boil now. It has to be, therefore, that the blood wasn't boiling before. In the Midrash there, this sentence that was attributed to the Kohanim is left out.

them on Zecharia's blood, causing their blood to touch his. The blood didn't stop boiling.

Then the *rasha* brought young men and women to kill on the *navi*'s blood. The blood wasn't pacified. He brought the *tinokos shel bais rabban*, the young children, and slaughtered them. And then **eighty thousand** *Pirchei Kehuna* were killed. The blood continued to boil.

When he saw what was happening, Nevuzaradan turned to the blood and said, "Zecharia, Zecharia, look at the good, exalted ones of the nation of Israel, the wise ones of the generation, the young men and women, the young children *Kohanim*, and even the small children – I've killed them already. Do you want me to slaughter everyone? I am letting you know that I will not stop my killing rampage until you rest from your fury!" After these words were said, the blood immediately rested.

By the end of the day, Nevuzaradan killed in the courtyard of the *azara* on one rock an immeasurable amount of people. One of the elders of Yerushalayim[48] said that the amount of people killed reached 940,000!

Besides this, Nevuzaradan killed another 2,100,000 people in a certain valley! All together, on that day, more than 3,000,000 people were killed[49] – in retribution for Zecharia's murder. The prophecy of the *navi* Hoshea[50] had come true, "Bloods touched bloods."

---

48. Gittin 57:

49. It seems like this is true from the Maharsha who adds that the blood rose from the valley because there were so many dead and reached the blood of the navi in the azara, as it says, "Bloods touched bloods."

50. Hoshea 4:2

74 | On Your Walls, O Jerusalem

The horrific killing spree was so terrible that even Nevuzaradan was shaken up and had thoughts of *teshuva*. He said to himself, "If because of the murder of one Jewish soul such a horrible decree was issued, that millions of men, women and children were slaughtered, it is unthinkable what my punishment will be for killing millions."[51]

Nevuzaradan actually did *teshuva* right then. He sent a gift[52] to his home with a detailed will[53] attached, and ran away to become a righteous convert![54]

As we mentioned before,[55] the Babylonians used the *bima* in the *azara* as the hub of their activities in planning how to destroy the *Mikdash*. They planned there for three days. In the meantime, they ate and drank in this holy place and even acted disgracefully and sinned.[56]

---

51. Even though the person who was killed was innocent and a prophet, judge and Kohein, and there was justification for killing the people that Nevuzaradan killed, there is still logic to the kal v'chomer that he drew. There must have been righteous people in the generation amongst the people that he killed. You can't assume that they deserved to die for Zecharia's death, as Zecharia was killed a number of generations previously (Eitz Yosef in the name of Yefas Toar).
52. Eitz Yosef and also Matnas Kehuna in the name of the editor
53. Rashi Gittin 57:
54. In a number of Midrashim, it says that Nevuzaradan led the captives to Bavel. (See Eichah Rabba 5:5 and others.) It is hard to reconcile this with the fact that he converted. It could be that he didn't decide to change his ways until later, after the exile, because until then he was caught up in the throes of war and massacre.
55. Pesikta 26
56. Taanis 29.

The Period of the Three Weeks | 75

All their planning proved unnecessary. While sitting there, they saw four angels come down from the heavens with torches in their hands which they used to set the four sides of the *heichal* on fire!

It was on the ninth of Av towards evening that they started the fire. The *Mikdash* wasn't burnt by humans. The Master of the palace Himself, God in heaven, destroyed His own house and lit in on fire when the time came and it was necessary.

Actually, Tisha B'Av was a day that had been readied for calamity already for many generations past.[57] It was on this day that the spies came back and spoke against the Land of Israel. On that day, the Jewish people sat and cried, every man in front of his tent. Hashem said to them, "You're crying for no reason today, crying that is inappropriate. I am going to cause you to cry for all generations on this day; I'll give you something to cry about!"

It was on the first day of the week[58] that the *Mikdash* was destroyed, right after a *shmitta* year, during the time that the guard of Yehoyariv was on call, while the *Leviim* were singing,[59] "And He brings upon them their own iniquity, and He cuts them off in their own wickedness".Hhh[60] Before they got to the final phrase of the verse, "Our God cuts them off," they were captured.

The *Kohein Gadol*, when he saw the fire catch in the *Mikdash*, took the keys of the *Mikdash* and threw them to the heavens. He called

---

57. Taanis 29.
58. Erchin 11:
59. Look in the Gemara there why the Leviim were singing this when it wasn't the shir shel yom, the song of the day, for the first day of the week. This certainly wasn't the song of the daily offering, as the daily offering had stopped from the seventeenth of Tammuz. It was the song sung on an olas nedava, an optional sacrifice.
60. Tehillim 94:23

out, "Master of the World, these are the keys to Your house. Apparently, I wasn't a worthy guardian, so You've taken away my position!"

The *Kohein Gadol* tried to go out to his fellow *Kohanim*, but the enemy didn't let him. They caught him and killed him near the *mizbeiach*, the place where he had brought the daily sacrifice.

His daughter, seeing what was happening, followed after her father, screaming, "Oh, Father! My beloved!" Her end was the same as her father's. She was murdered near the altar, and her blood mixed with that of her father, the *Kohein Gadol*.

They weren't the only two that died. The rest of the *Kohanim* were also killed, each with the people of his guard. Groups and groups of *Pirchei Kehuna*, the children, gathered on the roof of the *heichal* with the keys of the *Mikdash* in their hands. They said to God, "Master of the World, since we didn't merit to be faithful treasurers, take back the keys!" They threw the keys up to heaven and a hand came out and accepted them. They jumped into the flames where they found their deaths in the *Mikdash* they had served all their lives.

The *Leviim* who saw the *Mikdash*Bais HaMikdash being burnt threw their violins and trumpets into the blazing fire, jumping into the flames afterwards.

The maidens of Yerushalayim that had woven the curtain covering of the entrance to the *Kodesh Kedoshim* jumped to their deaths so that the enemies wouldn't defile them.

The fire burned in the Temple for the whole of the tenth of Av, until sunset. Most of the *Mikdash* was burnt on the tenth. Since the calamity started on the ninth, that day was established as the day of mourning.

The Period of the Three Weeks

The Temple that had been the joy of the Jewish people for four hundred and ten years was gone! The *Shechina* had left us!

We now have to learn about the long and bloodstained exile.

6

On the Shores of Bavel

Many of the people were killed in horrible ways. The rest of the people of Yerushalayim and the other cities of Yehuda were taken captive to Bavel.

Only a very small number of indigent people were left in Yerushalayim, to whom Nevuchadnezar left the vineyards and fields. Nevuchadnezar appointed Gedalia ben Achikam ben Shafan the scribe to rule over them. Gedalia had left the city before its destruction and went to Nevuchadnezar's camp at the advice of Yirmiyahu,[1] and Nevuchadnezar trusted him.

The rest of the people were taken down to Bavel. These people who had so recently trusted in their bows and swords now had their hands tied behind their backs with the sinews of their bows[2] as they were led to Bavel.[3] While they walked, bitter tears rolled down their cheeks. Because their hands were tied behind them, they couldn't wipe away the tears. The salty tears seared their flesh like the pain of boils.

---

1. Yirmiyahu 39:13, see Rashi there
2. Eichah Rabba 1:25
3. Pesichta 24

The travails of the trip were excruciating. They scraped their skin on thorns; their legs hit the mountain rocks. Many died on the way; others were maimed or lost limb after limb. Nevuzaradan wasn't moved by their plight. He continued to press them, not giving them a moment's rest. *Chazal* say that the Jews were not even allowed to rest one minute[4] from the time they left *Eretz Yisrael* until they came to the River of Peras. Nevuzaradan also didn't even allow them to bury the dead.

He was following the advice that Nevuchadnezar[5] gave him before he went up to fight Yerushalayim. "Know," Nevuchadnezar told him, "that the God of the Jews is waiting for His sons to return to Him. Even after you capture the city, you must know that there is a possibility that the Jews will repent. If they do, their God may be pacified and bring them back to their land, while kicking you out in disgrace. Therefore, be careful that you don't let them have even a moment's rest, to make sure they don't have the opportunity to pray and do *teshuva*!"

Even the horribly wicked man, Nevuchadnezar himself, realized the incredible power of *teshuva*.

Nevuzaradan took the advice to heart and didn't let the exiles rest at all. If someone asked to stay still for a moment, Nevuzaradan would chop him up limb by limb as a warning to the others. He wanted to make sure they had no time to call out to God.

It was only when they reached the shores of Bavel, the shores of the River of Peras, that Nevuzaradan told his soldiers to let up on the Jews. He was sure that they had gone far enough away from their land that their God would not have mercy on them and redeem them.

---

4. Pesikta 28
5. Eichah Rabba 5:5

80 | On Your Walls, O Jerusalem

Before they reached the shores of Bavel,[6] they passed the borders of Amon and Moav. The people of those countries came out to see what was happening. When they saw the Jews screaming and moaning in pain, they mockingly said, "Why are you upset? Why are you crying? You're going back to your father's house, after all! Your ancestors lived on the other side of the river, and now you are going to Bavel, which is on the other side of the river."

It wasn't only the way the Babylonians and the people along the way treated them that caused them to feel humiliated. The Babylonians made them walk to Bavel without clothing.[7] It was only when they reached the Peras River and the people of Bari saw their shame that they were given clothing. The people of Bari sent male and female slaves to Nevuchadnezar without clothing, saying, "Obviously the king prefers slaves without clothes!" The king then realized that he was degrading himself along with the captives and commanded that the Jews be dressed.[8]

They didn't find any peace near the Peras River either. The river itself killed more people than the Babylonians had killed. The Jewish people were used to drinking rain water and spring water. When they reached the turbid water of the river, incredibly thirsty, they began to drink. They died from the water.

The wicked Nevuchadnezar made sure to torture any survivors.[9] When he saw the captives were walking upright, he commanded the Torah scrolls they were carrying be taken and made into sacks. The

---

6. Tzefania 2:8, see Rashi there

7. Pesikta 28

8. See Yalkut Tehillim Remez 887 where it describes the reward the people of Bari got for the kindness they showed the Jews.

9. Yalkut Tehillim Remez 883

captives were forced to fill the sacks with sand from the beaches of Peras. The Babylonians then put the sacks on the Jews' backs in order to weigh them down and bend their backs.[10] The broken, miserable children of Zion finally cried out to Hashem and their weeping reached heaven.

At that time, when Hashem saw how the enemy was terribly mistreating His children, He wanted to return the world to nothingness. "I created this whole world for *Yisrael*! If this is how they are being treated, why did I create the world?" Hashem claimed. When the angels came to pacify Him, Hashem declared, "I don't need to be consoled! Go down and help My children!"

The angels went down to help the Jewish people with their troubles. Out of His love for His people, even Hashem went down, so to speak, to help them. His mercy was aroused even when they sinned and He was punishing them.

When they got to the shores of Bavel, Nevuchadnezar with all of his officers was sitting on a royal ship with an orchestra playing.[11] The *rasha* turned to the *Leviim* and said, "Sing to me from the songs of Zion![12] Play before the idols those songs you used to play before your God in His temple!"[13]

---

10. It says in the Midrash (Eichah Rabba 5:13) that Nevuchadnezar put grinding stones on the backs of the young Jewish men and that is how they were brought to Bavel. Until that time, one couldn't find large stones like the ones used for millstones in all of Bavel. After the churban, they were able to find these large stones – because the men carried them to Bavel on their backs!

11. As we said before, during the war Nevuchadnezar was in Dafne in Antiochia. It seems he returned to Bavel to celebrate his victory with his officers and parade in front of his people.

12. Yalkut Tehillim 883

13. Pesikta 28

The *Leviim* refused. Not only did they refuse, but, with tremendous strength of character, they all bit off their thumbs so they wouldn't be able to play on their musical instruments. It was an awesome sight. All of the *Leviim*, every last one, hung their violins on the willows that grew on the shores of the Peras River[14] and then put their fingers in their mouths and bit them off so as not to disgrace the honor of the King of kings in front of idols! When Nevuchadnezar repeated his request to the *Leviim*, they showed him their mutilated thumbs and said, "Look what happened – our fingers have been cut off!"

One can better understand what happened through a parable. There was a king who was married to a woman who was also of royal lineage. One day the king asked the queen to pour him a drink. She refused, and the king threw her out of the house. After she had left the palace, she married a simple, crass man who was ugly and covered in boils. One day, the man asked her to pour him a drink. The woman declared, "If I had only poured my first husband, the king, a drink, I would have remained until this day in the royal palace surrounded by luxury. And now that I have been sent away and lost my honor because I didn't pour a drink for the king, do you think I'll do it for an ugly, boil infested man?!"

This is what the *Leviim* said in their hearts, "If we would have sung to our God while we were still in our land, we wouldn't have been exiled and would have remained honorable. Now that we have been exiled because we wouldn't sing before Him, we should sing before idols? Never!" Resolutely, they cut off their fingers with their teeth!

Nevuchadnezar realized that it wasn't a coincidence that the *Leviim*'s fingers were cut off on the way to Bavel, but that it was the

---

14. Tehillim 137, see Rashi there.

Leviim's intention to make sure they didn't fulfill his request. He ordered many of them killed. Their corpses were piled high – all because they refused to sing the songs of Zion.

And the *Leviim*, as well as the rest of the Jews, were joyous! They were thrilled that they had passed the test and not desecrated the songs of their God in that foreign land. Because of their courageous act, the *Leviim* merited returning to see Yerushalayim rebuilt.

At the time the *Mikdash* was destroyed,[15] Yirmiyahu wasn't in Yerushalayim. He had gone to Anosos, at Hashem's command, to buy a field from his uncle Chanamel. As long as he was in the city, his merit protected it from being destroyed.

Yirmiyahu was sure that Hashem's mercy had been aroused and that He had decided not to fulfill the harsh decree, so he went happily to Anosos. When he returned, he found Yerushalayim destroyed and the Temple burning.

Yirmiyahu had actually known that Nevuchadnezar was going to destroy the Temple from long before. *Chazal*[16] tell us that Yirmiyahu and Nevuchadnezar knew each other for a very long time, from the time they were youths. At the time Nevuchadnezar was very poor. Nevuchadnezar had then declared, "If only I would be king of the whole world, I would go up to Yerushalayim and burn the Holy Temple and the whole city. I would kill the children of Zion, and whoever was left I would take into captivity."

---

15. Pesikta 26

16. Bais Akad Hagados part I, brought down in the book Koros Ameinu V'Hamikdashim

Yirmiyahu realized that all that Nevuchadnezar had spoken was going to come true! Yirmiyahu answered him, "If you do come to rule the whole world, at least give me Yerushalayim!"

Nevuchadnezar refused, saying, "I won't give you Yerushalayim!"

"If not, at least give me the *Bais Hamikdash*!" Yirmiyahu pleaded.

"I will definitely not give up on burning the *Bais Hamikdash*!" he declared.

"So give me the Sanhedrin!" Yirmiyahu suggested. When that request was also refused, he asked for the *tinokos shel bais rabban*, the young schoolchildren. This request was also denied. Nevuchadnezar would not give Yirmiyahu any of the things he requested when his dream came true.

There was one concession that Nevuchadnezar made. He agreed that on the day that he conquered Yerushalayim, he would let Yirmiyahu take out from the city whatever he wanted from midday until evening. That was all he would agree to. The two youths made a deal.

Time passed and Nevuchadnezar did conquer the holy city and burn the Temple. Had Yirmiyahu been in Yerushalayim then, he could have reminded the cruel conqueror of the promise of his youth. But Yirmiyahu wasn't in the city. By the time Yirmiyahu came back it was already towards evening. The time to ask Nevuchadnezar to fulfill his promise had passed.[17]

When Yirmiyahu saw smoke coming from the *Mikdash* in the distance, he assumed that the Jews had resumed offering sacrifices and

---

17. Although it says in the Midrash that Yirmiyahu rushed to get back to Yerushalayim to have him fulfill his promise, he didn't manage to get there. The Midrashim of Chazal that are mentioned here seem to say that Yirmiyahu didn't know about the churban at all.

that it was that smoke that he saw. When he climbed on the walls, he saw what was actually happening and became aware of the great tragedy taking place.

"Master of the World! You seduced me into leaving Yerushalayim and I fell for it!" He immediately went to follow the path of the exiled. He knew which way they had gone by the pools of blood and pieces of limbs that were scattered along their path.

"My beloved children, how did this happen?" he cried bitterly as he caught up to them.[18]

Yirmiyahu followed the Children of Israel as they made their way into exile, his heart going out to them.[19] He was aware there was nothing he could do to help them. He knew that they could have avoided the tragedy had they listened to him and repented. He also knew that now it was too late. The decree had been fulfilled; there was no going back.

Yirmiyahu saw a group of young men shackled in collars, tied together with a rope, being led like animals. Yirmiyahu came and stuck his head in the rope. "I am with you in your trouble!" That was the message he wanted to give the downtrodden men.

Nevuzaradan, though, as we mentioned before,[20] had clear instructions from Nevuchadnezar about how to treat Yirmiyahu. He had to make sure nothing bad happened to him. He couldn't let Yirmiyahu continue – it went against the commands he had received. He removed the collar from the *navi*'s neck.

When he saw that Yirmiyahu was trying to put it back on, he said to him, "I don't understand. You are free. Why do you put a yoke on

---

18. Pesikta 26
19. Pesichta 34
20. See two chapters previous

yourself? It means one of three things about you. It could be you are a false prophet and you never thought that all the bad things you prophesized would come true. Now that you see how immense the tragedy is, you want to mourn with the rest of your people.

"It could be that you are trying to show that you are not impressed by all this suffering and that you are prepared to accept it on yourself.

"Or it could be you are a murderer. You want me to cross the command of my king Nevuchadnezar and thereby cause my death indirectly.

"These are the only three ways I can explain your behavior." When Nevuzaradan finished, he added, "If you want to go to Bavel with the rest of your nation, you are free to do so, but you have to know I will not let you suffer with them. I have clear instructions to that effect from my king. If you want to go back to the Land of Israel and stay with the remnant of the people under Gedalia's leadership, I will also permit you to."

Crying and with a heavy heart, Yirmiyahu returned to the Land of Israel to be a support for the people who were left.

There was actually another astounding reason why Yirmiyahu decided to go back to *Eretz Yisrael*. Hashem said to him, "You and I have to be at *Bnai Yisrael*'s side to support them. There are some that stayed in *Eretz Yisrael* and some that went to Bavel. You remain with one of the groups, and I will be with the other. You, Yirmiyahu, decide who you will go with."

It was a very hard decision for Yirmiyahu. He knew how desperately the Jews going into exile needed someone to encourage and support them. He understood, though, that whatever help he would be able to give was nothing compared to the protection and help that they would get if their loving Father, their King, whose love was limitless even during the time of punishment, went with them.

Yirmiyahu turned to leave. The exiles saw that he was departing. They now understood that all the years he had rebuked them it had been out of love, and that he had been correct. They cried out to him,[21] "Yirmiyahu the prophet, are you just going and leaving us?"

Yirmiyahu, pained, answered, "My beloved children, I bring heaven and earth as my witnesses, if you would have cried just once when you were in Yerushalayim, you never would have been exiled! Now it is too late, the decree has been sealed. Your God, though, is going with you to Bavel and is suffering with your pain… and He will bring you back!"

Thus, Yirmiyahu began his trip back to *Eretz Yisrael*. On the way, he encountered the awful scenes portraying just how great the tragedy was. He found body parts, fingers and legs that had been dismembered as the people suffered the tribulations of their journey.

Yirmiyahu, the prophet who had warned them of the upcoming catastrophes years before they happened and saw the people ignoring his exhortations, felt the tremendous pain of his brothers. He picked up the fingers he found on the way,[22] caressing and kissing them. He put them in his cloak and said, "*Oy*, my children! *Oy*, my children! Didn't I warn you? Why didn't you listen to me? Why didn't you mend your ways before this came to be?" That's how he walked back to *Eretz Yisrael* - picking up a limb, walking, picking up a finger, walking some more.

Finally, he reached the remnant of Jews that were under the leadership of Gedalia ben Achikam.

---

21. Pesikta 26
22. The commentators discuss at length how Yirmiyahu, who was a Kohein, was allowed to gather these limbs and why this wasn't subject to the prohibition of Kohanim coming in contact with the impurity of death.

Before they entered Bavel, Nevuchadnezar had treated the people with extreme cruelty. Many had died before reaching Bavel. But, once they arrived, Hashem made Nevuchadnezar have a change of heart. The captured Jews should have been slaves. Instead, Hashem had Nevuchadnezar grant them freedom and the choice to live and settle anywhere in the land of Bavel as free men.

The people were very poor, though. Besides the fact that they suffered tremendous hunger, they also did not have any belongings. They had no dishes and cutlery or pots.[23] Even when they could procure food, they didn't have the means to properly prepare it. They had no choice but to knead their dough in holes they dug in the earth. It's not hard to imagine how unappetizing that bread must have tasted, for as they mixed the dough, stones and dirt were mixed in as well.[24]

Actually, many years before the *churban*, Yechezkel the prophet had warned the people that they should prepare themselves for exile and organize possessions that would help them survive in a strange country. The people didn't believe him and didn't follow his advice. They said in their hearts, "The images he sees are for the very distant future. They are not something that will affect us!"[25] Now they were left unprepared.

Besides allowing the Jews to live as free men, there was another way that Hashem made their stay in Bavel easier. He made sure there would be the kind of food there that would allow them to continue to live the spiritual lives they were used to.[26] Forty years before the destruction of the Temple, Hashem had the Babylonians decide to plant

---

23. Eichah Rabba 1:22
24. Eichah Rabba 1:22
25. Yechezkel 12:27
26. Pesichta 34

sweet date trees. These date trees provided high quality food that gave the Jews the energy they needed to learn Torah. It is known that dates are good for *yishuv hadaas*, clear thinking, in Torah. These dates helped the Jews establish the greatest Torah community that ever existed outside the Land of Israel.

Furthermore, Hashem sent the animals of *Eretz Yisrael* to Bavel with the Jews. 700 species of fish went from the Land of Israel to Bavel through underground water channels! 800 species of kosher grasshoppers went with them! Countless numbers of fowl flew with *Bnai Yisrael* to *galus*. This was all done to make sure the Jews had the type of food they were always accustomed to.

When *Bnai Yisrael* later returned to *Eretz Yisrael*, all the animals returned with them, except one. The Shibuta fish was not able to go back. Its soft spine didn't allow it to swim to *Eretz Yisrael*, which is the highest country.[27]

We see how great Hashem's love for the people was! They were being sent to exile as a punishment, but still He prepared the ground for them so they would have what they needed to survive spiritually in a strange land. It was an awesome sight to see the Jews being led into exile with hoards of birds flying over them and thousands of grasshoppers jumping behind them. Hashem's love for them, even in their darkest hour, was tangible.

It wasn't just the food that Hashem worried about; there was a great expression of compassion in the date the exile took place and the way they were exiled.[28] Yehuda was exiled on the ninth of Av, as we know, in the hottest part of the summer. It was a gift to the Jews that they were not exiled during the rainy season. It would have meant

---

27. Eitz Yosef
28. Eichah Rabba 1:42

certain death to many more people had they had to deal with the cold weather. Their punishment was mixed with mercy. They were exiled, but not in inclement weather.

There were also two ways to reach Bavel. One was via the desert, the other via Armenia, a settled area. Hashem arranged it that they would travel through settled lands, where food was available, and not through the desert. This saved many people from dying of starvation.

The exile not only affected the people who were being brought from *Eretz Yisrael*, but also the people who had been exiled with Yechanya[29] eleven years earlier. They were forced against their will[30] to go out and greet the king with the rest of the Babylonians. They, too, had to join in the cheering, "Our king has won over the barbarians, empty nameless people!"

They had to wear holiday clothes and act as if they were thrilled that their courageous king had won, but under their white clothes, they wore the black clothes of mourning. In their hearts, there was nothing but mourning for the destruction of the Temple and the suffering of their people. They raised one hand in congratulations to the king, while the other hand hit their thigh in a sign of mourning.

Further, the people who had been exiled with Yechanya left behind family who suffered with the conquering of the land. This one left a father, this one a brother, that one a friend. When the newly expelled people reached Bavel, they hurried to find out what had happened to their relatives and loved ones.

The people had no good news to share. Most of the people of Yerushalayim had been slaughtered. They had no choice but to relate the horrible news of murder, starvation and captivity. Many of the

---

29. Pesichta 23
30. Eitz Yosef

people who had been exiled previously suddenly found themselves bereaved with nothing to cushion the blow!

It was a terribly sad time. On the other hand, it was good for the people that they had brethren in Bavel who could comfort them.[31] Hashem had sent them early to pave the way.

The Torah world, *Bnai Yisrael*'s guarantee of survival, had come before them with the exiles of Yechanya. They were the *choresh v'masger*, the scholars and leaders of the generation.[32] When the exiled people reached Bavel, they found a blossoming Torah community ready to absorb them. There were houses of study and *yeshivos* in the foreign land they had just come to.

Again, the people of the generation deserved punishment. But while they were being punished, Hashem made sure they would not suffer a spiritual breakdown. He prepared the ground before in order to soften the blow of the punishment. He made sure there were leaders and scholars brought down before them. Houses of study were established, protecting their Torah and their faith, making sure it would be preserved until it was time to return to their land.

Nevuchadnezar destroyed the *Bais Hamikdash* and exiled the people, causing untold suffering. If you think, though, that there was no retribution for what he did, you are making a grave mistake!

Daniel had already prophesized[33] that for seven years Nevuchadnezar would lose his throne and even lose his place in the company of people. During those years, he would take on the characteristics of animals, stripped of all human nature. The dictatorial

---

31. Gittin 88.
32. See the introductory chapter.
33. Daniel 4, see Rashi and Mali.

king,[34] who destroyed the Temple that had been built in seven years, was to live seven years torn from his kingship, living a pitiful life amongst the animals.

Daniel,[35] who saw the poverty and destitution that his people lived in, suggested[36] to Nevuchadnezar that he take upon himself to support the Jews he had exiled. He told him it would be an atonement for the sins he had committed and would push off the punishment due to him.

For a year, Nevuchadnezar listened to Daniel's advice and actually did support the Jewish exiles. Divine retribution was pushed off for that year.

When he stopped, though, the punishment was swift to come. One day, out of the blue, Nevuchadnezar went mad. He started to vomit in public and do other disgraceful things. The two heads of his army, Koraish and Daryavesh, understood what was happening and quickly removed him from the throne, taking off his crown and royal robes.[37]

From that day on, for seven full years, Nevuchadnezar was crazy. In place of a human heart, he now had an animal's heart. He ate animal food and lived amongst them. During those seven years, he suffered seven types of diseases. After, he became well again and resumed his kingship.

Although he went back to leading the people, his sins were not yet atoned for. He ended his life in a very lowly, degrading way.[38]

During the seven years he had lost his mind, his son Evil Merodach ruled in place of him. When Nevuchadnezar heard that his

---

34. Megilla 11.
35. Sotah 21.
36. Daniel 4:24
37. Esther Rabba 3:1
38. Vayikra Rabba 18:2

son ruled in his place while he was suffering such horrible misery and living among the animals, he became enraged. He decided to punish Evil Merodach and sent him to jail, which in those days meant a life sentence. Anyone Nevuchadnezar sent to prison never saw the light of day again.

It was only after Nevuchadnezar died, ending his forty five year rule, that Evil Merodach was freed along with the other prisoners that Nevuchadnezar had imprisoned. The people again asked him to rule, but this time he refused. "I have enough troubles!" he said. "Last time, my father imprisoned me for taking the throne in his place. Who knows what he will do to me now if he comes back one way or another!"

The people really wanted him to rule. They decided to show him that there was no chance his father would come back. They took the great and powerful Nevuchadnezar out of his grave and dragged him in front of his son. They invited all the enemies of the dead king to stab his body, thus showing that he was certainly and permanently dead.

Evil Merodach accepted the proof that his father was really gone forever and took the throne. It was Hashem's hand that had the events unravel the way they did to degrade Nevuchadnezar even in his death.

Yes, the Jewish people deserved to suffer. But the one who agrees to be the instrument to bring that punishment will be subject to divine retribution. Here Nevuchadnezar lived seven years in total humiliation and even his death was undignified. It is because of Hashem's great love for the Jewish people that anyone who touches them will find himself the subject of His wrath.

7

Rachel Cries over her Children

We have absolutely no understanding what the holy words of *Chazal* mean when they describe Hashem's conversations with the forefathers of the Jewish nation and the angels. Still, there is much to learn from these Midrashim about the tremendous love that Hashem has for the Jewish people, a love that was not diminished at all during the time of punishment. The stories that are written in *Chazal* are going to be brought here, keeping in mind that we don't understand even the smallest iota of what awesome secrets they contain.

Here is what *Chazal* tell us:[1]

After the destruction of the *Bais Hamikdash*, Hashem said, "From now on, I have no place to live in the world. I will go back, therefore, to My original home in *shamayim*."

---

1. Pesichta 24

Rachel Cries over her Children | 95

Hashem then started crying[2] and mourning His children. "Woe unto Me! What have I done? I brought My presence to dwell on earth, even though My place is in the heavens. I did it only for the sake of the Jewish people. Now that they have sinned, I have exiled them and burned My house and left back to My original home in the heavens! Perhaps I have made Myself a mockery in front of the nations!"

The angels tried to comfort Hashem and stop Him from crying, but their words were of no avail. "Your words are blasphemy in My ears! Let us go down to My house and see what the enemies have done,"[3] Hashem answered.

And so Hashem went down with the angels, with Yirmiyahu leading the way to the *Bais Hamikdash*. When God saw what was done, He said tearfully, "Yes, this is My home, My resting place – to which the enemies did what they wanted!" He continued to cry about His children who were in exile, "*Oy*, My house! My children, where are you? My priests, where are you? The ones who love Me, where are you? What should I do? I warned you, but you didn't repent!"

Hashem's love is awe inspiring. Even after His children had committed atrocious sins, even after they didn't listen to the constant messages He sent them through His prophets, He still cried

---

2. We have already mentioned it, but it bears repeating. There is no real concept of crying with Hashem. Crying is a concept of the physical world. These types of words are applied to Hashem so that we, with our lowly understanding, can relate a bit to concepts that are beyond our grasp. The actions are described with their "parallel" in this world (Eitz Yosef).
3. As we stated, we have no concept of what these things mean. It's obvious that God didn't have to "go down" to the world to "check" what the enemies had done to His house. It could be that what is being expressed here is that there was a special hashgacha on the churban, that Hashem was very involved in paying attention to what was happening. But, again, we really have no idea what these things mean.

inconsolably when He had to punish them. The punishment was unavoidable, but the pain remained anyway. What good does it do for a father who has to hit his son to know that the son deserved it? The father's heart still melts at his beloved son's pain.

While Hashem was standing with the angels, looking at what had happened to His house and feeling sorry for His children who were there no more, He turned to Yirmiyahu and said, "Look, Yirmiyahu, at the situation I find Myself in! I am like a man who had an only son. He built for him a wedding canopy and married him off. While the son was standing under the wedding canopy – he died! I created the entire world solely for the Jewish people,[4] as a human king would prepare a wedding canopy for his son. And now my children are gone! Now what is My whole world worth? What did I make this whole incredible world for?

"You, Yirmiyahu, are having a hard time pleading for mercy for My children. You only know them in their present state of wickedness and sin. In your heart, you justify one way or another the horrible situation they find themselves in. Therefore, you can't plead their merit.

"I have no choice but to call the forefathers, Avraham, Yitzchak, Yaakov and Moshe Rabbainu, from their graves. They know the Jews from their glorious past. They certainly will be able to arouse My mercy and remind Me of the kindness they showed Me in their youth, the reason why I chose them forever. They will remind Me of their merits, the merits of the forefathers, so that they may be used as a merit for their descendants."[5]

Before Yirmiyahu went on his way, he tried to find out where Moshe Rabbainu was buried, as his burial place was not known to

---

4. See Beraishis Rabba 28:6.
5. Eitz Yosef

Rachel Cries over her Children | 97

anyone. He was told to go stand on the shores of the Jordan River and call Moshe, saying, "Son of Amram, son of Amram, stand and see your flock that has been swallowed by the enemies!"

First, Yirmiyahu went to the Cave of Hamachpela, where the forefathers are buried. "You are summoned to come before the Holy One!" he called.

He didn't tell them the reason for the summons, as he feared that they would fault him for what had happened, saying, "See what happened to our children in your generation!"

After he went to the other side of the Jordan River, the same scene repeated itself. Yirmiyahu called Moshe and told him that Hashem requests that he appear before Him. Moshe asked what the unique invitation was about, but Yirmiyahu didn't tell him since he was worried that Moshe would hold him responsible.

When Moshe saw that Yirmiyahu wasn't going to give him the information he wanted, he turned to the angels. They knew each other from the time he went to heaven to get the Torah and stayed there for forty days. He asked the angels why he was being called before God. They answered, "Son of Amram, don't you know? The *Mikdash* has been destroyed and the Jewish people have been exiled from their land!"

Moshe immediately burst into bitter tears. He went on his way sobbing until he met the *Avos*. Together with Moshe, they tore their clothes in mourning, put their hands on their heads and went to the gates of the *Mikdash*, which are parallel to the gates of the *Mikdash* in heaven, the conduit of blessing to the world.

There, the *Avos* and Moshe met Hashem in mourning – crying and wearing sackcloth.[6] The angels weren't familiar with what it meant for

---

6. This is how the Navi describes it in Isaiah 22:12.

the heavens to mourn. They were only used to seeing Hashem act strong and joyous. But Hashem taught them to mourn and all of the heavens began to grieve.

The *Avos* then came to ask for mercy, to find a merit for the people. First Avraham stood up. He cried and pulled out his beard and the hair on his head, slapped his face and ripped his clothes. He put dirt on his head. In this state of grief, he walked around the destroyed Temple and cried out, "Master of the World, why have I been so disgraced and humiliated?"

Avraham hadn't even yet begun to state his claims to Hashem when the angels, moved by Avraham's pain, lined up in rows and said to Hashem, "Master of the World, the streets that You made in Yerushalayim were always filled with passerby. Look how desolate they are! These roads that the Jews used to come up to Yerushalayim for the holidays, they are empty! Avraham was the one who brought the world to know of Your existence and taught them that You created the world. You made a promise to him and now it is broken! This Yerushalayim that You chose as Your city, how can You be so disgusted with it? How is it possible that You are not even acting with Your own children like You acted with the children of Enosh? In those days, even though they introduced idol worship to the world, You only destroyed a third of Your world.[7] In Yerushalayim, though, there is no one left!"[8]

Hashem answered the angels, "Why are you mourning? You always wanted Me to return to the heavens, and now I have. Why are

---

7. The Eitz Yosef explains that the generation of Enosh was in a better situation than the people of Yerushalayim here. The people of Enosh's time were washed away with water, but here Bnai Yisrael went through many calamities by human hands.
8. Maharzav

Rachel Cries over her Children | 99

you suddenly crying now, but you were silent when the *Bais Hamikdash* was burning? And, really, why are you upset over the suffering of Israel when they have sinned before Me and deserve the punishment they got?"

The angels explained that they never would have said anything, but they feel Avraham's pain as he stands in the *Mikdash* and laments the fate of his children. Hashem then turned to Avraham and asked, "Why are you, My friend, in My house?" With that question God gave Avraham the opening to ask for mercy for His children.

Avraham said, "Why have you exiled my children? Why were they given over to the gentiles who have slaughtered and tortured them terribly? And why were they doubly punished? It should have been enough of an atonement to destroy their Temple – they didn't need to be massacred also. If You decided to kill them in such horrible tortuous ways, then that should have been enough and the *Mikdash* should have been left alone. The *Bais Hamikdash* stands where I brought my son as a sacrifice to You. That merit should have been enough to save them from both punishments!"[9]

Hashem answered him, "Your sons did two things[10] wrong – not only did they not learn the Torah, but they also didn't keep the *mitzvos*. They served idols, a sin that is equal to the rest of the prohibitions of the Torah, in addition to not keeping the other commandments. They deserved a double punishment! They deserved to be completely destroyed! Killing them, destroying the Temple, even the *akaida*, were not enough to atone for what they did! It was out of mercy that I had

---

9. Eitz Yosef

10. Maharzav explains that this is the meaning of the two things Hashem answered Avraham, "Your children sinned and violated the entire Torah and the twenty two letters that it contains."

them killed and destroyed the Temple! It was to save them from complete destruction."

Avraham Avinu wasn't satisfied with that answer.[11] "Maybe they sinned by accident." Hashem answered that it had been on purpose.

"Maybe it was only the minority of the people that sinned," Avraham tried a second time. Hashem answered that it was most of them.

"Why don't You remember the *bris*, the covenant, that they have incised into their flesh?" Avraham asked. It was then that he was told that they had violated that commandment also.

"Okay, I accept that they sinned," Avraham continued. "But are they worse than the nations of the world? Is there anyone who is willing to stand up and testify that that is the case?[12] Even if they didn't keep the Torah, they were the only ones who were willing to accept it in the first place! Just for that alone, You should have pity on them!"

The Torah got up and testified that *Bnai Yisrael* sinned more than the nations of the world.

Avraham spoke to the Torah, "My daughter, aren't you embarrassed to testify against the Jewish people? Don't you remember how Hashem went from nation to nation and no one was willing to accept you but the Jews? How can you bear witness against them?" The Torah stood on the side, rebuked, and would no longer testify.

In place of the Torah, the letters of the *Aleph Bais* were called to testify. When the Aleph was about to bear witness, Avraham reminded her that, after all, the Jews were the only ones who accepted the Ten Commandments that begin with the letter Aleph.

---

11. Menachos 53:
12. Eitz Yosef

Bais came to bear witness, when Aleph decided to stand quietly on the side. Avraham told her to consider that even if the Jews did not keep the Torah, they were all experts in its five books, which begin with the letter Bais.

Avraham had an answer for Gimmel also. *Bnai Yisrael* are the only ones who keep the *mitzvah* of *tzitzis*, whose *pasuk* begins with Gimmel (*"Gedilim taaseh lecha"*). Gimmel stood aside without testifying. So it went with every letter. Avraham mentioned a reason why it wasn't appropriate for that letter to testify against the Jews.[13]

Avraham now mentioned his own merits, hoping they would help the Jewish people. "Master of the World, when I was one hundred years old, after I was finally given a son, You told me to bring him as a sacrifice to You. I took my thirty seven year old son to kill, in order to do Your will. I didn't have mercy on him. I tied him down with my own hands, to sacrifice him in honor of Your name. Can't You remember that now and have compassion on my children?"

Yitzchak came after Avraham. "When my father said to me, 'God will show us the sheep, as a sacrifice, my son,' I understood that I was to be brought as the sacrifice. I didn't hold him back from fulfilling Your will. I willingly allowed myself to be tied on the altar. I stuck out my neck under the knife! Can't You remember this at all and have mercy on my children?"

Yaakov, the father of the twelve tribes, was also not quiet. "Master of the World, for twenty years I worked in Lavan's house. After I left, my wicked brother Eisav came to try to kill my sons. I gave myself up to die for their sakes. Was all my effort for naught?[14] Isn't it right that

---

13. It didn't really help that they didn't testify. Since they came to testify but didn't due to Avraham's arguments, it was as if they did testify (Eitz Yosef).
14. Eitz Yosef

You should have compassion on the children for whose sake I suffered so much?"

Moshe, Hashem's trusted servant, tried next. "Master of the World, wasn't I a faithful shepherd to Israel for forty years in the desert? After all my devotion and effort, You told me I could not go into the land with them. Now You tell me I have to cry over them! I didn't enjoy the good with them, it isn't right that I should have to cry and suffer from the bad."

Moshe turned to Yirmiyahu, "Lead me to the path where they were exiled. I will go after you and see who dared raise their hand against them. I will bring them back from their exile!"

Yirmiyahu said, "I can't go to Bavel. The path is full of dead bodies, and I am a *Kohein* and can't become impure." Moshe didn't accept his argument. Moshe explained that since this is a matter of *pikuach nefesh*, life and death, the other *mitzvos* of the Torah are pushed aside, including the prohibition for a *Kohein* to become impure.[15]

So Yirmiyahu, with Moshe Rabbainu behind him, went after the exiled. They came to the shores of Bavel where *Bnai Yisrael* were crying. The people saw that Moshe Rabbainu was there and became very happy. "Moshe Rabbainu has come to redeem us!" they exclaimed.

A heavenly voice told Moshe that the decree had been sealed and that he would not be allowed to redeem them. Moshe told the people that he was unable to save them. He left them with words of comfort and a blessing that God should return them to their land soon.

---

15. Radal

Rachel Cries over her Children | 103

The people's disappointment was enormous. The redemption was almost tangible and then it disappeared in an instant. Their cries reached the heavens, but the decree was sealed.

When Moshe came back to the *Avos*, they hurried to find out what had transpired. He only had a dreadful report to share. "Holy fathers, you must know, part of your children were killed, part are standing with their hands tied behind their backs. Part are shackled with iron restraints. Some are being forced to work, unclothed, rowing ships. Some have died on the way to Bavel and their bodies are lying on the road as food for the birds and animals. Some are simply prey to the elements, exhausted and starving."

The *Avos* lamented over what they had heard. "Woe that this is what has happened to our children! Woe that our children are like orphans, that they are under the midday summer sun without clothing or protection. Woe that they have to walk in the rocky mountains without shoes, that they have to carry sacks of sand just so they should suffer more. Woe that their hands are tied behind them, that they are being tortured so much that they don't even have a chance to swallow the saliva in their mouths."

Moshe added, "Cursed is the sun that didn't darken when the enemies entered the Temple!"

The sun answered him, "Moshe Rabbainu, Hashem's trusted servant, do you think I was able not to shine? They didn't leave me alone! I was beaten with sixty whips of fire, and I was forced to light the way for the enemies."

When Moshe heard the answer the sun had given him, he began to lament, "Woe that the *Bais Hamikdash* is dark! Woe that the time has come for the *Mikdash* to be destroyed! Woe for the schoolchildren that were killed, with their parents being led to exile and the sword!"

Moshe then warned the Babylonians, "I caution you not to kill Israel in cruel ways and not to completely wipe them out. Don't kill children in front of their parents! The day of vengeance will come and God will seek retribution!"

The Babylonians didn't listen. They did kill in cruel ways; they did kill children in front of their parents. They even went so far as to command fathers to kill their children while in their mothers' arms!

The pleading of the *Avos* wasn't enough to save the Jews. After, though, Rachel tried to plead for her people.

"Master of the World, You know Yaakov had a special deep love for me. You know he worked for my father for seven full years for me. It was after those seven years, when it was time for me to be married to him, that my father the swindler planned to switch me with my sister Leah. When I found out about it, I told Yaakov and we made up certain signs between us so that Yaakov would know it was me and not my sister that he was marrying.

"But when it was time for Leah to go under the wedding canopy, I regretted my decision. I thought of the incredible shame that my sister, who had done nothing wrong, would suffer. I gave over the signs to her. By doing so, I was overcoming my natural desires and character traits and my jealousy. I did it all so that my sister would not be embarrassed.

"Yaakov did indeed marry my sister instead of me. That night, I joined Leah on her way to her new home, that home that should have been mine. I hid. When Yaakov spoke to Leah, I answered in her place so that he wouldn't recognize that she wasn't the woman for whom he had worked for seven years. I made sure she wouldn't be embarrassed. Can you imagine how emotionally difficult the situation was?

"If I, a human being, nothing but dust and ashes, was able to act that way, all the more so that You should have! You are the eternal

Rachel Cries over her Children | 105

King! You are the merciful One! Why were You jealous, so to speak, of the worthless idols that Your children served? Why did You punish them so harshly?"

These were the words that were finally accepted by Hashem. Hashem answered, "Know, Rachel, that it is because of you, only because of you,[16] that I will bring the people back to their land!"

This is what the Navi prophesized,[17] "Thus says the Lord: 'A voice was heard in Rama, lamentation and bitter weeping, Rachel weeping for her children. She refused to be comforted for her children, for they are not.' Thus says the Lord, 'Stop your voice from weeping and your eyes from tears, for your actions shall be rewarded,' says the Lord. 'And they shall come back again from the land of the enemy. There is hope for the future,' says the Lord, 'and your children shall come back again to their own border.'"

---

16. In the Gemara (Menachos 53:) it says that Hashem promised Avraham that their hope was not lost completely.

17. Yirmiyahu 31:14

8

Gedalia ben Achikam

As previously mentioned, Nevuchadnezar left a small group of people in Yerushalayim to work the vineyards and fields. They were under the leadership of Gedalia ben Achikam who lived in Mitzpeh. The fact that someone was left in the Holy Land was a consolation to the people.

The strong fighters who had escaped during the fighting to the mountains and deserts now returned to Yerushalayim. They were Yishmael ben Netanya, Yochanan ben Korach, Seraya ben Tanchemas Hanetafti, and Yozniya Hamachti. They came with their followers.[1]

The people were unsettled. They worried that Nevuchadnezar might come to fight them again. "Besides," they said to Gedalia, "Nevuchadnezar left his followers here. Perhaps we are going to be slaves to them."

Gedalia assured them, though, that if they didn't rebel and paid their taxes, they would be left alone and not have to serve the

---

1. Melachim I 25:23

Babylonians.² "I am watching from Mitzpeh," he continued, "to make sure I can stop any trouble that begins from the Babylonian army. Go gather any wine and oil and dry fruits that you find were left in the captured cities and settle peacefully in any city you want."³

The warriors mentioned above, as well as some people who had found refuge in neighboring countries, along with the remnant of people that were left originally in *Eretz Yisrael*, numbered about six thousand people.⁴ They listened to Gedalia and gathered food as he had said.

It could have been that this settlement of Jews would have lived peacefully for many years. Bailis the king of Amon, though, planned the downfall of the Jewish settlement of *Eretz Yisrael* by turning Yishmael ben Netanya against Gedalia ben Achikam.

Yishmael was from royal lineage. He wasn't worthy to rule, though, because he was the sixteenth generation from a freed slave.⁵ He was also a wicked man, son of a wicked man,⁶ a scoundrel and a murderer. Still, the king of Amon convinced him to kill Gedalia and take his place. "Why should Gedalia rule and not you?" he asked. "After all, you are of royal lineage!"

Yochanan ben Korach heard of the plan to assassinate Gedalia. He hurried to inform Gedalia about what Yishmael was plotting. "You have to listen! Bailis, the king of Amon, has incited Yishmael to kill you!"⁷

---

2. Malbim on Melachim I 25:24
3. Yirmiyahu 40:10, see commentaries there.
4. Toldos Am Olam in the name of the sefer Shilsheles Hakabalah
5. Yerushalmi Horios 3:8
6. Megilla 15.
7. Yirmiyahu 40:14

The righteous Gedalia refused to believe him. He thought it was merely a plan to ruin Yishmael's reputation in his eyes. Yochanan offered to clandestinely kill Yishmael to save Gedalia. He explained that if Yishmael succeeded in his plan it could have grave repercussions for the people left in *Eretz Yisrael*. Gedalia would not be convinced. "You are lying!" He forbade Yochanan from hurting Yishmael and totally ignored the information he had heard.

Gedalia was held responsible for ignoring what Yochanan told him. Although he was right in not assuming that the story was one hundred percent true, he should have at least considered the possibility that it was true.[8]

Gedalia didn't, though. He even sat down to a meal in Mitzpeh with Yishmael and ten other men who were Yishmael's followers,[9] along with other officers who were jealous of Gedalia's position.

It was during this meal, which took place on the third of Tishrei, that Yishmael and his ten cohorts got up and stabbed Gedalia.

The remnant of Israel had only been living under Gedalia's rule for fifty two days.[10] The murder of Gedalia was considered equal to the burning of the *Mikdash*.[11] It symbolized the final stage of the destruction of the land and Israel's exile.

Yishmael and his men also killed the Babylonian officers that were present at the time. The Jewish warriors were murdered as well. The only people left were the Jewish inhabitants of Mitzpeh, whom Yishmael took captive.

---

8. Yalkut Yirmiyahu 247:328
9. Yirmiyahu 41:1
10. Yalkut Yechezkel 343
11. Rosh Hashana 18:

Yishmael killed many other people. He killed eighty people that were coming from Shilo and the Shomron to Yerushalayim. They knew the Jews had been exiled, but assumed the *Bais Hamikdash* was still standing,[12] and they were on their way to bring *mincha* and *levona* sacrifices. When, on their way, they heard the Temple had been destroyed, they tore their clothes and shaved their heads and scratched their skin in mourning. They continued on their way, though, to join Gedalia.

Before they reached Gedalia, he was killed. When Yishmael met these people the day after Gedalia was killed, Yishmael kept the death a secret and pretended to be one of Gedalia's men, mourning over the Temple's destruction. He offered to take the group of people to Gedalia.

He waited until the people had entered the city and then he killed them also. He threw their bodies into a big pit that had been dug by King Assah when trying to protect himself from King Bassah. Yishmael only left ten men from this group from the Shomron alive, as those men had told him that they had hidden food in the fields. Yishmael left them alive in order to be able to get the food.

Those ten men and the rest of the captives were taken by Yishmael to the king of Amon, in whose name Yishmael had acted.

Yochanan ben Korach heard what had happened and gathered his men to avenge Gedalia's assassination and free the captives. Near the water pools of Givon, his camp met up with Yishmael's camp. The captives Yishmael had taken joined the fight to help Yochanan's side and they won a resounding victory. Yishmael ran away with just eight men to his friend, the king of Amon.

---

12. Yirmiyahu 41:5, see Metzudos.

The people were still worried that the king of Bavel would be angry, even though they had chased Yishmael away. Gedalia, the king's appointee, as well as the Babylonian officers, had been killed.[13]

Embarrassed, they went to Yirmiyahu.[14] Yirmiyahu had been the prophet they had ignored for years, but they had no choice. "Yirmiyahu, please plead before God that He should not destroy the small remnant that is left in the Land of Israel. Ask our God what we should do now. Should we run to Egypt? Is it better to stay here in the Land of Israel? We will do whatever God says."

Yirmiyahu prepared to ask Hashem what to do, but he did not receive prophecy right away. For ten days, until Yom Kippur had passed, he was unable to get an answer. After Yom Kippur, though, Hashem did answer him. "Tell the people that if they stay in the land, I will build them up and they will not be destroyed. I will plant them and they won't be uprooted. Don't be afraid of the king of Bavel. I will save you from him. I will give you mercy and he will be compassionate and leave you in your land."

The answer was clear, but Hashem knew that in their hearts the people wanted to escape to Egypt. He therefore added, "If you decide to go to Egypt, the sword that you are afraid of will catch you there. The starvation you are afraid of will cling to you there. All the people who go to live in Egypt will die by the sword, starvation and disease. No one will survive."

The prophet explained to them, "If you go now you are in a worse predicament than if you had gone without asking first. Had you not asked, you could have claimed you didn't know that you weren't

---

13. Yirmiyahu 41:18
14. From here on, the source is Yirmiyahu 42.

Gedalia ben Achikam | 111

supposed to go. You now have a direct command from God not to go! Don't cross His words!"

They didn't listen. Since Yirmiyahu didn't receive prophecy for ten days, they lost trust in his abilities. They felt that, due to their sins, Yirmiyahu was no longer able to lead them.

Azaria and Yochanan claimed that the prophecy was fabricated.[15] They said to themselves, "Baruch ben Nerya, Yirmiyahu's close student, certainly knows that a prophet can only receive prophecy for the first time in the Land of Israel. He, therefore, doesn't want to leave the land and lose the chance he is pining for – to get a prophetic vision.[16] He must have convinced Yirmiyahu to state in Hashem's name that we should stay in *Eretz Yisrael*. It certainly wasn't a prophecy from God."[17]

Yochanan gathered all the people and, ignoring Yirmiyahu's words, went to Egypt. This was the complete end of a Jewish settlement in the Land of Israel.

Even though they were now in a strange land, Yirmiyahu continued to rebuke the people in the hope that they would repent. He warned them that they were acting in direct opposition to Hashem's words.

They didn't listen. The women began to offer incense to the sun and the moon. They declared that the Jews were a nation like all other nations and that they would never change their ways!

---

15. Yalkut Yirmiyahu Remez 329

16. In actuality, Baruch ben Nerya didn't receive prophecy. Neviim only get nevuah for the sake of the Jews. The Jews were in exile now; why should he get nevuah?

17. Yirmiyahu 43:3, see Abarbanel.

Eight years passed. Nevuchadnezar came with a great army to fight Egypt and conquer it. For eight years, Yirmiyahu exhorted the people to leave their evil ways. *Bnai Yisrael* didn't repent, and Egypt was conquered by Bavel. The Jewish community was wiped out. Only Yirmiyahu, Baruch ben Nerya, and a few people who only moved to Egypt because they were forced to, survived.

This was the final event of the exile. For seventy years, the Jews remained in exile until they returned to their land and rebuilt the *Mikdash*.

9

What We Lost When We Lost Yerushalayim

When the *Mikdash* was destroyed, we lost many things. We lost the *Bais Hamikdash* itself, Hashem's awe inspiring holy house. We lost the ability to bring sacrifices and be granted immediate atonement. We lost the glory of Yerushalayim and the magnificent sight of the *Kohanim* serving in the Temple. But, more than that, the Jewish people have been on a continuous downward spiral, becoming weaker and weaker, level after level.

When the *Bais Hamikdash* was in existence, the *Kohein* used to take the craw of the bird that was being brought on the altar as a sacrifice and throw it from the southwest corner of the *mizbeiach* to the southeast corner. This was a distance of thirty two *amos*. It took incredible strength to throw a light object such a far distance. This type of physical strength no longer existed after the destruction of the Temple.[1]

---

1. Pesichta 23

114 | On Your Walls, O Jerusalem

Our rabbis also teach us that, after the destruction, there were a number of things that became extinct.[2] The Shamir worm that was used to build the *Bais Hamikdash* is one of them. This was a worm the size of a grain of barley that was able to cut through even the strongest rock.

Also, an excellent type of silk and gorgeous white glass are gone. The very special wine of the Golan is no more. That wine was of such thick, high quality that it would turn into something similar to rings of figs. The flour before the destruction was so fine and rich that it seemed as if it had been kneaded with oil and honey.

Our rabbis say that since the *Bais Hamikdash* was destroyed there is no day whose curse isn't greater than the day before. Even the dew doesn't come as a blessing. The taste and richness of the fruit is gone as well.

The spiritual level of the people was also lowered. Before the destruction, the people had total belief in God. They did not worry at all about how they would find sustenance. This type of people is no more.

The wisdom of the generation before the destruction was incredibly vast. The people were able to delve into and connect full, detailed *masechtos*. The original orders of the *Mishna* included all the wisdom that is contained in the Talmud. After the destruction, Rebbi Hakadosh had to divide the longer tractates and condense them into six orders. He had to adapt the *mishnayos* to the learning ability of a generation whose abilities were lessened.

The gates of prayer in heaven that were opposite the gates of the *Mikdash*[3] were locked.[4]

---

2. Sotah 48
3. See Maharsha (Baba Metziah 59.).
4. Baba Metziah 59.

What We Lost When We Lost Yerushalayim

The greatest loss was the loss of *ruach hakodesh* and prophecy. There was no prophecy after this point; it was the end of the Jewish people's direct communication with Hashem and the guidance of His messengers, the prophets.

The Jews also went from being the most honorable of people to being downtrodden and scorned. When the gentiles would become drunk at their parties, they would mock the Jews.[5]

When the gentiles would want to tell each other not to be spendthrifts, they would use the Jews as an example. "Watch your money so you don't become like the Jews that have to eat carob because they are so poor," they would say.[6]

When wishing themselves long lives, they would mock the Jews. "May you last as long as the Jews' Sabbath clothes. They only wear them once a week, so they last forever."[7]

If in the circus they would see a camel covered in black, as was usual in those days, someone would crack a joke at the Jews' expense. "Why is the camel wearing black? Those Jews keep *shmitta*, so for a year they don't have enough food. They probably eat the thorns and thistles that the camels usually eat. The camel is mourning over the thorns he's lost."

The gentiles would bring mummified dead bodies[8] with their hair shaved off, as was traditionally done to the dead at the time, into their circuses.[9] This, too, was used as a joke against the Jews. "The Jew

---

5. Pesichta 17
6. Yifei Ainaim
7. Hamarich, brought in the Eitz Yosef
8. Eichah Rabba 3:5
9. Some say these were actual dead mummified bodies (Eitz Yosef). Some say they were people dressed like dead men (Matnas Kehuna).

works so hard all week to earn his Sabbath needs. When the Sabbath finally arrives, the poor fellow realizes that he spent all his money on meat and fish and there is none left to buy wood to make a fire and cook all the rich foods. What does he do? He chops up his bed to make kindling wood. That's why there are Jews that always sleep on the floor without bedding, rolling in the dirt that ruins their hair and causes painful sores on their scalps.

"But don't worry, the Jews know how to manage. They buy expensive oils and put them on their heads and they heal. The only ones who really suffer from the situation are the dead people. Since the Jews want the oils so badly, the price rises. The dead don't have enough resources to buy the oil, so they have no choice but to shave their heads so they won't need the expensive oil.[10] This dead body with no hair is proof of what I'm telling you!"[11]

The Jews were considered so lowly and despised that *Chazal*[12] tell of two sinful gentile women who were arguing. One said to the other in the heat of the fight, "Get out of here! You look like a Jew!"

After a while, the two women reconciled their differences. One said to the other, "I forgive you completely for the fight that we had, but I cannot forgive you for calling me a Jew! For that I will never forgive you!" The Jews were considered so lowly that there was no greater insult.

---

10. Yifei Ainaim
11. The Matnas Kehuna and the Eitz Yosef explain that there were two points of mockery here. The first was that the Jews' hair fell out because they had to sleep in the dirt, so the mummy was like a Jew's body. The second was that the price of oil skyrocketed because of the Jews' demand for it.
12. Eichah Rabba 1:39

What We Lost When We Lost Yerushalayim

The Land of Israel was also desolate. The roads were no longer needed to serve the *olei regel*, the people who were traveling to the *Bais Hamikdash* for the holidays, so they became desolate.[13]

The Land of Israel was no longer the same place it had been when the Jews lived there. Its special characteristics were lost. Even more so, it became worse than other lands. It was a land full of sulfur and salt,[14] to the point that a bird wasn't able to fly in its skies for fifty two years[15] – until it was conquered by Koraish of Persia and some of the Jews returned to the land.

There is a story in the Midrash that helps us understand what it means that the land was full of sulfur and salt. There was a man that plowed the valley of Bais Arbel after the destruction. He put his hand on the peg of the plow and touched some of the dirt... and burned his hand!

In the first years, the people living in the land didn't give up on eating the produce of the field. They tried many ways to grow things in this sulfur, but to no avail. Even when they turned over the soil to try and bring up dirt from deep down, and even when they fertilized

---

13. Eichah Rabba 1:30

14. This is the first way the Eitz Yosef explains it. He later explains that the reason the birds didn't fly over the land for fifty two years was because they followed the Jews into exile. The Barzav explains that the birds not flying over the land was because of the "curse of the Temple's destruction." It sounds like, according to him, it wasn't because of the sulfur and salt, but as a direct result of the curse.

15. There is an opinion that the land was only full of sulfur and salt for seven years. According to the second opinion in the Eitz Yosef (brought in the previous footnote), it could be that all agree that the sulfur and salt only lasted for the first seven years, as the issue of the birds not flying over the land was not necessarily connected to the sulfur and salt. That is the opinion of the Ap"l even according to the Razav.

118 | On Your Walls, O Jerusalem

the land, nothing was able to grow. All the new or fertilized dirt soon became sulfur and burned up the produce.[16]

There was no logical explanation for what happened. The land had produced a great yield for generations, but in one day became totally unusable. That is how the Land of Israel is. It saves its blessings for its children. This land flowing with milk and honey is only there for the Jewish people. If we look at these small rays of light in the darkness, we can get a glimpse of God's true love for His people.

---

16. There is another opinion that they were able to grow in the land when they brought up dirt from the depths and fertilized it well. See previous footnote that discusses that the sulfur and salt may have only lasted for the first seven years. It is possible to say that for those seven years, all the land was sulfur and salt, even the dirt from deep down. After seven years, until fifty two years had passed, although the land was still sulfur and salt, the dirt brought up from the depths was not sulfur and salt and was able to grow something when well fertilized.

10

The End of the Second Temple

The period right before the destruction of the Second Temple was not an easy one.[1] It is not within the scope of this book to discuss all the political issues that were taking place at that time. They are documented in Divrei Hayamim. We are focusing here on those issues that caused the destruction of the Second Temple and the exile that we remain in until today. In order to understand those

---

1. The description of the battles of the biryonim against the Romans is based on the writing of Josephus and the added comments of the book Toldos Am Olam. Therefore, we didn't mark the sources of each detail. Anyone who is interested should look in the history books of that period. The author is also not a historian and isn't expressing his own opinions on the events of that time. The history is brought down from those sources as long as it doesn't contradict what Chazal said. This history is brought to make it easier to understand what was happening at that time. This is based on the Mishna Berura's ruling (307:58) that one can study Josephus's writing even on Shabbos.

We condensed the events that are not mentioned in Chazal and focused on those events that are mentioned in the Gemara and the Midrash. The sources for those stories are brought.

points, we will touch upon what was going on in that period, but only briefly.

Nero was the emperor of Rome at the time. He was the sixth emperor of Rome, and a cruel, corrupt leader at that. He killed his own family and the leaders of Rome. He even burned the city of Rome itself, enjoying the sight of the flames eating up the better part of the city.

The power to rule in Rome's different provinces wasn't directly the emperor's. Rather, there were governmental representatives, each of whom was in charge of his area. Felix was in charge of Yerushalayim at the time. He, like his superior, was wicked and calculating. On whim, he would destroy whatever he wanted in Yerushalayim. No one could stop him, for he had the authorization of Emperor Nero, as did all the governmental representatives who were even given military power to do as they pleased.

The other ruler of Yerushalayim was King Agrippas. He didn't really have any authority, that was all given to the Romans. The only way Agrippas could accomplish anything was by pleading with and flattering the emperor and his men.

Those were the leaders. Now let's look at who the population of Yerushalayim was made up of.

There were three main camps in those days. The first was the Sadducees. They supported the Roman government. These Sadducees, or *tzedukim*, explained the Torah according to what the simple meaning seems to imply without considering the words of the sages, totally distorting its meaning. They even set up their own courts under Chanan ben Chanan, the "high priest."[2] Their courts judged based on the Sadducees' interpretation of the Torah, totally distorting the *halacha*.

---

2. Whenever we mention from this point on the title Kohein Gadol or High Priest, it doesn't necessarily refer to the glorious position of serving

The next group of Jewish people was the *sikrikim* (Sicarii), the bandits. They spilled much innocent blood in the streets of Yerushalayim and even in the Temple itself. These wicked people were called *sikrikim* because of the *sika* sword that they used to carry out their murders. This sword is short and curved and easily hidden. They were so sly about their killings that even people right in the vicinity of the murder couldn't say who had done it!

These people were part of the *sinas chinam*, baseless hatred, that was rampant in those days. The streets of Yerushalayim weren't safe. The people didn't know who they were supposed to be wary of and going out in the streets was actually endangering one's life! People who had to go out would wear armor to protect themselves from these bandits.

Amongst the people were many poor people who couldn't afford armor to protect themselves. These destitute people tried to escape the city to avoid the *sikrikim*.

When the *sikrikim* heard that people were running away from them, they became furious. They told the Roman leader Felix that these people were running out of Yerushalayim in order to plan a rebellion. Felix didn't need more proof than their words and sent a battalion of soldiers to kill every last one of those poor souls.

These *sikrikim* ruled with terror. In the political arena, they intended to get rid of the Roman rule by force.

The third group of people in Yerushalayim was the Torah scholars and those who followed them. Rabbi Yochanan ben Zakai was their leader. He was a student of Hillel the Elder. Rabbi Yochanan ben

---

God in purity and holiness. Many times in the period of the Second Temple, Sadducees and other wicked people were appointed to serve as High Priest, either through bribery or connections to the Romans.

Zakai's unfathomable greatness is described in the *Gemara*:[3] "It is said about Rabbi Yochanan ben Zakai that he had mastered Scripture, *Mishna, Gemara, halacha* and *aggadah* as well as scriptural exactitudes, rabbinic exactitudes, *kal v'chomer* arguments, *gezeiros shaveh* expositions, astronomical cycles and *gematrios*, the conversations of the angels and the conversations of demons and the speech of palm trees, parables of launderers, and parables of foxes...."

The scholars wanted peace. They didn't regard it as a positive thing that the Romans were ruling, as the *tzedukim* did, but they also didn't approve of using force to overthrow their rule, as the *sikrikim* wanted. They understood that rebelling against the Romans wouldn't work and would result in the destruction of Yerushalayim and the Holy Temple.

During all the years of bloody fighting between the Romans and their followers and the *sikrikim,* or *biryonim*, as they were also called, the Torah scholars tried unsuccessfully to stop the *sikrikim* from what they were doing.

The beginning of the fighting between the *sikrikim* and the Romans began under the leadership of a very powerful man named Elazar ben Anneni the *Kohein Gadol*. This Elazar gathered a group of young men and went to take revenge for the Jews from Felix and Filus his army commander. Elazar dealt a mighty blow to the Roman army, causing Filus and his men to run away to Egypt.

On the way to Egypt, Filus met King Agrippas, returning from Rome. At that time, most people were happy with Agrippas's rule. Filus told him what the Jewish men had done to him and, instead of continuing to Egypt, returned to Yerushalayim with Agrippas.

---

3. Sukkah 28.

The End of the Second Temple | 123

When Agrippas came back, the people gathered around him and begged him to help them throw off the yoke of Rome. Agrippas, just returning from Rome, had seen the incredible power of the Roman empire and its incredibly vast army. He explained to the people that trying to rebel was tantamount to suicide.

He announced, "If you are looking for peace, I am with you. The Roman emperor doesn't know what is going on in all of the countries under his rule. If I write to him that the heads of his army are mistreating the people here, I am sure he will replace them with others who will rule peacefully and it will seem as if you are free. If you want to rebel against the mighty Roman empire, I cannot join you. I won't be a part of something so futile!" He began to cry when he saw that the scholars and even Anneni the *Kohein Gadol* had joined him.

But Elazar, Anneni's son, and his cohorts were not pleased. Young blood boiled in their veins. They didn't listen to what Agrippas said, and which *daas Torah* agreed with. They drew their swords and killed all the Roman officers that were with Agrippas. They even tried to kill Agrippas and his men, but they managed to escape the city. This was the real beginning of the rebellion.

The meaning of rebelling against the great Roman empire was obvious to all. The Torah scholars, who understood what was going to happen as soon as the emperor heard about the events, hurried and left the city to show they had nothing to do with the killings. They established their community in Metzudas Tzion.

The young bandits were not happy that the scholars had run away. It meant that they didn't believe in their abilities and that they wouldn't cooperate. Consequently, the bandits became enemies with the Torah scholars. They even ran after them to Metzudas Tzion and killed many of them.

Agrippas wasn't satisfied leaving things as they were. He sent his army with about 6000 men to suppress the rebellion of these hooligans and to bring back social order. He also intended to restore his lost honor.

It wasn't simple to overcome these *biryonim*. They were very strong. The soldiers did manage to beat them when they fought on the outskirts of Yerushalayim. Later, the *biryonim* retreated to the *Bais Hamikdash* and even took shelter in the *heichal*. This was a clear defilement of the *Mikdash*.

The holiness of the site didn't stop Agrippas and his men from entering the sacred place to continue fighting. In the narrow *heichal*, the *biryonim* had the upper hand. In open spaces, such as when they fought in the outskirts of the city, the swords and long spears of the army were useful. This was not the case in the *heichal*, where there was no room to use them and they just weighed down the soldiers. The *sikrikim* used their small, short knives and killed many of Agrippas's soldiers.

This battle was won, in the end, by Elazar and his men. From then on, they ruled over Yerushalayim and the Temple freely through their brute strength and the gangs under their command.

They burned King Agrippas's palace, his treasure houses and the archives where the promissory notes of all the poor people were kept. This eased the burden of the poor people and drew many of them to place their loyalty with Elazar and his men.

Although until this point Agrippas had been a kind and caring ruler, from the time the *biryonim* rebelled he no longer cared about meeting the needs of the people. He concentrated on getting back his position. Agrippas was also worried about Emperor Nero's reaction to the fact that the bandits had killed Agrippas's army. He hurried and went to Nero on his own to tell him all that had taken place in the Land of Yehuda.

The End of the Second Temple | 125

Nero wasn't interested in being involved in a war in Yehuda. He therefore sent his army officer Cestius, who was in Aram, to initiate a peace treaty between the people of Yerushalayim and the emperor. Agrippas told Cestius that he had tried to bring peace but was unsuccessful. Cestius appreciated the information, as he had been looking for the opportunity to take revenge from the strong men of Yehuda who had caused him a number of setbacks in the past.

Cestius gathered his massive army and marched to the Land of Yehuda, wreaking destruction and havoc on the Jewish settlements he passed on the way. He swore to destroy every last Jew.

It wasn't to be, though. Cestius's army became embroiled in battle with the *biryonim* close to Yerushalayim, where they were soundly defeated. The *biryonim* killed 27,000 of Cestius's men. Only twenty seven men fell from the other side!

This was a gift from God. He was hoping that they would return to Him, allowing Him to avoid the *churban*.

Cestius lowered himself to ask for peace with Elazar. Elazar refused, because he saw how successful they had been in the last battle. Cestius had no choice but to return to Rome and shamefacedly tell the emperor about his defeat.

This was the end of the first stage of battle between the people of Yehuda and the Romans; the beginning of the rebellion. Instead of turning to God and changing their ways, they trusted in their might and the decree continued to hover over the city.

11

Political Turmoil

Time passed and the Roman representative in the Land of Yehuda, Felix, was replaced with someone by the name of Porcius Festus. He was Felix's opposite in goals and temperament. Whereas Felix had brought much evil and bloodshed with him, Festus wanted there to be peace. Festus waged a war against the *sikrikim*. Many were killed and many jailed. All in all, we can say that it was a tranquil time for the Jews of Yehuda.

During that period, Agrippas the king appointed Yishmael ben Fiabe to be the *Kohein Gadol*. He was an appropriate choice for the position. The position of *Kohein Gadol* at the time was one that had great influence on the people and societal issues. Yishmael contributed to the peaceful atmosphere in the city, as his interests were only for the good of the people.

The *Kohein Gadol* also had access to the vast treasuries of the *Mikdash*. Many of the *Kohanim Gedolim* in this period who were appointed by the Roman rulers took advantage of their power and misappropriated the funds, sharing the wealth with the rulers who had appointed them. The *tzedukim* also did what they could to get their hands on the treasures. Yishmael changed things. He allowed the God-fearing Jews to appoint a suitable treasurer and stopped the *tzedukim* from being able to plunder the wealth.

Political Turmoil | 127

Agrippas was constantly worried about a rebellion and wanted to show everyone that he was the monarch. He therefore built a balcony on his palace from which he could see the sacrifices being brought and what was going on in the area around the *azara*.

The wise men considered this a disgrace of the Holy Temple. They decided to build up the wall of the *azara* that faced the king's palace, using the Temple's treasury funds. When it was complete, the king was no longer able to see what was going on in the Temple. The wall even blocked the Roman watchtower that had always served as their lookout over the *Mikdash*.

Agrippas went wild. Festus was furious and ordered the wall to be destroyed. The Elders of Yerushalayim didn't give in. They advised that the matter be brought before the emperor himself, so that he could decide who was correct. And so, a delegation of the Elders of Yerushalayim and Yishmael the *Kohein Gadol* went to Rome. Hashem made the emperor agree to their position. The emperor agreed that the wall should be left in place.

As a result of this defeat, Agrippas was quick to replace Yishmael ben Fiabe with a *tzeduki* acquaintance of his, Yosef ben Shimon, who was called Kabi. This meant that the power over Yerushalayim and the Temple treasuries was again in the hands of the Sadducees. Later, Agrippas replaced Kabi with Chanan, another Sadducee who ended up being even worse than his predecessor.

The upright Roman representative Festus died in the interim. The emperor sent Luis Albinus to replace him. At the same time, Chanan the *Kohein Gadol* made a new "Sanhedrin" of *tzedukim*. They judged their cases any way they pleased. Their decisions had nothing to do with Torah law and showed great cruelty.

The Torah scholars were worried about the effect such a "Sanhedrin" could have, especially one that claimed it was acting in the name of Torah law. They quickly sent a delegation to Luis Albinus who was on his way to Yerushalayim. They posited that it was impudent of the Sadducees to appoint a court without getting permission from the ruling government. Albinus agreed with them and immediately sent a harsh letter warning them what the results of their actions might be.

Agrippas saw what Albinus was like. Determined to stay on the good side of the stronger party, he swiftly replaced Chanan the *Kohein Gadol* with Yeshua ben Damani. The Sadducee "Sanhedrin" was no more and the Torah Sanhedrin came back.

Albinus finally reached Yerushalayim after a delay. In the meantime, all the effort that his predecessor had invested in establishing law and order were lost. The *sikrikim* reared their ugly head. The Sadducees gained power and were even able to, later on, convince the Roman representative to side with them. There was a full-fledged civil war going on. Agrippas didn't take advantage of his position of power to help his brothers by influencing the emperor and his men.

To summarize what was going on, the power lay with the *sikrikim*. They ruled the streets and instilled fear in everyone, thereby being able to overcome the *tzedukim*'s plots. The *tzedukim* held the power, on the other hand, over the king's officers and the Roman representatives, as well as the *Kehuna Gedola* and the treasuries of the *Mikdash*. The *tzedukim* were loyal to Agrippas, who was fast losing the admiration of the inhabitants of Yerushalayim.

Albinus the Roman appointee was totally corrupt. He imposed all sorts of taxes on the people. He stole and oppressed the people. He was glad to accept bribes from anyone who offered them. This fact strengthened the position of the *biryonim* who were determined to overthrow Roman rule. They gained strength daily and there was no one to stop them.

Political Turmoil | 129

The people lost out on both sides. The Roman appointee sowed havoc in the city, as did the *biryonim*. The people were caught in the middle, doubly hit with murder and thievery.

The emperor decided to replace Albinus at some point, sending Gessius Florus in his stead. Before Albinus left his position, he left the people of Yerushalayim with a "goodbye present." He freed all the people in jail, thus freeing murderers and thieves. Yerushalayim became a ghost town. Between the *biryonim* and the criminals who were on the loose, the people feared for their lives when they went out.

The people were very excited when they heard that Albinus was being replaced. Their joy was premature, though. When Florus reached Yerushalayim, the situation only got worse!

Albinus had at least tried to cover up his vices, but Florus took pride in them. He levied unbearable taxes and killed and stole just to fill his coffers. Florus did all he could to start up with the Jews under his rule. He plundered the treasuries of the *Mikdash*, as one example. This only further encouraged the people to rebel. "It's better for us to die in war than to die due to the indulgences of Florus!" the people said in their hearts. They were getting ready for a major rebellion against the Roman rule.

The situation went from bad to worse in Yerushalayim. Because Florus plundered the treasuries of the *Mikdash*, the people began to scorn him, wanting to defend the honor of the Temple. In response, Florus commanded his men to arrest the people who were against him. When his request went unfilled, he randomly picked people off the street to vent his anger on. Many thousands were killed that day. The Jews got angrier.

The rebellion didn't erupt yet, though. The people still hoped to be able to find a diplomatic solution towards peace. They therefore sent a delegation headed by the *tzeduki Kohein Gadol* with a message of peace to greet the Roman army that was making its way to Yerushalayim.

The plan didn't work. Florus heard about it and made it clear that he would not speak to the Jews at all. He threatened that if they would complain that they had been disgraced, he would attack them. And that is exactly what happened.

The Jewish delegation came to greet the legionnaires to offer their blessings. Their greetings weren't returned. When the Jews started to complain, the soldiers waited for the signal and then hurried to kill them!

Running after the escapees, the soldiers burst into the city. Their intent was obvious; they wanted to capture the *Mikdash*. The army of Florus that was already stationed in Yerushalayim aided the soldiers, greatly hoping to take charge of the *Mikdash* and its treasure houses.

Their plan was foiled. The people of Yehuda fought fiercely for the honor of their Temple. All the inhabitants of Yerushalayim gathered, ready to fight the Romans. They blocked their paths in the bending alleyways, until the army had no choice but to retreat and leave the city walls.

Florus decided, at this point, that he needed backup. He sent a letter full of lies to Cestius, the president of Syria. He described how he was up against an intense rebellion that he managed to suppress, but that he doesn't have enough soldiers and needs help.

Cestius was a moderate character. He refused to accept Florus's claim without investigating the facts. In order to see what the situation really was, he sent Neopolitanus to Yerushalayim. Here was the Jews' chance to be saved, assuming he would describe the facts as they were. It could have been the beginning of their salvation, if Agrippas hadn't been a traitor!

Political Turmoil | 131

Agrippas met Neopolitanus on the way to Yerushalayim. Instead of telling the truth about how evil Florus was, he placed the guilt squarely on the people's shoulders. The people of Yerushalayim sent a delegation to greet Neopolitanus and tell him about Florus. When they arrived, Agrippas, in Neopolitanus's presence, accused the people of being unwilling to bow to Roman rule and live in peace and order.

When Neopolitanus reached Yerushalayim, he did find out the truth. The crying widows of the men who had been killed came to meet him. They showed him the destroyed marketplace and the ruined houses that Florus's men were responsible for. The message back to Cestius, the Syrian president, was positive regarding the Jews.

Even though Florus didn't get the backup he had been hoping for, he continued to rule as the Roman representative. The people turned to Agrippas, begging him to send a letter to the Roman emperor to describe Florus's deeds and ask for his replacement.

Agrippas was not willing to do anything that jeopardized his power in any way. He acted as if he was willing to fulfill the request, but at the same time he soundly rebuked the people for considering rebellion. He asked them to be patient in waiting for the emperor to answer their request, and, in the meantime, to allow Florus and his men to rule.

Thus, Agrippas made it perfectly clear to the people that he sided with the decadent Florus. They understood through his comments what Agrippas was planning. He became their enemy and was even forced to leave Yerushalayim, angry and snubbed by the people he was supposed to govern.

It seemed that at this point, the Jews had real hopes for tranquility. The villain Florus and Agrippas the traitor had left the city. It seemed all the people had to do was explain to the emperor what had happened so he wouldn't be angry with them and then there would be real peace in Yerushalayim!

The Sadducees weren't happy with the situation. They feared their standing might be hurt and that the people might bring them to task for the damage they had done in the previous years. They sent a letter to Florus and Agrippas, asking them to quickly return with their soldiers to put down the rebellion that was brewing in the city.

There was nothing sweeter to their ears than hearing that civil war had broken out in Yehuda. Instead of them starting war, the Sadducees had done it for them. All Florus and Agrippas had to do was sit and wait and let the people fight amongst themselves.

Agrippas knew, though, that if he wanted the most benefit out of the infighting, the Sadducees, who were his allies, would have to win. He decided to send 3000 cavalry from his army to help "restore order."

The cavalry blew new life into the Sadducees. They overtook the upper city, while Elazar and his men controlled the lower city and *Har Habayis*.

For seven days, war raged in Yerushalayim, but neither side made progress in overtaking the other's territory. Many lives were lost on both sides.

This week of warring ended on the fourteenth of Av. The following day was Tu B'Av, a joyous holiday in the Jewish calendar. It was on this day that the tides turned. Elazar and the *sikrikim* chased the Sadducees out of the upper city.

When the zealots led by Elazar saw that they were winning, they laid siege on the Fortress of Antonia where the Roman legions that remained after Florus left had taken refuge. After two days of holding them under siege, Elazar and his men captured the tower and killed the Roman soldiers.

They also besieged the fortress where Agrippas's men were. Elazar's army was reinforced by Menachem Haglili, who came from the Galilee with arms he had taken from Masada.

In the end, Elazar's men made peace with Agrippas's soldiers and let them leave the fortress. Actually, the *biryonim* had also made a treaty not to hurt the Roman soldiers who were in their fortress, but the treaty was broken and they killed the Roman soldiers.

Once the enemies from the outside were taken care of, the infighting began. Menachem Haglili, who had come with his soldiers to help Elazar, started to force his rule upon the group. Elazar and the people didn't appreciate his grab for power. Menachem went too far when he entered the courtyard of the *Bais Hamikdash* like a king with his entourage. The people stoned him until he ran away. In the end he was caught and killed by Elazar's people.

We have to stress at this point that all the events we are describing here were not done with the agreement of the Torah scholars. The Torah leaders were adamantly against bloodshed and war. Their opinion was that the people should pledge their loyalty to the Roman emperor and ask for peace. The young, hot blooded people ruled, though, and they didn't listen to the advice of the sages.

Here we close another chapter in the days of war that came upon Yerushalayim. The civil war quieted down. The Roman army retreated. There was quiet. But not for long.

At this point, Cestius, the Roman army general, came up to Yerushalayim to put down the rebellion. His path was not easy. All along the way he had to fight tough battles against the Jews who tried to stop him from entering their borders. Finally, after absorbing great losses and killing many, he reached the gates of Yerushalayim.

134 | On Your Walls, O Jerusalem

The people of Yerushalayim, under Elazar, were ready for battle. The Sadducees, their enemies in the past, joined forces with Elazar's men. They understood that if the city would fall, they too would suffer. They saw the utter destruction Cestius had inflicted on the communities that had fought against him on his way to Yerushalayim.

Agrippas now stepped into the picture, intent on helping the Roman conquest and realizing that the Romans would never be successful if the people were on alert. Agrippas sent two of his friends to come in Cestius's name and ask for peace, offering a pardon for the past if they would put down their arms and accept Rome's rule.

Elazar and his men and the residents of the city weren't tricked by Agrippas's deceitful message. They understood that Agrippas was trying to mislead them into giving themselves up to the Romans, who would then kill them. Agrippas's friends, the Sadducees, fell for the plan. Agrippas managed to start civil war again between the Sadducees who wanted to give in and the zealots who were completely against it.

During the civil unrest, Cestius succeeded in advancing almost up to Yerushalayim itself. The Sadducees wanted to give up Yerushalayim to him, but their plan was discovered, and Elazar and his men managed to get them away from the walls of the city. Cestius tried for five days to overtake the city, but the men bravely defended themselves.

On the sixth day of fighting, the fighters of Yerushalayim lost strength. The stones the Romans had catapulted on them forced them to abandon their posts on the walls of the city. Cestius now had a way to conquer the city. He planned to dig under the wall and burn down the gates in order to enter the city itself.

It wasn't time, though, for the city to be destroyed. Illogically, Cestius suddenly became weak-hearted. He didn't understand that the Jewish fighters had retreated. He didn't know that the Sadducees were waiting for their chance to open the gates and help the Romans conquer the city. Against all reason, Cestius gathered his commanders and told them they were withdrawing.

When the Jewish warriors saw that Cestius was withdrawing, their bravery returned to them and they followed the Roman army, dealing them a mighty blow. The tired Romans, weighed down by heavy artillery, couldn't fight the light-footed Jewish men. Seeing no other option, they threw down their weapons and ran away, leaving the loot for their enemies. Many of the Sadducees had to run away also.

This temporary setback in the fall of Yerushalayim was just another chance for the Jews to maybe, just maybe, turn to their God and ask Him to remove the baseless hatred in their hearts. But the fire of baseless hatred raged on in them, and they closed their hearts to the entreaties of the sages. The destruction was getting closer.

12

On the Verge of War

Everyone realized that war was inevitable. The emperor wasn't going to ignore the fact that his powerful army led by Cestius was defeated by the Jewish fighters. The people of Yerushalayim, therefore, called a public gathering to decide what they could do to mitigate the oncoming trouble.

All the factions of the city participated in this gathering. Even the *tzedukim* came, acting as if nothing was more important to them than the welfare of the city.

The meeting concluded with resolutions to fortify and build up the city walls and appoint leaders over every section of the Holy Land to protect them from the emperor's wrath.

The people did not try to overthrow the Roman rule. They were just preparing themselves in self-defense in case the emperor considered what had taken place as a revolution against him.

Unfortunately, that's exactly what happened.

Chazal explain to us what led the emperor to conclude that the people were in fact rebelling. It is well known that the *Bais Hamikdash*

On the Verge of War | 137

was destroyed because of the sin of baseless hatred.[1] The events that led up to the destruction also came about through an incident based in senseless hatred.[2] The following story describes what happened.[3]

One of the wealthy men of Yerushalayim had a friend whose name was Kamtza and an enemy whose name was Bar Kamtza. Their names were very similar and that fact is what led to a mix up with horrible ramifications.

The wealthy man decided one day to host a banquet. He wanted to invite the Torah leaders of the generation and his friend Kamtza. Of course, he had no intention of inviting his sworn enemy, Bar Kamtza.

The rich man sent his servant to invite his guests, as was done in those days. The servant didn't hear right and instead of writing Kamtza on the list of invitees, he wrote Bar Kamtza.

Perhaps the servant raised an eyebrow when he heard his master instruct him to invite his enemy Bar Kamtza, but he didn't see fit to question the invitation. In any event, he went to extend a royal invitation to Bar Kamtza for the meal.

Bar Kamtza accepted the invitation as a gesture of reconciliation.[4] If not, why would his enemy have invited him? He was delighted with the invitation and arrived at the party ready to end their fight.

He soon realized that there had been a mistake when the host turned to him angrily in front of the other guests and said, "If I'm not mistaken, we are enemies! Perhaps you could explain to me what you

---

1. Yuma 9:
2. Maharsha on Gittin 55:
3. Gittin 55:, Eichah Rabba 4:3 (with small changes that will be listed)
4. The Maharsha explains that Bar Kamtza was Kamtza's son. When Bar Kamtza got the invitation, he assumed that the man wanted to make up with him due to his love for his father.

are doing at my banquet?" He insisted that Bar Kamtza immediately get up and leave!

Bar Kamtza was perplexed. What should he tell him, that he was specifically invited to the party by the rich man's servant? That would make him look like a naïve fool for believing that the invitation was meant for him. Bar Kamtza didn't try to explain himself. Instead, he searched for a solution to the uncomfortable situation he found himself in.

"You're right. I really shouldn't have come," Bar Kamtza humbled himself. He added, "But since I came by mistake, I beg of you not to embarrass me by asking me to leave in the middle of the affair in front of all your guests! Let me stay. I give you my word that I will pay you back for the portion I eat."

The arrogant host refused the offer. "No way! You must leave immediately!" he said forcefully.

Bar Kamtza offered another suggestion. "I understand that my presence is marring your enjoyment. I ask of you not to humiliate me, in any case. I'll tell you what I'll do. You let me stay, and I'll pay for half of your whole banquet. This way, even though you'll be enjoying the party less, it will cost you less."

The man still refused. "I don't want your money, and I don't want you here!" he insisted.

Bar Kamtza tried one more time. "I'll pay for the entire affair. It won't cost you anything. This way, you don't have to feel you spent money on something you didn't enjoy." Again his offer was turned down. The host's patience was over. He grabbed Bar Kamtza by his garment and escorted him out of the hall.

Bar Kamtza was mortified. The humiliation of being shepherded out in front of all the guests was branded on his heart. He demanded revenge.

Since the Torah leaders of the generation were also present at the party,[5] Bar Kamtza was furious with them and blamed them for his disgrace. He felt that if they had cared that he was being shamed, they would have stood up and protested.[6] He included them in his plan for revenge.

Bar Kamtza came to the terrible decision to act as an informer and fabricate that the Jews were planning a revolt against the emperor.

That day, Bar Kamtza set out for Rome. After he arrived, he stated his claim to Nero the emperor. "My master the emperor! I have come from far to reveal to you that the Jews of Yerushalayim have rebelled against you!"

The emperor was not convinced so fast. "How should I know that you are telling the truth?" he asked.

Bar Kamtza had an answer ready and waiting. "Go check the validity of my words yourself.[7] Send a sacrifice to the Jews of Yerushalayim for them to offer in their Holy Temple. See if they will fulfill your request! I am sure the Jews will disgrace your sacrifice!"

---

5. The Midrash explains that Zecharia ben Avkulus was the one that was at the party and didn't protest.

6. The Maharsha explains that it might have been that they couldn't protest.

7. The Midrash says that the main issue in the tale-bearing of Bar Kamtza was that he said the Jews would not sacrifice the emperor's animal, but would bring another in its place and eat that one themselves. The Midrash doesn't mention the discussion about killing Bar Kamtza so that he wouldn't badmouth them to the emperor. According to their opinion about what Bar Kamtza said (that they would switch the animal), had Bar Kamtza not returned to the emperor, the emperor would have wanted to know why he didn't come back and would have found out what happened.

His suggestion was accepted. That day, the emperor sent with Bar Kamtza[8] a healthy, beautiful lamb to the *Bais Hamikdash*. He even decorated the lamb with a golden crown and a cloak of royal purple studded with precious stones. He also covered his ears with gold.[9]

There was no reason the sacrifice shouldn't be accepted. Besides the Jewish sacrifices, sacrifices of gentiles who wished to serve the true God were offered in the *Bais Hamikdash*. Bar Kamtza, though, had a plan to make sure the sacrifice was not accepted.

At one of their stops on the way to Yerushalayim, without anyone noticing, he made a small blemish on the upper lip of the animal that the emperor had sent.[10] It was the type of flaw that made the animal unacceptable as a sacrifice according to the Torah, but the gentiles would not consider it a fault at all.

The sages were now in a difficult predicament. On one hand, according to Torah law, they were forbidden to bring the animal as a sacrifice. On the other hand, they couldn't explain to the emperor why they were refusing his sacrifice. If they would tell him that the animal was blemished, he would claim that such a thing was not considered a flaw.

The sages debated the issue. In the beginning, they decided to sacrifice the animal, even though it was blemished. They decided to forgo the law in order to make sure there was peace with the ruling power. They understood that refusing the sacrifice would place the

---

8. In the Midrash it seems that the emperor did not send the lamb with Bar Kamtza himself, but with a messenger who was supposed to report how the events unfolded, i.e., whether the sacrifice was brought or not.
9. Tzemach David
10. According to another opinion in the Gemara there, the blemish was in the eye.

On the Verge of War | 141

Jews in significant danger. In a case of life and death, one is allowed to ignore Torah prohibitions.

Rabbi Zecharia ben Avkulus, one of the greatest sages of the generation, disagreed. "Although there is place to allow the sacrificing of a blemished animal to ensure peace, there is a greater danger involved in bringing the sacrifice. Someone might learn from our ruling that it is permitted to bring blemished animals as sacrifices and not understand it was an exceptional ruling made for that time only."

"If so, it is best that we assassinate Bar Kamtza so he won't be able to tell the emperor what happened," argued the sages. "If we make sure he is killed and hide the fact, the emperor will assume that his sacrifice was brought in an honorable fashion. He'll assume that Bar Kamtza never returned because he was ashamed that his lie was uncovered."

Zecharia ben Avkulus again disagreed. "If so, people may say that someone who blemishes a sacrifice deserves to die. They will say that all Bar Kamtza did was make a blemish on the animal. Killing Bar Kamtza can lead to grave misunderstandings in Torah law."

We find in *Chazal* that Zecharia ben Avkulus is taken to task for being overly patient. Patience is a wonderful quality, but not when it is overdone. Then it can lead to tragic results, as it did here. Our rabbis phrased it thus: "The humility of Rabbi Zecharia ben Avkulus destroyed our Temple and burned our *heichal* and exiled us from our land!"[11]

---

11. Even though the decree had been issued, it is possible that the emperor would have left the Temple where his sacrifice had been brought (Maharsha).

142 | On Your Walls, O Jerusalem

Be that as it may, the sages decided to refuse the emperor's animal. Bar Kamtza went[12] and told the emperor that his sacrifice was turned away, and that it was proof of the mutiny of the Jewish people.

Adding to the impression[13] that the Jews were about to revolt was the fact that Elazar and his men made a new rule forbidding sacrifices from non-Jews to be offered in the Temple. Because of the civil war that had taken place, they were worried that the Romans, with the aid of Agrippas and the Sadducees, would try to take control of the Temple when they came to offer sacrifices. Again, the Torah allows sacrifices from the nations, but Elazar, with the backing of the people who were oppressed by the Romans, forbade them.

This new edict did not find favor in the Romans' eyes nor in the eyes of the sages. The sages tried to explain to the *Kohanim* who were following Elazar's directive that what they were doing was against *daas Torah*. The Torah allows the offering of gentile sacrifices. Their words had no effect.

Wind of this new edict reached the emperor, who took it as another proof that the Jews were trying to revolt. He decided to send his army, under the command of Nero[14] the army general, to stop the insurgency.

---

12. The Midrash says that it was the emperor's emissary who told him his sacrifice was refused. On the first day, in order to buy time, the Kohanim said they would bring the sacrifice the next day. The same thing happened on the second and third day, at which point he went and told the emperor that they had replaced his sacrifice.

13. This section is based on historical books.

14. In the Gemara it says that Nero Kaisar was sent by the emperor to conquer Yerushalayim and he was the one who converted. It seems from the Midrash (1:31) that Nero was the emperor himself. It says in the book Midrashei Koros Ameinu V'Hamikdashim that it is possible that the

On the Verge of War | 143

Even when he reached Yerushalayim, Nero the general still doubted the wisdom in waging a war. The nations of the world knew that the Jews were God's beloved sons, and He didn't let them fall to their enemies easily. Passed down in tradition were stories of kings who had started up with the Jews and suffered a strong defeat. Nero decided to set up a short experiment to see what his chances of success were.

The first stage of the experiment had already been used by Nevuchadnezar hundreds of years before. He shot arrows to the four directions. All the arrows, no matter in which direction they had been aimed, turned towards Yerushalayim.[15]

That wasn't enough for Nero. He then asked one of the children of Yerushalayim what he had learned that day. The child quoted a verse

---

emperor and the army general had the same name – Nero as was common in those days. This is what it also says in the Tzemach David. Both the emperor and his underling were called Nero, and it was the second one who went to Yerushalayim. It is brought there from Seder Hadoros (Davar Acher 829) that Nero was the emperor and not the army general. The Maharam Shif says that Nero was the army general, not the emperor. From the Gemara and the Midrash it seems that they both had the same name and that it was the army general who went to Yerushalayim. In the Tzemach David there are different opinions saying that it was the emperor who went to fight Yerushalayim and even converted. His conversion was only private, on the outside things remained the same and he continued to sit on the throne until he died.

15. The Maharsha explains that this was the point of commenting on the arrows that were shot in every direction. If not, there was nothing learned from the arrow that was shot towards Yerushalayim and reached it. See the next chapter where it is explained that it was a good sign the arrow test worked.

from Yechezkel,[16] "And I will lay My vengeance upon Edom by the hand of My people Israel. They shall do to Edom according to My anger and My fury and they shall know My vengeance, says God."

Nero was intelligent and understood the message. Hashem wanted him to destroy His Temple, but at the same time vowed to take revenge on whoever did it. "I don't want to be the one to destroy God's house and then afterwards be punished for it," Nero said to himself. He left his vast army and converted. Amongst his descendants was Rabbi Meir, the holy *tanna*!

The emperor heard that Nero had defected from the army and converted. He also heard about the tremendous defeat Cestius had suffered around the walls of Yerushalayim. The emperor worried that this would be the beginning of a series of revolutions in different areas that Rome had captured. He decided that the matter had to be taken care of.

He sent another very talented army general, Vespasian, to take Nero's place in his quest to stop the rebellion in Yerushalayim.

Vespasian made his way to the city via the Galil and the lowlands along the shore, leaving death and destruction wherever he stepped foot. In a number of places, including the fortified city Yudfas, he came against heavy opposition. He lost many men, but in the end he managed to conquer the city, killing tens of thousands.

We are not going to describe all the battles that took place in the Land of Israel, but *Chazal* mention the fall of Tur Malka, which was Har Hamelech in Efraim. From what happened there we can learn a lot about what was going on in general at the time.

---

16. Yechezkel 25:14

On the Verge of War | 145

Chazal[17] tell us that in Har Hamelech, King Yannai built 600,000 villages![18] *Chazal* say that each of these villages[19] had as many inhabitants as the number of people that left Egypt, that is to say, 600,000 men![20] If you multiply the number of villages by the number of inhabitants in each, you reach the astronomical number of 360,000,000,000 people!

If you would go to the location of Har Hamelech today, not only would you wonder how so many people lived there, but it would be hard to see how even six hundred thousand people could live there. The sages have already explained that when the Jews were exiled, the land shrank, just as the skin of a deer shrinks when it is removed and can no longer cover the body of the animal.

Another *Chazal*[21] about the wondrous size of Har Hamelech teaches that one of the villages there produced 600,000 vessels containing salted fish to feed the workers who harvested the figs every

---

17. Gittin 57.

18. In the Yerushalmi (Taanis 24.) it says that there were "only" 10,000 villages in Har Hamelech, of which 1,000 were owned by Rabbi Elazar ben Charsom.

19. Besides three villages that had double that many inhabitants. They were Kfar Bish (The Bad Village), named after the bad character of the people that wouldn't host guests, Kfar Shachlayim, named after the employment of the inhabitants who made a food called Shachlayim, and Kfar Dachria, where the women gave birth mostly to boys, and would cease giving birth after having one girl.

20. We have to clarify if the number means 600,000, the number of men over twenty that went out of Egypt, or the millions who went out of Egypt if we count the women and children. If so, the number of people living there is astounding.

21. Berachos 44.

week. This wasn't the food for the entire population of the village; it only fed one type of worker!

There were also three villages in Har Hamelech[22] whose notebooks recording the taxes they owed the king had to be loaded on wagons because they were so heavy!

Another story in *Chazal* describes one of the cities of Har Hamelech in which eighty pairs of *Kohanim* married eighty pairs of daughters of *Kohanim* in one night. That means there were eighty affairs in which two *Kohanim* married two daughters of *Kohanim*. And that was in one city in one night, and only takes into consideration the *Kohanim*! This story also only accounts for a unique situation. Additionally, there were *Kohanim* who married daughters of *Kohanim* who were not sisters and *Kohanim* sisters that married *Kohanim* that weren't brothers and *Kohanim* who married *Leviim* and *Yisraelim*. There were also *Leviim* and *Yisraelim* who married *Kohanim* women. And all this in one night in one city!

Har Hamelech was completely destroyed in the end. *Chazal*[23] teach us that the destruction was the result of an incident that happened with a rooster and a hen.

It was the custom that when a groom and bride went to the wedding canopy, the guests would take out a rooster and a hen, symbolizing their blessing to the couple, "May you multiply like chickens!"

One night, in one of the villages in Har Hamelech, a troop of Roman soldiers passed by when the groom and bride were about to be married. They decided to hassle the Jews whom they hated so much and took their chickens.

---

22. Yerushalmi Taanis 24.
23. Gittin 57.

On the Verge of War | 147

The Jews didn't take the incident sitting down. They fought against the soldiers and killed many of them. When the emperor heard about it, he considered what the Jews had done a rebellion. He didn't know the circumstances surrounding the incident, and, even if he had, probably wouldn't have considered the stolen chickens ample reason for going out to battle.

The emperor sent his army to Har Hamelech to avenge the blood of his fallen troops.

It turned out to be not so simple to conquer the mountain. The Jews had a very strong and courageous man called Bar Daroma on their side. He was so strong that he could jump a *mil* in one jump. He caused the Romans great damage and was too swift for them to catch. The Roman emperor realized that he could lose his whole army to one man!

At this point, the emperor decided to pray to Hashem. He put his crown on the ground and said, "Master of the entire universe, if it is good in Your eyes, I ask You not to deliver me and my whole army into the hands of one man! It would be too much of a shame and a disgrace!"

The emperor's prayer, even though it wasn't with good intentions, aroused a prosecution in heaven against Bar Daroma. The negative power of that prosecution caused him to say[24] the wrong thing. "You, our God, have left us and will no longer go out with our troops!" Bar Daroma said arrogantly. He had the feeling of *kochi v'otzem yadi assa li es hachayil hazeh*, i.e., it is the strength of my own hands that brings me success. His arrogance was sinful, and it was decreed he should die.

---

24. David Hamelech said something similar, but Chazal teach us that David said it as a question. Bar Daroma was making a statement that it was because of his own strength and not Hashem's providence that he was winning the war.

148 | On Your Walls, O Jerusalem

None of the mighty soldiers could capture him, but Hashem subdued him. When he went to use the bathroom, a snake came and pulled out his innards. He died on the spot.

The emperor understood that he wasn't saved through the prowess of his army. Had Hashem not killed Bar Daroma, his whole army might have fallen to that one man! The emperor decided to retreat and to leave the Jews in Har Hamelech alone for the time being.

Hashem, though, had decided that it was time for Har Hamelech to be destroyed, so the story unfolded in an unexpected way.

. When the emperor turned to leave, the Jews began celebrating their miraculous victory. They lit candles and celebrated joyously. The light from the candles was so powerful that one could see a coin a *mil* away from the city!

They didn't thank God for their victory, though. They attributed it to their great strength. It was decreed, as a result, that they would not be saved from their enemies.

The emperor heard of their celebrations. Instead of understanding what anyone would, that they were celebrating their victory, he decided that they were mocking his downfall! He decided to come back and fight with 300,000 sword-bearing soldiers. He fought the Jews for three days and three nights. Since we understand how many people lived in Har Hamelech, we can see why it took so long to kill them out, even with such an enormous army.

Har Hamelech was so large that people on one side didn't hear about the war that was taking place on the other end. Ironically, as blood was being spilled like water on one end of the mountain, the people were still celebrating their victory on the other, not knowing how near their end was.

Har Hamelech is a good example of what was going on at the time. Millions were killed, brave and powerful warriors fell because of

Hashem's decree, and the cities were conquered and destroyed by the powerful and cruel Romans.

While Vespasian was busy destroying the Galil, subduing city after city, things were heating up in Yerushalayim. Yochanan Haglili, a man from Gush Chalav, arrived in the city, having escaped the Romans when they destroyed his city. He sided with the zealots who were intent on vanquishing the Romans through force. He quickly moved up through the ranks to become one of the heads of the zealots.

At the time, the Yerushalmi people were divided into two camps. The first wanted to subjugate themselves to the Romans and avoid war. The Sadducees were in this camp, as they were similar in philosophy and viewpoint to the Romans. Also in this camp were the Torah scholars who understood that the rebellion against the Romans couldn't be successful and would end in calamity.

The other camp was the camp of the zealots, the *biryonim*, headed by Elazar and Yochanan Haglili. They were ready to die in battle, and their goal was to chase the Romans out of Yerushalayim and the Land of Yehuda. They paid no attention to the position of the Torah scholars and their warnings.

The *biryonim* from all the cities in Yehuda that had fallen to the Romans gathered in Yerushalayim, hoping at least to protect Yerushalayim.

There was bloody fighting between the two factions of Jews. The scholars took no part in these clashes, but the *tzedukim* did.

At one point, the *tzedukim* managed to garner followers amongst the inhabitants of the city who were afraid of war with the Romans. When the zealots saw that they weren't strong enough to win, they did something unheard of. They sent messengers to Edom, asking them to help. The Edomites, fond of fighting in general, happily complied.

Tens of thousands were killed in these battles of one brother against the other. There was even fighting within the *Mikdash* grounds. The Temple Mount was covered in blood.

Not only did the zealots murder without mercy, kill anyone who seemed to be against them, and torture people to force them to join their side, they even desecrated the bodies of those who had died and would not let the people eulogize them or bury them. They killed anyone who tried to uphold the dignity of the dead.

Throughout this period, the *Kohanim* still performed the service in the Temple. People were killing each other left and right, but the *Kohanim* still continued to bring the *korbanos*.

At one point, the Edomites realized that they were just a tool being used by the zealots to destroy, and so they left. Before they left, though, the zealots managed to take control of the city streets. Many joined them, either willingly or out of terror. They gathered around Yochanan Haglili, the unofficial leader of the masses of *biryonim*.

Yochanan now left Yerushalayim on a killing rampage against the cities that had given in to the Romans. Many fell in this unnecessary civil war, but this became a turning point in the downfall of Yochanan and his men.

One of the cities that Yochanan came against sent a letter of peace to Vespasian asking for his help. He gladly acceded to their request and killed much of the riffraff that made up Yochanan's group.

Another facet of the war in Yerushalayim was Shimon ben Giyora, a man from Geresh. He was a young and extremely powerful man who had a small militia. He was brought in by the *tzedukim* to try and strengthen their cause.

Eventually, the camp of the *biryonim* also split into two. One side was headed by Yochanan Haglili and the other by Elazar ben Anneni. Both were stationed on the Temple Mount. Yochanan's group was on the mountain itself; Elazar's group was positioned in the gates of the Temple.

The *Kohanim* continued to perform their service without stop. Many fell due to the infighting between the two factions of the zealots that was taking place in the *Mikdash* itself.

People were dying everywhere, whether at the hands of the zealots or at the hands of the Romans. Hundreds of thousands lost their lives. Vespasian continued to advance, slowly reaching his destination, Yerushalayim. He besieged the city with his mighty army, a siege that was to end in the destruction of the Temple.

13

Under Siege Again

Vespasian did as the emperor Nero commanded him and laid siege on Yerushalayim for three years.[1]

Actually, the Jews would have had no problem dealing with a siege on their city.[2] There were three wealthy men[3] at the time, each of whom agreed to support the city for twenty one years![4] Their names were Nakdimon ben Gurion,[5] Ben Kalba Savuah[6] and Ben Tzitzis

---

1. Gittin 56.

2. Gittin 56.

3. Eichah Rabba 1:31. The Midrash lists four wealthy men, naming ben Gurion and ben Nakdimon as two separate people.

4. In Eichah Rabba it says that each of these wealthy men could support the city for ten years.

5. He was called this name because nikdah lo chamah, meaning the sun shone again for him. This is referring to the incident (Taanis 19: through 20) where he borrowed cisterns of water for the people who were olei regel and promised to pay back the water or its value if the cisterns didn't fill up. On the day the debt was due, Hashem answered his prayers and sent rain to fill up the cisterns. He also made the sun go back in the sky to an earlier hour since the due date had already passed.

6. He was called this because anyone who came into his house hungry as a dog (kalba) left satisfied (savuah).

Hakeses.[7] Each of them agreed to support the city in one area. One was to supply the wheat and barley, one the wine, salt and oil and one the wood needed for cooking.

Had things gone as they should have, the siege would not have affected them. There is no army that can hold a siege for twenty one years! Not having to worry about starvation, the Jewish people would have held out as long as it took.

The *biryonim*, though, were intent on doing whatever it took to force the people to wage war against the Romans. These *biryonim* believed in their great strength and did not listen to the sages. Although some people had joined the cause out of fear of the zealots, most people preferred to live a tranquil life. The *biryonim* knew that as long as there was food in the city, they would not be able to advance their plan.

The zealots came up with a plan. They burned down the storehouses of the three philanthropists! They destroyed 1,400 storehouses![8] They assumed that the resulting food crisis would bring more people to side with them.

It is incredible to think what horrible decisions a person can come to when he doesn't take the advice of the Torah leaders and instead does whatever seems right to him at the time. In one fell swoop, the *biryonim* destroyed the Jews' chance of surviving the Roman onslaught. The zealots brought about the *churban* with their own hands!

---

7. He was called this because his tzitzis used to drag on pillows when he walked through the streets because he was so wealthy. The poor would collect these pillows (keses) and sell them, thus supporting themselves. According to another opinion in the Gemara, it was because his kess, his place (as they used to recline on pillows), was amongst the leaders of Rome.

8. Tzemach David

Soon enough, the people felt the shortage. In the beginning[9] they were able to bribe the enemy soldiers by sending them a container full of gold, which the Romans returned full of wheat. After a while, the Romans returned only barley for the gold. Later, the Romans sent only straw. It was hard for them to satiate their hunger with the straw, but the cooked straw gave off a little starch that helped them survive. In the end, the Romans returned their container of gold... empty. Starvation became rampant.

A story is brought in the *Gemara* that shows us what was happening at the time.[10] There was a woman named Marsa bas BaisusBaisus. She was a very wealthy woman who was used to the lifestyle of the affluent and dined on delicacies.

During this period of starvation, she had to make do with less. She sent her maidservant one day to the market to get some fine flour to bake bread. The maidservant went to the market, but there was no fine flour left, only white bread.

She returned to her mistress, explaining that there was no fine flour available, but that there was plain white bread. The mistress sent her back to get the white bread.

By the time she returned to the marketplace, that too was gone. She hurried back to Marsa to tell her that now there was only black bread.

With instructions to get the black bread, so at least there would be something to eat, the maidservant went to the market, only to find that that too was gone.

---

9. Eichah Rabba 1:39

10. Gittin 56.

The maid returned to explain to her mistress that there was no food at all to be bought! She told her mistress that her only option was to go out herself in search of something to stave off her hunger.

Marsa bas BaisusBaisus went out to the streets, having no choice. When she went out, she stepped on something filthy that was lying on the ground. She was so disgusted and distraught that she perished on the spot. When Rabbi Yochanan ben Zakai heard the story, he ascribed the *pasuk* to her: "The tender and delicate woman among you, who would not venture to set the sole of her foot up on the ground for fastidiousness and delicateness, her eye shall be evil towards the husband of her bosom and towards her son and towards her daughter… towards her children whom she shall bear, for she shall eat them for want of all things in secret, because of the siege and distress wherewith your enemy shall distress you in your gates."[11]

This is one version of how Marsa bas Baisus Baisusdied. The *Gemara* brings another version that is a bit different. In this account, Marsa found one of the figs that Rabbi Tzadok had sucked on and discarded between his fasts.[12] She tried to eat it, but because she was so finicky, she passed away.

Before she died,[13] she managed to take out all her gold and silver and throw it into the marketplace, claiming, "What good are all my fortunes if I am to die of starvation?!" About her the verse states, "Their money they will throw outside."[14]

---

11. Devarim 28:56-57
12. When he fasted for forty years before the churban.
13. It's hard to understand how she could have done this if she died suddenly from being disgusted. It's possible that she threw her money out before she left to wander the streets, when she realized money wouldn't buy her anything.
14. Yechezkel 7:19

The famine raged on. The Romans weren't satisfied with letting the starvation run its natural course of destruction. They roasted goats near the western part of the city so that the eastern wind would bring the smell into the city and make the people feel even hungrier. Many people who were on the brink of survival expired due to the mouth-watering smell.[15]

The situation was so severe that the fighters positioned on the walls of the city would challenge each other, wagering food.[16] They would announce that anyone who could bring five heads of Vespasian's soldiers would get five dates. And the men took the challenge successfully. It was worth it for them to go down into the enemy's camp and kill five men just for five dates.

When Vespasian saw how brave the Jewish fighters were, he understood what a wise decision it had been to make sure they didn't have food or drink. He would examine their bowel movements, seeing that they didn't contain any remnants from grains. He understood, therefore, that the famine was brutal. He said to his men, "Look how brave the warriors of Yehuda are – and they are surviving on almost nothing! Imagine what they would be like if they had proper nutrition – they would kill seven times the amount of us at least!"

The man who was in charge of the storehouses and burned them down in the end was ben Batiach.[17] He was the head of the *biryonim*[18] and a relative of the *gadol hador* Rabbi Yochanan ben

---

15. Eichah Rabba 4:12
16. Avos D'Rabbi Nosson, end of 86
17. Gittin 56. and Eichah Rabba 1:30-31
18. In Chazal it says that ben Batiach was the head of the biryonim, but in the history books it mentions Elazar ben Anneni the Kohein, Yochanan

Zakai. Not only was ben Batiach not interested in considering his illustrious relative's opinion on what to do about the Romans and how it was wrong to destroy the people of Yerushalayim's food supplies, he was even willing to kill Rabbi Yochanan over his opinions.

Chazal[19] tell us that when Rabbi Yochanan ben Zakai heard that the food storehouses were burned down, he let out a cry of pain. "Woe!" he said. His sister's son, ben Batiach, heard about the *gadol hador*'s reaction and called him in to see if what he heard was true.

It was obvious that if ben Batiach was able to verify that Rabbi Yochanan was upset about what he had done with the stores of food that Rabbi Yochanan would be killed. The *biryonim* had no mercy on anyone who might threaten their control.

Rabbi Yochanan, therefore, had to deny that he had been distressed to save his life. He claimed, "I didn't say 'woe,' I said 'wow!'"

"What were you so happy about?" ben Batiach asked his uncle. He couldn't believe that his uncle would be happy with what he had done.

Rabbi Yochanan ben Zakai said, "I was happy that you burned down the storehouses of food. Now the people will have no choice but to get up and fight against the cursed Romans!"

Haglili and Shimon ben Giyora. If ben Batiach wasn't mentioned at all, it's hard to say that he was the main leader over all the biryonim. We do find in the Midrash (Eichah Rabba 1:31) that ben Batiach was in charge of the treasury. Therefore, perhaps we can say that although ben Batiach was appointed to be in charge of the treasury only, since it was such an important position it was as if he was the main leader.

19. Eichah Rabba 1:30-31

158 | On Your Walls, O Jerusalem

Ben Batiach believed him and sent him on his way. Thus, Rabbi Yochanan saved his life. The rabbis apply the *pasuk,* "Wisdom saves his owner," to him.

It seems, though, that although ben Batiach acted tough and threatening to his uncle, it was because he was afraid of his fellow *biryonim*. Privately, he would have acted differently, as *Chazal* describe a different incident that shows another side of ben Batiach.

Three days after the stores of food were set aflame,[20] Rabbi Yochanan ben Zakai walked through the streets of Yerushalayim. He saw the people drinking water that straw had been soaked in, hoping to consume the little starch that was left in it.

Rabbi Yochanan wondered, "People who are living off straw water can fight against the awesome Roman army?" He decided that he had to find a way to contact Vespasian and come to some sort of settlement.

Rabbi Yochanan sent a secret message to his nephew ben Batiach, who was also known as Abba Sirka, the head of the *sikrikim*. He asked for a clandestine meeting.[21]

Although ben Batiach didn't listen to his uncle's opinion on how to deal with the Romans and was even willing to kill him out of fear of his companions, he still had too much respect for his uncle to refuse his request.[22]

When ben Batiach came to the meeting, Rabbi Yochanan came right to the point. "Tell me, why are you doing this? Why are you

---

20. Eichah Rabba 1:31
21. Gittin 51., Eichah Rabba 1:31
22. It could be that Rabbi Yochanan realized that ben Batiach was speaking in such a negative way during their first meeting because he was afraid of his compatriots. He therefore asked to meet with him privately to try and work out a way to save the people with him.

hurting the people? Why did you burn their stores of food when by doing so you are causing their death by starvation?" he asked.

Abba Sirka answered, "Look, my uncle, personally I think you are right. I have changed my opinion now that I have come to the realization that the *biryonim* are not out for the good of the people. But what can I do? I can't influence them at all! If I criticize them at all, I am sure to find myself dead!"

What he was saying was true, and Rabbi Yochanan ben Zakai agreed that there would be no purpose in Abba Sirka losing his life in protest. He asked his nephew to help him get out of the city so that he could come to some sort of agreement with Vespasian.

Abba Sirka came up with a plan. "I can only think of one way to get you out of the city," he began. "You have to have your students spread a rumor that you are very ill, on your deathbed. After a few days have passed, have them announce that you have died.

"Have your students ask permission of the *biryonim* to take you out of the city limits for burial. As we know, according to Jewish law you can't leave a dead body in Yerushalayim.

"Then, you have to make sure of two things. Take something that smells putrid, like an animal carcass, and put it in the coffin with you. This way, no one will wonder why the usual bad smell isn't emanating from the dead body. Finally, make sure that no one carries you in your coffin except your students. This is to ensure that no one will notice that the coffin is too light to contain a dead body, as live people are lighter."

Rabbi Yochanan agreed to Abba Sirka's plans and followed them exactly.

When the time came, Rabbi Eliezer and Rabbi Yehoshua carried the coffin, with Abba Sirka leading them. When they reached the city gates, they realized that it was not going to be simple to convince the guards to let them out. If Abba Sirka hadn't been with them, the plan probably would have been foiled.

The guards were worried, and rightly so, that the whole scene was a trick to get Rabbi Yochanan out of the city so that he could make peace with the Romans. The position of the sages on the Roman issue was well known – they wanted peace.

In order to make sure that Rabbi Yochanan was actually dead, they decided that they would stab the body. Abba Sirka objected. "Do you want our enemies who are watching our every move to say that we disgrace the bodies of our *gedolim* by stabbing them?" he protested.

The words spoken by the leader of the *biryonim* hit their mark. Instead, they decided to shove the body, assuming that if Rabbi Yochanan was alive he would groan in pain. Abba Sirka again disagreed with what they intended to do. "Do you think that's much better than stabbing him? It's also a disgrace, and one that the Romans will surely note!"

The guards let the casket through. Rabbi Yochanan's two students put the coffin down far away from the guards in a burial cave outside the walls. They returned to the city, whispering a prayer for Rabbi Yochanan's success.

Rabbi Yochanan didn't waste a minute. As soon as the gates of the city were closed with his students back inside, he got up and went to the Roman camp, asking for an audience with the army general.

Vespasian assumed that Rabbi Yochanan wanted to announce the surrendering of the city and immediately agreed to see him. Rabbi Yochanan greeted the general, "Peace unto you, king! Peace unto you, king!"

Vespasian answered him, "You deserve death for two reasons. First of all, you called me king when I am not king, but just the army commander. What you said smacks of being a rebellion against the king.

"The second reason you deserve to die is that you didn't come until now to greet me and make peace. If according to you I am king, then you certainly should have come out of honor to my throne!"

Rabbi Yochanan wasn't put off by his words. He answered him, "In response to your first argument claiming that you aren't king, I am here to tell you that you are and if you are not you will be in the very near future.[23] If you ask how I know this, I will tell you that a verse in our Torah[24] reveals that Yerushalayim will only fall by the hands of a king, and it seems that Yerushalayim is destined to fall in your hands.

"Regarding your second argument, that if you are king I should have come to greet you earlier, you are right. I would have come a long time ago if it were possible, but there are zealots in the city who don't allow anyone to leave. It was only now that I managed to fool them and come out.

"And now that I have explained the situation in Yerushalayim, that it is controlled by zealots, I would like to request that you don't fight against the entire city's inhabitants. Most of them want peace. The

---

23. Rashi. Even though Vespasian wasn't the one in the end who conquered Yerushalayim, but Titus, it says in Tosafos that since he was the one who laid siege on the city for three years, it was as if he conquered it. The Yefeh Anaf adds that since Titus conquered the city at the command of Vespasian, it was considered as if Vespasian conquered it.

24. Yishayahu 10:34, "The Levanon will fall by a mighty one." A mighty one always refers to a king, as it says (Yirmiyahu 30:21), "And their mighty one (their king) will be from them." Levanon always refers to the Bais Hamikdash, as it says (Devarim 3:25), "This great mountain and the Levanon."

biryonim are forcing them through terror not to greet you in peace and surrender," concluded Rabbi Yochanan.

The Roman ruler began a philosophical argument by way of a parable.[25] "Tell me, if there is a barrel of wine with a snake in it, what should you do?" He was hinting at the fact that even though Yerushalayim was full of people wanting peace, the *biryonim* were calling for war. They are the snake.

Rabbi Yochanan knew what to answer. "You should call an expert at trapping snakes. Have him catch the snake and leave the barrel alone." He was telling the general to focus his efforts on catching the zealots and to leave the city in peace.

During their meeting there were four representatives of other countries. One was from the Arab countries. One was from Africa. One was from Alexandria, and one from the Philistines.

The name of the Arab representative was named Kilus or Panger. He interrupted the conversation at this point to give his opinion. He

---

25. The conversation is paraphrased from the Midrash. The Gemara says that Vespasian himself thought the barrel should be broken to kill the snake. Rabbi Yochanan didn't answer him back. About this, the Gemara brings the pasuk (Yishayahu 44:25), "He sets the wise back," that hints that since the decree was set against Yerushalayim, wisdom was taken away from the wise men and he didn't have a fitting answer that would result in the Jews being saved.

Another difference in the versions of the Gemara and the Midrash is that in the Gemara Rashi explains that Vespasian's intention was to convince Rabbi Yochanan that those who wanted peace should have broken the walls to let his soldiers in and, thus, chase the biryonim away. Rabbi Yochanan should have answered that they thought in the end they would chase the biryonim out of the city by peaceful means or trickery, and the city would be left whole. He didn't answer anything, though, as his wisdom was removed.

said that certainly the barrel should be smashed. Everything possible must be done to kill the snake. He was clearly hinting to the fact that he felt Yerushalayim should be destroyed.

Vespasian asked **Rabbi Yochanan** another question. "What about a wooden cabinet where precious items are stored but there is a snake inside?" Here, he was hinting at the *Bais Hamikdash*, where the zealots were stationed. Again, Rabbi Yochanan said the best idea would be to hire someone to catch the snake and leave the cabinet whole. Panger disagreed. He said the cabinet should be burned in order to kill the snake!

At this point, Vespasian, impressed with Rabbi Yochanan's intelligence, let Rabbi Yochanan answer Panger. "You should know," Rabbi Yochanan said, "that anyone who harms his neighbor harms himself! You Arabs are our neighbors. Instead of defending us and convincing Vespasian to leave us alone, you are advising him to destroy the city, including our Holy Temple!"

With feigned innocence, Panger answered, "I would never do such a thing! I am not against you; I am trying to help you. I know that as long as your Temple is standing, everyone comes to fight you out of jealousy. I suggest that it be destroyed so you will finally be able to live in peace and tranquility!"

Rabbi Yochanan replied with only one sentence. "Your heart knows what your true intentions are, for good or for bad!" He was hinting at the fact that in the end he would get his just dues. We will soon read about what happened to him in the end.

In the meantime, though, Vespasian took Panger's advice and continued with his plan to destroy Yerushalayim. What happened next made Vespasian gain tremendous respect for Rabbi Yochanan.

164 | On Your Walls, O Jerusalem

While they were speaking,[26] a special messenger arrived from Rome saying that the emperor Nero[27] had died and that, after much debate, it was decided that Vespasian should be appointed in his stead. Vespasian now saw clearly that the words of Rabbi Yochanan ben Zakai had come true.

Right after this, Vespasian again saw the wisdom of Rabbi Yochanan. When the messenger came, Vespasian was in the middle of putting on his shoes. He only had one shoe on when the messenger told him that he was now to be the emperor. He tried to put on his other shoe, but wasn't able to get it on his foot.

Confused, Vespasian looked to the people who were present, asking, "What is going on? Why is such a strange thing happening?"

Rabbi Yochanan answered him,[28] "The wisest of all men told us in the book of Proverbs[29] that when someone hears good news, his limbs

---

26. The Midrash brings a slightly different version. There it says that Rabbi Yochanan wasn't present when the messenger came. He was locked up in a room within another room seven times. They were trying to see if he was smart enough to tell day from night. He passed the test by following his regular learning schedule. He knew how much time passed based on how many chapters he was able to review in that time.
It's also brought in the Midrash that the messenger didn't come right away, but only after three days, when Vespasian was busy washing himself under a grapevine.
27. According to historians (Tzemach David part 2, 830 and more) there were a number of emperors between Nero and Vespasian. We rely on Chazal, though, who show us the truth of the events through their divine inspiration.
28. According to the Midrash, Rabbi Yochanan wasn't present. Apparently, he was summoned to offer his opinion on the strange occurrence with the shoe. Rabbi Yochanan's brilliance really shone through now. He correctly explained the event through his Torah wisdom without even knowing that Vespasian had heard good news.
29. Mishlei 15:30, "A good report makes the bones fat."

naturally swell. You just heard good news, so your foot is swollen. Ask that someone you hate be brought before you and you will see that you will be able to put on your other shoe. Misery makes a person's limbs shrink, as the wisest of all men said, 'A broken spirit dries the bones.'"[30]

Vespasian acted on Rabbi Yochanan's advice and it worked. The shoe suddenly fit again. Awed by Rabbi Yochanan's great wisdom, he decided to give him a gift. "I am going back to my country now, but I am going to send someone else to fight Yerushalayim until it falls. I am granting you a chance now to ask me for anything, and I will give it to you."

Rabbi Yochanan asked for three things. First, he asked that Yavne and its scholars should be spared. At that time, when the Sanhedrin exiled itself from Yerushalayim to Yavne, Yavne became the largest Torah center outside of Yerushalayim. Once Rabbi Yochanan saw that Yerushalayim was going to be destroyed and its inhabitants killed, he wanted at least to save the Torah.

The second thing he asked for was that the family of Rabban Gamliel the Nasi, who was from the royal family of Yehuda, be saved. He wanted to ensure that the royal line would survive.

Thirdly, he asked that physicians heal Rabbi Tzadok, whose body was severely weakened due to his fasting for forty years as he pleaded with God that Yerushalayim not be destroyed.[31] His extended fasting resulted in the fact that he could no longer eat.

The emperor granted those three requests.

---

30. Mishlei 17:22
31. The Gemara describes the recovery of Rabbi Tzadok. First he was given water that had bran soaked in it. He was then given water with coarse bran soaked in it and flour mixed in. After that he was given water with a higher percentage of flour mixed in and so on, until he became stronger.

166 | On Your Walls, O Jerusalem

Rabbi Akiva[32] felt that Rabbi Yochanan should have asked that Yerushalayim should be spared,[33] but Rabbi Yochanan felt that if he

---

The Midrash brings a totally different version. When Vespasian conquered Yerushalayim, he told Rabbi Yochanan that he could save someone who was dear to him before his soldiers entered and the situation went out of control. We have to look into the order of events further. It seems clear that Titus was the one who conquered the city. It could be that Vespasian was on the scene also, even if he wasn't commandeering the war. In that case, he could have told Rabbi Yochanan to take out whoever was dear to him, and Rabbi Yochanan chose Rabbi Tzadok.
Rabbi Eliezer and Rabbi Yehoshua were then sent to bring Rabbi Tzadok. They found him in the gates of the city on the outside. They brought him to Rabbi Yochanan and Vespasian. Vespasian then saw an astounding sight. Rabbi Yochanan, the leader of the generation, stood up before Rabbi Tzadok, who looked horrible due to his extreme thinness and weakness.
"Before this old man you stand up?" he asked.
Rabbi Yochanan answered Vespasian, "You should know, honored emperor, that if there had been one other man as righteous as Rabbi Tzadok in Yerushalayim, even double your soldiers would have been helpless and you never would have conquered the city."
He then explained that he was so thin because he would suck out the insides of a fig and then learn one hundred chapters.
It also says in the Midrash that after they healed Rabbi Tzadok, his son said to him, "Father, give them your reward in this world so that they won't get reward in the World to Come for helping you." Rabbi Tzadok agreed and told them two important pieces of wisdom in those days. He explained to them the wisdom of doing arithmetic on one's fingers, where one can figure out the multiplication tables just using his fingers, and the wisdom of a special kind of scale that was known to him but not to many others. This was enough payment for what they did. After all, they hadn't been able to return him to full health, as Rabbi Eliezer his son commented (Eichah Rabba 4:11).
32. Or Rabbi Yosef, according to another opinion in the Gemara.
33. According to the Midrash, Rabbi Yochanan did try to ask for

had asked for too much, his wishes wouldn't be fulfilled and he would have lost the opportunity completely.[34]

Before we close this topic, we need to mention what happened to Panger, the Arab representative who called for Yerushalayim to be destroyed.

After Yerushalayim was conquered, Vespasian divided the four walls of Har Habayis amongst the four representatives. Each one was in charge of destroying his wall. Panger was in charge of the Western Wall, what is known today as the *Kosel Hamaaravi*. This is the wall that Hashem's divine presence never leaves and which will never be destroyed.

All of the other representatives destroyed their walls easily, but Panger was unsuccessful. He knew he would have to face the emperor Vespasian's wrath. When called on the carpet for not fulfilling what he was commanded to do, Panger answered, "Oh great and powerful emperor, know that what I did was for your honor! I worried that if I destroyed the western wall, future generations would not know the incredible strength of Yerushalayim and what you captured! I decided to leave one little wall so that people will learn of your glory!"

Vespasian was not impressed. "No problem. It was a good idea. But since you neglected to fulfill a direct command, you need to be punished. Since you were worried about my glory, I will not punish

---

Yerushalayim to be spared, but the emperor explained to him that although he was now emperor, he was only appointed because of the war he waged against Yerushalayim. Chazal tell us that the verse, "Her enemies will be leaders," (Eichah 1:5) describes Vespasian. Because he fought against the Jews, he became a leader of the people.

34. It's brought in the Midrash that he asked for something else, that anyone who exited Yerushalayim from the western gate that faces Lod for four hours after the conquest of the city would be spared.

you, but you will punish yourself in my honor. Go up to the top of the tower and jump. God will be the judge. If you remain alive, then you deserve to live. If you die, though, that means that you deserved to."

Panger jumped and died, his body shattered. Thus, Rabbi Yochanan ben Zakai's curse came true.

Anyone who indicts his neighbor, the Jews, ends up destroyed!

14

The City is Conquered

Since Vespasian had to return to Rome to take the throne, he sent his son Titus to lead the battle against Yerushalayim. At the time, Titus was in Alexandria with his soldiers. At his father's command, he gathered all the troops from the surrounding countries and went to fight Yerushalayim. Titus was much more malevolent than his father and his campaign against Yerushalayim was sown in cruelty.

Before he even began to fight, he suffered a great loss. He thought that no Jews would be outside of the wall, and he therefore went on a tour of the walls of the city. There was a group of *biryonim* waiting in ambush for him, and they managed to kill many of the Romans. It was only by a miracle that Titus himself escaped.

This was Titus's first taste of Hashem's involvement in the destiny of His holy city. Hashem showed him how even a small group of Jews could have wiped him out. But he saw that God saved him, as he still had to do his job of destroying the *Bais Hamikdash*.

He prepared his men for ruthless battle, instilling in them a deep hatred of the Jews. He reminded them how Yaakov, their forefather, had "mistreated" the Romans' forefather, Esav. He also commanded that anyone who finds a Jew out of the city walls and doesn't kill him, will be killed himself. He made his goal clear: he wanted the Jews of Yerushalayim and Yehuda completely annihilated.

In Yerushalayim, when the Jews saw the vast Roman encampment, the different groups of *biryonim* made peace and united. Since their sinful baseless hatred was gone for the moment and instead peace reigned, they were able to stop even the mighty Roman army. The fighting was fierce and left many dead on both sides, and in the end the enemy army retreated. They were frightened by the incredible strength the Jews had. It even got to the point that many of Titus's fighters defected to the Jewish side and helped them out of fear!

The atmosphere of brotherhood was short lived, though. When the heat of the battle had passed, Yochanan Haglili, the leader of the group of *biryonim* that controlled the Temple Mount, decided to take over the entire city. His ambitions included being in charge of the *Bais Hamikdash*, which was now under the jurisdiction of the zealot Elazar ben Anneni.

During the fighting between the two groups, many innocent people lost their lives. In the end, the two factions decided to unite against the third group of zealots under Shimon ben Giyora, who ruled the lower city. Their treaty didn't do much to compensate the thousands who had been killed and wounded.

This pact didn't last either. When Shimon ben Giyora went out to fight Yochanan and his men, Elazar joined Shimon in his battle against Yochanan!

Hundreds of thousands of people lost their lives in those miserable days, many of whom didn't even merit burial! In addition, the *biryonim* stole the last bit of food out of the mouths of the people of the city. When they saw a home that was locked, they assumed that there was some food inside and broke in and mercilessly emptied it. If they saw someone on the street who didn't seem as gaunt as he should have looked, they would beat him to death to get him to reveal where his food stores were!

Many, many residents of the city left its borders in a desperate search for food. They faced the dangers of meeting up with a Roman who would kill them on the spot if caught, and being robbed by the *biryonim* upon their return if they were lucky enough to get back with food! Besides, the only food they had a chance of finding outside the city walls was some wild grass. Many even died from the internal damage caused from eating the plants that weren't appropriate for human consumption and the dirt stuck to them.

Titus used the hiatus of their internal fighting to prepare his men properly for war, unhampered by the Jews who were too busy with their domestic clashes. The Romans built ramparts to stand on while fighting the men on the walls. They fortified stations for their men and prepared the ground for the iron battering rams they were going to use to smash down the walls. Each of the machines was manned by archers and soldiers to protect them against the zealots who might escape and try to destroy their work.

Within four days, Titus completed his preparations. Titus concentrated on the outer of the three walls. He used his battering rams in three positions.

Meanwhile, the *biryonim* united again against the enemy. They concentrated on burning down the wooden equipment that the Romans were using. From time to time, the *biryonim* scored an impressive victory. Once, they managed to burn a number of the Romans' ramparts, another time they cut off the legs of a tower that was used to fire arrows at them, killing the many Romans inside. They managed to destroy many of the fifty battering rams that Titus had brought to destroy Yerushalayim.

The decree against the Jews was sealed, nonetheless. Hashem didn't allow the *biryonim* to overcome their enemies. On the seventh of Iyar, the iron battering rams broke through the third wall! The zealots retreated to the middle wall as the Romans advanced. The Romans completely destroyed the third wall.

The war now focused on the middle wall. Even though the Jews fought bravely and caused the Romans losses, the wall was broken through after five days, on the twelfth of Iyar.

A mass of Roman soldiers entered the breach in the wall. Titus thought that he now had the whole city in his hands. He soon realized how wrong he was.

The Jews were fighting with light weaponry and knew the narrow streets and alleyways like the back of their hands. Both of these facts were to their advantage. Also, the number of Jews fighting swelled from moment to moment. People who had never held a weapon joined the cause against the Romans; everyone united to drive them out.

The Roman army had to retreat. The Jews chased after them as they tried to make their way out of the city through the breach in the wall. The breach was small. On the way in, it didn't matter. The Roman troops were able to wait their turn to enter. However, now that they were running for their lives, there was no time to wait. The Jews took advantage of the situation and killed countless Roman soldiers. The Romans suffered a massive defeat.

The victory of the Jewish side infused new hope and strength in the people. They thought they could overcome the Roman army.

They didn't understand how vast the Roman army was. No matter how many soldiers they would kill, the losses were almost not even noticeable. Secondly, the Jews were weak from starvation; they couldn't survive a long, drawn out battle. Most importantly, they didn't realize that as long as the reason for the decree still existed, they were going to lose. Had they repented for the sin of baseless hatred and changed their ways, they might have stopped the destruction.

After a few days, the Romans stormed the city again. The Jews were prepared and blocked the breach in the wall with their bodies. They didn't hold out long. After three days, the Romans entered the city.

Intent on not repeating the same mistake, Titus made sure to destroy the northern part of the wall and take control of the other parts. This way, the Jews lost the advantage they had of knowing the narrow alleyways. The entire lower city was now in Roman hands.

Although they had scored a great victory when they overcame the second wall and took over the lower city, the Roman soldiers had not had an easy time in battle and were exhausted. Having no choice, Titus declared a hiatus in the fighting for a few days so the men could rest and reorganize.

Titus used the time well. It was time to pay the soldiers. He made the receiving of their salaries into a grand ceremony that took place over four full days. He had each of the men pass before him, his armor shining in the sun. They made an incredible impression, enough to instill awe in anyone's heart.

Almost anyone's. The *biryonim* were not put off. The sages begged them to call for a truce and save the rest of the city and the Temple, but they refused. They didn't realize that there was no way to win if Hashem was not on their side.

The zealots did not surrender. Titus prepared for war. He started building four ramparts in order to break the last wall. The zealots did not make his work easy. They struck the Roman workers again and again.

On Your Walls, O Jerusalem

Titus now understood that it wouldn't be simple to follow the plan he had mapped out for himself. He realized the third wall was not like the other two. The Jewish fighters understood that they were fighting for their lives and fought like lions, paying no attention to their exhaustion and starvation.

Titus decided to offer the Jews a chance for peace.[1] "The city has almost been conquered!" he announced. "Why are you forcing me to completely destroy it along with your Temple? Turn the city over to me, and I will offer you a peace treaty!"

The zealots turned down the offer. "We will fight to the death!" they claimed. "We will chase you out like we did before!" They continued to taunt[2] the soldiers and disrupt the building of the ramparts.

Others, though, when they heard Titus's words, despaired. They escaped to Titus's camp. He let them live and settle anywhere in the country. He also changed the law requiring his men to kill any Jew they found out of the city walls to allowing them to kill the Jews if they wanted to, offering a reward of four *zuz* for every dead Jew.

Titus used the defectors to garner information. He learned from them that the amount of people who had died from the fighting and famine had passed 600,000, and that didn't include the hundreds of thousands killed by the zealots!

---

1. It's important to stress that even though Titus was offering peace, it was only after he figured that he wouldn't be able to conquer them in battle. In his heart, this evil man didn't want the city to be saved. He wanted the city destroyed, as Chazal tell us his wickedness was extraordinary.
2. Avos D'Rabbi Nosson 84

The City is Conquered

It took seventeen days to finally finish the ramparts, due to the constant disruption by the city's defenders. In the end, under careful watch, the four ramparts were completed.

Titus now focused on organizing the soldiers. Besides his regular troops, masses and masses of people from surrounding countries came to fight, rejoicing in the downfall of Yerushalayim. Men came from Macedonia. Tarmod sent 40,000 archers, and as a result will forever be remembered in shame.

The zealots were ready to fight. They were willing to do anything, anything but listen to the *chachamim* and ask for a peace treaty. They continued to cause trouble to the Romans. One attack caused tens of thousands of casualties on the Roman side, but only seven fallen on the Jewish side.

The Jewish men found a daring and ingenious way to destroy the ramparts. In the dark of night, they dug a tunnel from their side of the wall to the area under two of the four ramparts. They strengthened the tunnels with thick wooden planks, covered with pitch, kerosene and sulfur. They then went back into the city and lit a fire at the entrance of the tunnel. This fire would spread down the tunnel, burning the supporting beams and causing the tunnel to collapse. The ramparts on top would collapse into the tunnel, their wood burning in the flames. Two of the ramparts were destroyed this way.

The other two were destroyed when the brave men of Yerushalayim went out in the middle of the night with torches. They were unafraid of the Romans and the catapults that were hurled at them. Their friends remained on the wall, engaging the Romans in fierce battle to help their compatriots. They burned down the ramparts, staying to make sure the fire reached a point where there was no way to save them.

176 | On Your Walls, O Jerusalem

The watchmen over the ramparts ran to their camp, but the Jewish men ran after them, fighting them with all their strength. They continued the bloody battle within the Roman camp, the Romans losing many men. If Titus wouldn't have come personally to strengthen his men and scold them for letting the Jewish men run wild, those few men might have wiped out the whole camp.

With Titus's arrival, the tides turned. The Jews lost many men and retreated into the city.

From that day on, the Romans were terribly afraid of the Jews. They didn't know how to handle their bravery and strength. One day, the Jewish fighters went out to battle face to face with the Romans who were camped outside the city. 500 men managed to kill 8000 Romans, almost without opposition. The Romans were too afraid to come close to the Jews and would only fight with arrows and catapults. Not one Jew was killed in that battle!

Titus and his officers now realized that they were not going to win the war with direct combat. He decided to build a dyke around the entire city, meaning a high mound of dirt.

This served two purposes. First, it gave the Romans the advantage of height. They could now make sure that there were no Jewish infiltrators like the ones that had caused them so much damage. Secondly, the dyke would increase the starvation. Some people in the past had managed to sneak out and find something to eat, but no more. Now there would be absolutely no way to leave the city.

Titus devoted the whole army to the cause. Normally, it would have taken a number of months to build the dyke, but the job was completed in only three days. It was time for the decree to be fulfilled, so Hashem helped the enemy do the job. The Romans were so eager, they worked nonstop to finish the task at hand.

The City is Conquered

The famine did get worse and worse. It got to the point that the people would eat anything they could swallow. Anyone who could find a dead snake or mouse to eat was considered a lucky man. These vermin were disease-ridden. Besides the hunger, they also had to deal with disease plaguing the city. More corpses littered the streets.

The people even searched through animal excrements and sewage, picking out anything they could! This, of course, led to a further decline in health.

There was also a severe water shortage. The Romans had diverted their water source. There was almost not a drop of water left in the city to wet their parched lips.

It should be mentioned that even during this horrible period, when the curses of the Torah came true,[3] the people helped each other. As an example, *Chazal*[4] tell us of a woman who didn't have anything left in her house but a loaf of bread that was enough food for her and her husband for one day. Showing a greatness of spirit, instead of eating her portion herself, she went to give it to a neighbor whose son had died of starvation. She hoped the bread would help console the woman over her loss.

As time went on, thousands of dead bodies piled up in the streets. No one cried over them or eulogized them. Everyone was just waiting for their own turn to come. People who were on the verge of death would dig their own grave and sleep in it for a couple of days until they died. It was the only way they knew they would be buried.

---

3. Josephus, one of the great recorders of history at the time, said that he couldn't write even one thousandth of the horrifying results of the starvation, and that is after the descriptions listed here....

4. Eichah Rabba 4:13

600,000 bodies were thrown over the walls. This didn't include the bodies that lay dead in the streets. There were so many bodies that the zealots had a difficult time getting out of the city to cause the Romans trouble. They ended up having no choice other than climbing over the bodies of their friends and neighbors to get out.

At one point, the Jews stopped throwing the bodies outside the wall and piled them up in their houses, locking the doors behind them. They were hoping to stop the effects of the decaying bodies that were thrown outside. It was not enough, though, to stop the horrible stench that emanated from them in the heat of the summer. The situation was worse than impossible.

While the Jews were suffering the pain of starvation and tens of thousands were taking out their dead every day, Titus and his men were busy building new, larger ramparts. There were no longer trees in the vicinity, so in order to find wood, the Romans had to travel ninety *ris* from the city to find some trees.

In the meantime, amongst all the suffering, the ugly face of civil war reared its ugly head again. Shimon ben Giyora went on a killing rampage against the higher-ups in the city, accusing them of helping the enemy. He even killed many of the righteous sages who protested the spilling of innocent blood. Those who dared cry or eulogize the people who were killed for no reason were beaten to death.

Even some of the *biryonim* were horrified by the iniquity that was being perpetrated. One of these people was Yehuda ben Yehuda, one of Shimon ben Giyora's army generals. He took ten of his followers and sequestered himself with them in a fortress he was in charge of. From there he called to the Romans for peace. He was ready to give up the city to the enemies in order to save the people from Shimon ben Giyora's whims.

The Romans were used to the zealots' tricks and assumed this was one of them. Instead of taking them seriously, they ignored Yehuda ben Yehuda and his men. In the intervening time, Shimon ben Giyora found out what they were doing and murdered them, throwing their bodies over the wall in front of the Romans.

Yochanan Haglili, another leader of the zealots, sinned in another way. He plundered the stores of the *Mikdash*, even giving consecrated wine and oil that was meant for lighting the *menorah* to his fellow zealots.

Many pretended that they were going to fight the Romans, when in actuality they just wanted to give themselves up. Titus allowed these people to live. Unfortunately, starved, they were excited to see food for the first time and ate with great appetite. Their stomachs couldn't deal with the food and they died.

The people who didn't have that problem were still not sure of their safety. There was a rumor amongst the Roman soldiers that the Jews hid their money in their stomachs by eating gold coins before they left the city. Numerous soldiers ripped open these poor people's stomachs, leaving thousands to die a gruesome, excruciating death.

No matter what was happening, the service in the *Bais Hamikdash* continued as usual. Every day, the Jews sent two baskets of gold from the donations given to the *Mikdash* over the wall. The Romans sent up two year-old sheep to be used for the daily sacrifices. It is just amazing that with the war raging everywhere, even in the courtyard of the Temple, the *Kohanim* performed their service and the *Leviim* sang.

The new ramparts were finished at the end of Sivan. They were now ready to launch their attack on the third wall. The Roman soldiers were petrified of the Jews at this point, though, having seen what they were capable of.

The Jewish warriors were also terrified. They knew they were incapable of destroying the new ramparts. They were worn down by their own fights and could not put up a united front against the enemy. Small groups would launch little attacks against the Romans, but these attacks were not well planned and were done out of desperation. The Romans had no problem dealing with these attempts at ruining the ramparts.

The Jewish people didn't turn to Hashem in repentance, so the day of the attack finally arrived. The Roman army stormed the Antonia fortress using every means at their disposal,[5] such as iron rams and other war machines and noisemakers.

The other side fought back by hurling torches, sulfur, arrows and stones at the Roman men who tried to climb the walls. Breaking the wall was not as simple as the Romans thought it would be. The third wall turned out to be stronger than the other two. An iron battering ram didn't even make an impression on it.

The Roman fighters' spirits fell and they decided to retreat. "There's no way to conquer this city," they said to each other, and turned their backs to the city walls. This was Hashem's way of giving the Jews one final chance.

The people were ecstatic when they saw the Romans retreating. "Our city will never fall!" they said to themselves. They didn't stop to

---

5. They didn't have much left. Of the 500 battering rams that Titus brought with him, only one remained. The rest had been burned by the zealots. Titus had appointed 1000 watchmen over each one, but it didn't help. Titus found that the Jews would bravely leave the city walls, sometimes even one man alone, and overcome the thousand guards. When they destroyed the last battering ram, they even went so far as to throw the experts who knew how to build them into the fire. This was to ensure they wouldn't be able to make any more.

think why they were being threatened at all, and that that reason hadn't changed. As long as they clung to their sins and as long as baseless hatred lodged in their hearts, the decree would remain.

After a short break, the tired Roman soldiers got a new wind. "It is a disgrace to run away from those starved Jews!" They tried a new tactic and dug under the walls to weaken the foundation. They labored to remove four stones from under the wall and continued to attack the wall. The third wall fell!

It actually wasn't the removal of the four stones that made the wall unstable, but rather the tunnel that Yochanan Haglili had dug when his men had burned the ramparts in the past. Hashem showed the zealots that, though they trusted in their strength and bravery, if Hashem willed it, their own work would be what would cause their downfall.

The Romans assumed the city was theirs. It wasn't that simple. While the Romans were working on breaking through the wall, the Jews had built a new wall in the area where the Romans had concentrated their efforts.

Not only was this new wall a technical difficulty for the enemy soldiers to overcome, it weakened their morale. They had been disappointed so many times that this finally convinced them that the city was invincible. They decided it was time to retreat and give up their plans of conquering the city.

Hashem decided that the city would be destroyed, so the plan to give up never came to fruition. Instead, Titus came up with another plan. "It doesn't make sense to try and break this wall. They will just build another one in its place again. We have to climb over the wall," he said.

They tried, but the Jewish fighters fought ferociously. They could not get over the wall. The soldiers despaired, but the heavenly decree was still in place!

A few days passed during which no one had the heart to try and climb over the wall again. But then a few brave fighters decided to "be zealous for the honor of the emperor and his army!" Silently, in the middle of the night, they advanced, as the Jewish warriors slept the deep sleep of starving men.

They reached the top of the wall and killed the Jewish guards. They then blew loud trumpets to alert their people that the path was clear. The Jews didn't realize that there were only a few Romans that they could have overtaken easily. They were startled by the trumpets. They began to be chased away by their enemies, announcing as they ran, "The Roman army has come up over the walls!"

Titus, hearing the trumpets, organized his soldiers in the middle of the night and brought them to the wall. They chased the starving Jewish soldiers, not stopping even when they took refuge in the Temple Mount. Titus's men tried to get in the walls of the Har Habayis through the tunnel that Yochanan had dug to destroy the ramparts.

All the Jews now joined together in a common purpose. Shimon ben Giyora's men fought shoulder to shoulder with Yochanan Haglili's men. They knew this was the deciding moment. If they couldn't stop the enemy's onslaught, Yerushalayim would be in Roman hands.

Both sides lost many men. Rivers of blood flowed in the streets, the blood of the Jews mixing with the blood of the Romans. At the end of the day, the Jews managed to push the enemy to the Fortress of Antonia, where the wall had been breached, stopping them from going into the streets of the city and capturing the Har Habayis.

This day, when the city was broken into, was the seventeenth of Tammuz. Besides the breaching of the Fortress of Antonia which let the Romans into the city, another terrible incident took place that day. The Romans decided not to allow the Jews to continue their service in the Temple. They were following the advice of a Greek man who had told them that as long as the Jews continued serving their God in the Temple, there was no chance that they would be able to overtake them.[6]

It was easy enough for the Romans to stop the sacrifices. They simply did not send them the two animals they had provided every day in return for the gold the Jews sent them. At first, they sent two kid goats that were not yet a year old and, therefore, not fitting to be used as sacrifices. Later, brazenly, they sent up two pigs when the Jews sent down their baskets of gold.[7] The Jews hadn't managed to pull the baskets with the pigs even halfway up the wall when one of the pigs stuck his nails into the wall and the Land of Israel shook 400 *parsa*.[8]

The seventeenth of Tammuz was the first time since the Temple had been rebuilt that the daily sacrifices weren't brought. The Jews had lost the merit of the sacrifices that had protected them. The path was now paved for the Romans to conquer the city and destroy the *Bais Hamikdash*!

At this point, Titus set aside seven full days to completely destroy the walls of the Fortress of Antonia, down to their foundations. He was preparing a wide path for his soldiers to storm the city. The path still wasn't wide enough for the masses of soldiers, so Titus selected his strongest and bravest men only to be involved in the conquest.

---

6. Sotah 49.

7. This is what is brought in the Yerushalmi (Taanis 22:). In the Talmud Bavli (Sotah 49:) we find that they only sent up one pig.

8. This is how the Bavli (Sotah 49:) explains it. The Yerushalmi says that it only shook forty parsa.

184 | On Your Walls, O Jerusalem

The worst of the fighting was not yet over. The closer the soldiers got to the Temple Mount, the more determined the Jewish fighters became not to let strangers profane their holy place. They fought like wounded animals, determined to give up their lives to protect what was most dear to them.

Their horrible hunger also forced them to attack Titus's soldiers and take their animals and eat them. These attacks became par for the course, and sometimes they would net a particularly good catch, as they once did when they overcame the watchmen over the Roman property. They procured for themselves horses, donkeys and other animals.

The Romans understood from these attacks and the success of the people in pushing them away from the Temple Mount that the Jewish spirit wasn't broken. Titus decided that the only way to successfully conquer the city was through a proper attack, including ramparts that would help destroy the walls.

Titus got to work right away. He sent workmen to wander as far as they had to until they found the wood they needed. If they had to travel ninety *ris* to find wood before, they now had to travel one hundred *ris*, as the closer trees were already used up.

In the end, wood was brought to Yerushalayim. The building of the ramparts began. The Jews fought back. They weren't successful in stopping the building altogether, but they managed to delay the progress.

In the meantime, on the twenty seventh of Tammuz, the fighters of Yehuda set a trap for Titus's men. In the west, there was a tall hall that King Shlomo had built. The kings during the period of the Second Temple raised the walls even higher and covered them with cedar and cypress trees. The Jewish fighters filled the space between the walls and the ceiling and the trees that were covering them with branches and

The City is Conquered | 185

kerosene and other flammable materials. They also covered the trees with kerosene, sulfur and tar.

The Jewish fighters then pretended that they were running away from the Romans into that hall. The Romans went into the hall, assuming they would catch the Jews inside, and even took ladders to climb on the roof, yelling calls of triumph. They were sure they had the Jews trapped.

When the hall was totally full, even the roof, one of the Jews shut the door and lit a fire which quickly spread, due to all the flammable things inside. 22,000 Roman soldiers burnt to death, locked in that hall. Besides the men who perished, the ploy also caused the Romans' morale to plummet. They ran out of the *heichal* and out of the city, back to their camp, thinking all the time how they would never be able to conquer the Jews by force. They decided to wait until the Jews all starved themselves to death.

Titus didn't have patience to wait. "We must conquer the Temple Mount with brute force!" he commanded his men. The soldiers followed orders and battled the walls of the *heichal* for six full days. These walls were fortified very well and withstood the onslaught. There wasn't even a crack in the walls after the attack! They used up the ramparts and iron battering rams, but the walls were not damaged.

Titus then, in a change of tactics, told them to climb over the walls and then go into the city and fight. This plan also met with fierce opposition. The Jews pushed the men who managed to climb up the walls to their deaths. They also pushed over the ladders, killing the men who were in the middle of climbing. The Romans died right and left. In the end, they were left with no choice but to retreat and wait to see what would develop.

This was *Bnai Yisrael*'s last chance to do *teshuva*. Hashem was calling to them, "Repent! Remove the hatred in your hearts! Submit your will to *daas Torah*!" Tragically, they didn't listen. And so, the tides now changed.

Suddenly, Titus had the idea to ignite the gates of the *azara* that were covered with silver. The silver melted and the wood caught fire, and the flames spread to the halls of the *Mikdash*. The Jewish fighters felt despairing and weak. They didn't even bother to try and put out the fire. The Romans went from gate to gate and burned all the chambers of the *Mikdash*.

The next day, Titus ordered that the fires be extinguished and a path made for the soldiers to go and destroy the *heichal*. The men then stormed the *heichal*. After a short battle with the zealots, they took control of the *heichal*. It was time for the decree to be fulfilled; the *biryonim* were ineffective.

Titus desecrated the *mizbeiach* by throwing a swine's head on it. He brazenly entered the *azara*, pointed to the altar and called to it, "Fox, fox, You're king and I am king. Come and fight me!"[9] He thus mocked God. He continued his scoffing and said again to the altar, "Tell me, how many bulls were slaughtered to be brought on you? How many chickens had their necks broken off? For what purpose? How much wine was poured on you? How much spice was burnt on you? You destroy and use up the whole world!"

Titus continued on his rampage. He went into the Holy of Holies with his sword drawn.[10] He spread the Torah scroll on the ground and committed a very heinous sin on it. After, he took his sword and cut the curtain that separated the Holy and the Holy of Holies. When he

---

9. Avos D'Rabbi Nosson 81
10. Gittin 56:

The City is Conquered | 187

cut the curtain, it began to bleed. Hashem was giving Titus the chance to err in thinking that he had actually killed God.

Titus's soldiers followed suit. They didn't just destroy the Temple and desecrate it; they disgraced and mocked God by bringing sacrifices to their idols on the holy altar. They brought their despicable icons into the Holy and the Holy of Holies.

Titus took the *paroches*, the curtain he had cut down, and made it into a sack to hold the spoils of the Temple. He put in the holy vessels and the other gold items he found. He took these wrapped items with him to Rome, using them to demonstrate his great victory.

The soldiers also wanted their share of the booty. As reward for their dedicated service to the Roman army, they were allowed to grab whatever they could find. There was so much gold there that the price of gold dropped radically and gold could only be sold in Syria for half the price it was worth before!

There is an interesting story brought in *Chazal*[11] that shows us that Titus's supposed bravery[12] when he did the horrible acts mentioned above was really non-existent.

Originally, Titus was scared to enter the Holy of Holies himself. He was worried about what Hashem would do to him. He therefore had the idea to have a Jew go in and give him the spoils. He announced that whichever Jew went in first would be allowed to keep whatever he took out.[13]

---

11. Yalkut Beraishis 115

12. This description is taken from the drashos of Hagaon R' Shabsi Yudelevitch, zt"l.

13. According to the records of the time, Titus didn't talk to the Jews at all. He entered Yerushalayim after the conquest with the express purpose of slaughtering the people. It is possible, therefore, that this Yosef Meshisa

One man of weak character named Yosef Meshisa went in and started gathering the spoils. While the young *Kohanim* were jumping off the roof, he agreed to enter the holiest place in the world because of his lust for money! He took out the *menorah* which he wanted for himself.

The Romans didn't keep their word, though. "This stunning *menorah* doesn't belong in a private home! It is only fitting to be in a palace! We are not willing to leave it in your possession!" they told the shocked Yosef. They told him to go in again and take out something that would be more appropriate.

This time, Yosef Meshisa refused. The holy spark within him suddenly blazed to life and he declared out loud in a sure voice, "Wasn't it enough that I angered my God once? I should anger Him a second time?" He wouldn't go back in.

The Romans wouldn't let him off the hook. Since he refused, they wanted him to do it even more. They were also afraid of God's wrath and needed to send in a Jew before they would dare step in the sanctuary.

First they tried to speak to him nicely. They promised him whatever he brought out and all the taxes of the Yerushalayim residents for three years, enough to make him filthy rich for generations. Yosef Meshisa still refused. He repeated his words again and again, "It's enough that I angered God once. I will not anger Him further!"

When the Romans realized that bribery wouldn't work, they tried other means. They put him in a wheat threshing machine. It was made

---

was one of the Jews who escaped to Titus before the city was captured. They had been granted their lives and perhaps entered the city with him after it was conquered.

of two boards full of sharp protrusions. They turned the boards, causing the protrusions to rip Yosef Meshisa's body to shreds!

Yosef Meshisa screamed as he was being tortured to death, but not screams of pain. He yelled from the depths of his soul that was now aflame with holiness and purity, "Woe unto me that I have angered my Master! Woe unto me that I have angered my Master!" He yelled again and again until he expired.

From this tragic incident we can learn the greatness of the Jewish people. We also see that Titus's pomp was artificial. The mighty Roman general wasn't even willing to step into the sanctuary until he had sent a Jew in first.

Unfortunately, Yosef Meshisa's story wasn't unique. There were *Kohanim* who showed Titus the hidden treasures of the *Mikdash*, where, amongst other things, the holy garments and spices were kept. We don't know if they did *teshuva* like Yosef Meshisa did, and it's painful to think to what levels some of the people sank.

Going back to the events of that time, it was the bitter day of Tisha B'Av that Titus destroyed the Temple. The fire burned from the ninth of Av through the tenth, burning the *Mikdash* to its foundations.[14] Only the Western Wall, the *Kosel*, was left standing, along with the gates[15] of the *Bais HaMikdash*. Those gates sank into the ground. Since

---

14. Yerushalmi Yuma 1.

15. In the books of the history of that period it is brought that the gate of the heichal was set on fire. Because Chazal say something different, we have to say that it looked like the gate was burnt, but actually it sank into the ground

they were the handiwork of King David,[16] no foreign hands were allowed to touch them.

Just as the First *Bais Hamikdash*, this one was destroyed on the first day of the week,[17] at the end of a *shmitta* year. It happened during Yehoyariv's guard, while the *Leviim* were singing! They sang,[18] "And He brings on them their own iniquity; and He cuts them off in their own wickedness."[19] They didn't get to finish the verse, "The Lord our God cuts them off," before the gentiles entered and conquered them. The Temple had stood for 420 years.

The *Kohanim*, each in their guard, acted as their ancestors did during the destruction of the First Temple. The *Pirchei Kehuna* gathered in groups on the roof with the keys to the *Mikdash* in their hands. They said to Hashem, "Master of the World, since we didn't merit to be trustworthy treasurers, take back the keys!" They threw the keys up to the sky and some type of hand came out of the heavens and caught the keys. The *Kohanim* then jumped into the flames that were destroying the Temple they had served faithfully their whole lives.

They weren't the only ones who found their death. The children of Esav, drunk with their success, killed tens of thousands of people. You couldn't even see the ground of the Har Habayis. It was

---

16. This is what it says in Sotah 9. about the gates. I also saw in the name of the responsa of the Tzitz Eliezer (18:1) the same thing about the Kosel which was built on the foundation that King David laid.

17. Erchin 11:

18. Look in the Gemara to see why the Leviim sang this if it wasn't the proper song for the first day of the week. Either way, this wasn't the song sung over the daily sacrifice, as the sacrifices were no longer offered since the seventeenth of Tammuz. It was the song offered over a nedava sacrifice.

19. Tehillim 94:23

The City is Conquered | 191

completely covered with corpses, whose blood ran in rivers down the streets of Yerushalayim.

Even now, the zealots didn't concede defeat and surrender to Titus.[20] The end of these people who had caused so much suffering to their brethren in their arrogant refusal to bow to *daas Torah* was very bitter indeed.

Yochanan Haglili and Shimon ben Giyora were captured after hiding in Yerushalayim's trenches. They were paraded in front of the Roman camp in disgrace. Yochanan was then killed in a very tortuous manner while Shimon was decapitated and thrown to the dogs.

Elazar ben Anneni the *Kohein* and the 40,000 men he led took shelter in a fortress in the upper city before it was captured. They continued to war against the Romans even after the *Bais Hamikdash* was destroyed. When they realized there was no hope, every man killed his own family so that the enemy wouldn't take them captive. 8,000 of them went out to battle, knowing they would never survive. Before they died, though, they managed to kill 95,000 Roman soldiers!

All the other Jews were killed, besides the few thousand that Titus had let free because they surrendered before the city was conquered. Nothing was left of the city. Many of the captives were sold as slaves, mostly the younger people who were not yet seventeen. The price a slave could fetch was not very high, as there was such a tremendous supply!

Titus brought 90,000 people from Yerushalayim to Rome, including mostly the most impressive ones, so that he could show off his victory. Many others were slaughtered by the Roman soldiers.

---

20. In the beginning the zealots had sent a message asking for peace, but they weren't agreeing to subjugate themselves to Titus, they were asking to leave the city and leave it in his hands. Titus refused their offer.

Others were forced to wrestle with wild animals, or even their own brethren, to provide a sick sort of entertainment. There they found their deaths.

The people who were freed didn't fare all that much better. The extended famine had left its mark permanently on their health. It is told in the Midrash[21] by Rabbi Eliezer the son of Rabbi Tzadok of a woman who came to her father's house to ask for some food. At first glance, you couldn't even tell she was a woman. Her hair had completely fallen out because of the starvation. Her face had changed, also. The only thing she could manage to eat were the insides of cooked figs.

Those who had run away soon saw how happy their neighbors were to turn them in. If they tried to escape to the east, the people of Tzur turned them in to the Romans. If they tried to run north, the Philistines turned them in. In the west, when they tried to board boats to escape into the Mediterranean, the Ishmaelites chased them and gave them over to the Romans.[22]

The tortured, downtrodden people remained faithful to their God throughout all their tribulations. We will discuss more about that later. First we have to see what became of Titus. We certainly know that someone who destroyed God's Temple was not going to remain unpunished.

Titus was swollen with pride. He declared that not only had he conquered God, but that he had done so in God's own house, a much greater feat.

Already on the boat on the way back to Rome, God began to show him that his pompous arrogance was out of place. A storm brewed in

---

21. Eichah Rabba 4:11
22. Eichah Rabba 1:56

the sea and almost sank the ship.²³ After all the wars, when he had finally won, Titus was about to die, lost at sea with no one even knowing where he was buried.

Titus was not humbled by what he realized was the beginning of divine vengeance. He stood at the helm of the ship and declared, "It seems to me that the Jews' God only has power in the water. Pharaoh, who enslaved His children, was drowned in the Yam Suf. Sisra, who made war against the Jews, was drowned in the Kishon River. Now God is trying to drown me in the Mediterranean. If God is mighty, I invite Him to fight me on dry land! Then we will see who is mightier!"

"Wicked man, the son of a wicked man, the descendant of the wicked Esav," a voice called out, "if you want to fight Me on land, so be it. The war between you and God, so to speak, will take place on land. For this war, the Creator of the world will send a tiny little creation of His, a mosquito. Let's see how you deal with this light creature!"²⁴ The heavenly voice finished speaking and the sea calmed down.

When Titus reached the shore, a mosquito went into Titus's nose, settling in his brain. It pecked at his brain for seven full years! Titus suffered from horrible headaches for those seven years, with the pain constantly increasing.

Titus finally thought he found a solution to his problem. He was in the marketplace one day and passed a blacksmith store. The blacksmith was hitting iron with his hammer. Titus's headache stopped completely. The mosquito was bemused by the banging of the hammer

---

23. Gittin 56:

24. The mosquito is classified as a "light creature" because it has no excretory system. It eats, but doesn't produce waste.

and was still. Titus summoned a blacksmith to his palace to hammer every day and keep the mosquito in his head quiet.

When a non-Jewish blacksmith would come, he would pay him four *zuz* for the job, but when a Jewish blacksmith would come, he would get nothing. "It's enough that you see your enemy suffering! You don't deserve more than that!"

This setup went on for a month. It certainly wasn't pleasant to listen to a hammer banging all day, but it was the lesser of two evils. The headaches without the banging were unbearable.

The mosquito slowly got used to the banging. After a month, he began pecking at Titus's brain again. Until his dying day, the mosquito continued to vex him day and night. When seven years had passed, Titus died. After his death, the doctors opened his head to see what had caused him the headaches for so many years. To their surprise, they found a gigantic mosquito who had reached the size of two *litrin*, the size of a year-old bird![25]

Before Titus died, he had left instructions how to deal with his body. He asked that his body be cremated and that his ashes be spread over the seven seas.[26] He thought that that would be enough to stop God from bringing him to judgment….

In the end, Titus finally realized who won. He was so afraid of God's vengeance that he preferred not to have a respectable burial in his birthplace. He would do anything he felt would help save him from having to meet up with God.

---

25. This is one opinion. Another states that the mosquito weighed two selaim, as much as a sparrow.
26. It had been decreed that Titus should fall to the depths of the sea. Because he blasphemed, he didn't drown. Hashem first made him experience His greatness and punished him harshly for seven years. After, he ended up in the depths of the sea.

Years later, one of his nephews, Onkelus, wanted to convert. He called up his uncle Titus from the dead using sorcery called Ov. He wanted to know his uncle's opinion about his possible conversion to Judaism. Titus, still the same wicked man, advised his nephew to fight the Jews. He told him that anyone who fights against the Jews becomes a leader.

At the same time, though, he told his nephew about his punishment. "Every day," he told Onkelus, "they punish me with something I decreed against myself. They gather my dust from the seven seas and put my body back together again. They judge me as one body. Then they burn me and scatter my ashes again in the seven seas."

Even after his death, a wicked man stays a wicked man. All the more so a righteous man will remain righteous even in the hardest of times, as we will see in the next chapter.

15

The Spiritual Strength of the Children

Throughout this dismal period of exile under Roman rule, we find many instances of incredible spiritual strength. Even the children understood that the only thing of lasting value is serving God and that life without that is worthless.

We are told of four hundred boys and girls[1] who were taken captive by Titus and led to Rome. It was clear to the children that they were to be used in disgraceful, sinful ways. It was also clear to them that death was much more preferable than a life of iniquity. They ignored their natural will to live and subjugated their wants to *daas Torah*.

There was no Torah authority on the ship that was taking them to Rome. There was no one with whom they could share their doubts and fears. That being the case, they gathered together to do their best in understanding God's will under the circumstances. "If we throw

---

1. Gittin 57:, Eichah Rabba 1:45

The Spiritual Strength of the Children | 197

ourselves into the sea, will we merit life in the World to Come or will we be held responsible for taking our own lives?" they asked each other.

In the end, the oldest of the children got up and said to his friends,[2] "In the book of Tehillim[3] King David said in God's name through his divine spirit, 'From Bashan I will bring them back, from the depths of the sea I will bring them.' Hashem promises that He will bring back those who drowned in the sea in honor of His great name. Here is the answer to our question."[4]

When the children heard the answer, the girls immediately jumped into the sea. They didn't make calculations, didn't hesitate. The boys followed, thinking, "If the girls jumped to save themselves from being given to sin, should we not?" They too jumped, in front of the astonished soldiers.[5]

We also find the story of Chana or Miriam[6] and her seven sons.[7] She was called with her sons to come before the Roman emperor where they were ordered to bow to an idol.

---

2. The Midrash says that it was through special divine assistance that the boy found a proof from this verse.
3. Tehillim 68:23
4. See Tosafos Avodah Zara 18., the words beginning "v'al yechbal." There it is explained that a person is allowed to take his own life if he is worried he will be forced to sin.
5. The Midrash doesn't mention the difference between the boys and girls. But there it says there were three groups that jumped in the sea, each calling out a different verse before they did. It could be the Gemara and the Midrash are referring to two different instances.
6. In the Midrash her name is listed as Miriam. The Gemara simply calls her "a woman."
7. Gittin 57:, Eichah Rabba 1:50

198 | On Your Walls, O Jerusalem

The children refused. The emperor was not satisfied with the negative reply he received from the children with the encouragement of their mother. He separated the children,[8] calling them in one at a time.[9] He told each one that they must bow to the idol or they would die. He was sure that, standing alone, they would not be brave enough to defy him.

When he called the first son, the child told him, "It says clearly in the Ten Commandments,[10] 'I am Hashem your God!'" He would not bow, and he was summarily executed.

The second son, when called in and threatened the same way, said, "My brother did not bow and neither will I! It says in the Ten Commandments, 'You should not have another god before Me.'" The emperor killed him.

The third brother[11] explained his refusal with the verse,[12] "He who sacrifices to a false god shall be utterly destroyed." He was killed.

The fourth brother quoted the verse,[13] "Do not bow down to another god." He suffered the same fate as his older brothers.

The next brother explained his refusal, quoting,[14] "Listen Israel, Hashem is our God, Hashem is One." The sixth brought the verse,[15]

---

8. This is what it seems like from the Midrash.
9. The Maharsha says that each child was brought in on a different day. See there for an explanation why the verses each child picked were appropriate for that day.
10. Shemos 20:2
11. From here on we find a different order of the verses they quoted in the Midrash and the Gemara. The above follows the order of the Gemara.
12. Shemos 22:19
13. Shemos 34:14
14. Devarim 6:4
15. Devarim 4:39

The Spiritual Strength of the Children | 199

"You should know today and put on your heart that Hashem is the God. In the skies above and the earth below there is no other." They were both executed in order.

Only the seventh son was left. He was exactly two and a half years old[16] at the time. He, too, refused the request to bow to the idol. He quoted the verse,[17] "You have distinguished Hashem this day to be your God, to walk in His ways and to keep His statutes and His commandments and His judgments and to hearken to His voice. The Lord has designated you this day to be His special people as He promised you and that you should keep all His commandments." He said, "We have already sworn to God that we will not switch Him with any other god!" The young boy refused to bow to the idol.

The emperor would not give up on him so easily.[18] He knew what a disgrace it was that the boys didn't listen to him, even with all his threatening and punishments.

He said to the young boy, "Your older brothers already enjoyed this world for a number of years. It's not so terrible that they gave up their lives because of their stubborn refusal to bow to the idol. You are so young, on the other hand. You haven't yet enjoyed the world! I'll make you a deal. You bow to the idol and I will give you all the good this world has to offer!"

The boy answered him, "Honored emperor, it says in our Torah,[19] 'Hashem will rule forever.' It also says,[20] 'Hashem is the King forever.

---

16. Two years, six months and six and a half hours according to the Midrash there.
17. Devarim 26:17-18
18. From here on is from the Midrash. The Gemara is written in much shorter form.
19. Shemos 15:18
20. Tehillim 10:16

The nations will be destroyed out of His land.' Therefore, your offer doesn't seem too worthwhile.

"You, God's enemies, are going to be destroyed from the world, but Hashem will rule forever. You, man of flesh and blood, don't know if you will even be alive tomorrow, but Hashem is eternal. You can't be sure of your wealth even for one day, but Hashem is in charge of the entire universe. You tell me, whose reward is more valuable? The reward you promise which isn't at all certain or the reward God promises me?"

The emperor still did not give up on the child. "Look at your dead brothers! Listen, I'll compromise. I don't want to see you die. I'll throw my ring in front of the idol. You bend down to pick it up. In your heart you don't have to have even a drop of intention of bowing to the idol, but it will look like you did to the people who are watching. This way, you will live and I will save myself from the embarrassment of you and your brothers not listening to me."

The boy answered, "*Oy*, it's a shame you are not using your head. Who are you afraid of – people! You are worried about your honor and reputation in their eyes. If you are so worried about what people who are just like you will think, shouldn't I worry so much more about what the King of kings thinks? How can I arrogantly sin before Him, even if it's just giving the impression that I am?"

At this point, the emperor entered a philosophical debate with the child, which the child clearly won, basing his arguments on unshakeable principles. However, based on what the child said, the emperor decided that he had such a strong question that the child certainly would have no answer. "If your God is so great," he asked, "why doesn't He save you and your brother, from me as He saved Chananya, Mishael and Azarya from Nevuchadnezar's hands hundreds of years ago?"

He answered, "There is a great difference between the two situations. First of all, there is a vast difference between you and Nevuchadnezar. Hashem doesn't do miracles through just anyone. Nevuchadnezar was a great and mighty ruler. You are not as great and it would be inappropriate for God to do a miracle through you to save me from your hands.

"Secondly, Chananya, Mishael and Azarya were righteous and pious men. They had the merits to be saved. We don't have those merits. We deserve to die. If you don't kill us, Hashem will find another way to give us what we deserve. There are plenty of bears, lions, tigers, snakes and scorpions around to kill us if He wants. Hashem wants the bad to come through you, though, so He can punish you later!"

On the spot, the emperor decided to put him to death. Before the decree was fulfilled, the boys' mother fell before the emperor and asked to be killed before her son, so she shouldn't witness his death. The emperor refused. In his cruelty, he wanted the mother to suffer.

"It says in the Torah,"[21] the emperor quoted, "'A bull or sheep, you shouldn't kill him and his son on the same day.'" That was how he justified his refusal to kill the mother before her child.

When the mother saw her request refused, she pleaded, "If you are not willing to kill me before my son, at least let me say goodbye."

The emperor agreed. With tears in her eyes, the mother hugged the child and said, "My beloved son, when you get to heaven above, go to Avraham and tell him, 'My mother says not to be so proud that you built an altar and brought your son as a sacrifice. You only built one altar and my mother built seven! You withstood the test, but in the end

---

21. Vayikra 22:28

you didn't have to complete the deed and kill your son. My mother saw her children actually killed.'"

The enemy got up while she was still hugging him and slaughtered him in her arms. After, the woman went mad due to her tremendous suffering and went up to the roof and jumped to her death.

A voice came out of heaven and declared,[22] "The mother of sons is joyous!"

Chazal[23] also tell us about the son and daughter of Rabbi Yishmael ben Elisha the High Priest. They were both taken captive and sold as slaves. After a while, their two masters met in an inn. After each saw the other's slave, they came up with an idea.

The slaves from Yerushalayim were known to be of unrivaled beauty. They decided that it would be a good idea to match up their two slaves, and the children that came out of the marriage would certainly be as beautiful as they were. They were sure those children could be sold for a lot of money, and they agreed to split the profit.

That night, they brought the two slaves together, who were acually brother and sister. No one knew of their relation.

When they were alone, they began to cry and didn't come near each other. Each stood in his own corner, the tears flowing down their cheeks. In the dark, they didn't recognize each other, and the night passed in deep pain for both of them.

---

22. This is what it says in the Gemara. In the Midrash it says the pasuk, "The poor woman gave birth to the seven." In the Gemara it says that the mother went up to the roof and died. The commentaries explain that she was allowed to do what she did because death was better to her than life. The Midrash, though, says that she went crazy and jumped off the roof in her madness.
23. Gittin 58.

The Spiritual Strength of the Children | 203

The son said, "I am a *Kohein,* the son of *Kohanim Gedolim*. I should marry a slave?"

The girl similarly said, "I am a *Kohenes,* the daughter of a *Kohein Gadol*. I should marry a slave?"

In the morning, when they recognized each other, they fell on each other's necks and cried very bitterly until their souls expired.[24]

---

24. Eichah Rabba 1:46 brings a similar story about the son and daughter of Rabbi Tzadok the Kohein Gadol. According to that story, the siblings didn't recognize each other because of the time that had passed. When the girl told the boy about her troubles, complaining that a bas kohein like her had to marry a slave, the boy understood it was his sister. In order to make sure, he asked her questions about where her family lived in Yerushalayim and if she had siblings. She told him about her brother and described a birthmark he had on his shoulder. The brother then showed her the birthmark on his shoulder. After, when they both knew the truth, they fell on each other's shoulders, staying that way until morning when their souls left them.

16

The Fall of Beitar

After the destruction of Yerushalayim, its Temple, and the exile of the people of Yerushalayim to Rome, there were still settlements remaining in the area surrounding Yerushalayim. Beitar was one example. After Titus returned to Rome, Hadrian Kaiser, a cruel and wicked man, was put in charge of these settlements.

Beitar lasted for fifty two years after the *churban*, until it was decreed in heaven that it, too, should be destroyed. The reason[1] that it was destroyed was due to a certain happiness the residents of Beitar had shown over the destruction of Yerushalayim, lighting candles when the *churban* happened.

The people of Beitar were certainly miserable over the destruction of the *Mikdash* and the suffering of their fellow Jews, but they had a certain hatred for the people of Yerushalayim. The reason for this animosity was a particular type of ruse that some people in Yerushalayim used to swindle the rich community of Beitar.

---

1. Yerushalmi Taanis 24., Eichah Rabba 2:4, Eichah Rabba 4:21

The Fall of Beitar | 205

When a man from Beitar would go to Yerushalayim in the period before the *churban* to pray, these people would ask him, "Is the rumor that you want to be a ruler true? If you want, we can get you a high position if you give us your field."

The man would answer them, "I have no interest in power, and I am not interested in giving up my field."

The swindlers would then offer[2] a more respectable position of leadership to him in exchange for his field. When they were refused a second time, they offered to pay the full value of the field. If again they were turned down, they had a more devious way of getting the field.

They would write a forged contract selling the field to them and get one of their friends to falsely sign the contract. They would then send the contract to Beitar, saying that the field no longer belonged to the original owner and requesting that they make sure that the previous owner doesn't enter the field.

When the defrauded Jew would come back to Beitar after his trip to Yerushalayim and find out what happened, he would say, "Too bad I didn't break my leg and not make the trip to Yerushalayim." He would then add some curses against the people who lived in Yerushalayim.

This kind of thievery was common during the period before the destruction, mostly, it seems, against the wealthy people of Beitar. This is what caused the Beitar Jews to feel somewhat happy when Yerushalayim fell. Their joy at the destruction of the holy city was what sealed the judgment against them.

The verdict was executed as follows.[3] There was a custom in Beitar that when a baby boy was born a cedar tree was planted; when

---

2. See Eitz Yosef
3. Gittin 57.

a girl was born a pine tree was planted. When the children grew up and married, branches of the trees that were planted in their honor were cut down to make their wedding canopy.

One day, the emperor's daughter[4] was passing through Beitar when the wheel of her carriage broke. Her servants cut down some trees that had been planted in honor of the births of children to fix the wheel. Even though this could have been done in all innocence, it infuriated the local people and they beat the servants that had cut down the trees.

The beaten, wounded servants went to Hadrian and told him what had happened. It could be the Roman servants reported the incident because they saw it as a rebellion, or it might just have been their way of taking revenge against those that had struck them. Their words were enough to encourage Hadrian to wage war against Beitar, with the express purpose of killing every last man there!

It wasn't so simple to attack Beitar successfully. In Beitar, there was an incredibly strong man named bar Koziba. He had an extremely powerful army of 400,000 men.

The test one had to undergo to be accepted into his army was to stick one's finger in fire until three drops of blood dripped out![5] When bar Koziba was criticized for making too many disfigured people, he changed his initiation test to having the man uproot a cedar tree while riding on a horse! In his army of 400,000, 200,000 had passed the thumb test and the other 200,000 had uprooted a tree.

---

4. It seems this was the daughter of Aidrianus Kaiser and not of the emperor in Rome.

5. Yerushalmi Taanis 24. In the Midrash Eichah Rabba 2:4 it is brought that they had to cut off their thumbs with their teeth.

The Fall of Beitar

If his soldiers were that strong, we can imagine how strong bar Koziba was himself. *Chazal*[6] tell us that he would catch the stones that were catapulted at the city with his lower legs and then throw them back on the enemy, killing many.

He had such supernatural might that some of the greatest of the Jewish sages at the time thought he was *mashiach*![7] *Chazal* tell us that Rabbi Akiva assumed he was *mashiach* until Rabbi Yochanan ben Torsa explained to him that it wasn't true.

Hadrian knew that he didn't have a chance to win in direct combat. He therefore besieged the city, hoping to win that way.[8] After three and a half years of siege, Hadrian gave up. "If the Jews of Beitar didn't surrender yet, it's hopeless," he thought.

Hashem didn't let him give up. Bar Koziba and his men were too arrogant, so Hashem decreed that they should fall. Before they went out to war, they used to say to Hashem, "Master of the World, don't help us but don't fight against us! That's all we ask!" They were so sure they could win the war without Hashem's help. Their lack of understanding that people have no strength besides what Hashem gives them caused their downfall.

Even though it was decreed that they should fall, they still had the merit of Rabbi Elazar Hamodai helping them. Rabbi Elazar Hamodai used to sit in sackcloth and ashes and pray every day that Hashem shouldn't sit in judgment and destroy Beitar. Beitar could only fall after Rabbi Elazar Hamodai had been killed.

---

6. Eichah Rabba 2:4

7. Yerushalmi Taanis 24. See Rambam chapter 11 of Hilchos Melachim in *halacha* 3.

8. From here on, the description is according to the Midrash and Yerushalmi as brought above.

This is how it happened that he was killed, paving the way for the destruction of Beitar. After the three years of siege, Hadrian was about to despair of conquering Beitar and begin his retreat, as we mentioned. Just then, a Kuthite man came and whispered a secret in his ear, "You should know that as long as the hen is rolling in the dirt (he was referring to Rabbi Elazar Hamodai who sat in the dirt in sackcloth) you have no chance of conquering the city. If you want to take over the city, you've got to get rid of Rabbi Elazar Hamodai first. Then it will be no problem!"

When Hadrian asked if he had any idea how to go about getting rid of Rabbi Elazar Hamodai, the Kuthite offered his services to make sure that Rabbi Elazar was killed, and immediately went to put his plan into action.

The Kuthite snuck into Beitar through the sewage system. He approached Rabbi Elazar, who was immersed in his prayers, and acted like he was whispering something into his ear. The Kuthite was known as a collaborator with Hadrian. When the people saw that he had gone to speak with Rabbi Elazar, they quickly went to bar Koziba to report what they had seen.

Bar Koziba summoned the Kuthite right away to find out what the conversation was about. This was the moment the Kuthite had been waiting for. "I don't know what to do!" he exclaimed. "If I tell you what the conversation was, Hadrian will kill me. But if I don't tell you what the conversation was about, you will kill me!

"I suppose it's better to risk dying later than a certain death right now, so I will tell you what happened. I came as a messenger from Hadrian to discuss Rabbi Elazar's plan to surrender the city without fighting in order that the siege be lifted."

Bar Koziba was irate! He immediately called Rabbi Elazar and asked him the contents of the conversation he had had with the Kuthite.

Rabbi Elazar honestly had no idea what he was talking about. He had been totally involved in his prayers and didn't pay any attention to what the Kuthite was whispering in his ear.[9]

When Rabbi Elazar told him that, bar Koziba didn't believe him. He kicked him once, and Rabbi Elazar died on the spot.

Now the decree was sealed. A heavenly voice announced, "You killed Rabbi Elazar Hamodai, who was the arm and eyes of the people. Therefore, your arm will dry up and your eyes will darken!" Since Hashem decreed, although it was unnatural, bar Koziba[10] and the city of Beitar fell to the enemy!

Hashem didn't let the Romans take pride in killing bar Koziba. *Chazal*[11] tell us that after Beitar fell, the enemies found bar Koziba's body. They cut off his head and brought it to Hadrian. "Who killed this mighty man?" he asked, astounded. A Kuthite who was there claimed that he had.

---

9. This is what is brought in the Midrash. The Yerushalmi says that Rabbi Elazar knew that the Kuthite hadn't said anything at all. This is what he told bar Koziba.

10. This is what it says in the Rambam. A similar version is found in the Pesikta (30). The *Gemara* and Midrashim say that a snake was found wrapped around his body, seemingly implying that the snake bit him, but not necessarily. It could be that he was killed by the enemy and then, only after he died, Hashem sent the snake so that the enemy would not take pride in killing bar Koziba.
In the *Gemara* (Sanhedrin 93:) it says bar Koziba was killed by *beis din* since he himself claimed that he was *mashiach*, but he didn't stand up to the test when they checked if he really was *mashiach* or not. Therefore, bar Koziba was a false prophet. The Radvaz said that the *beis din* didn't kill him, but removed their support from him. This gave the enemies the power to win over him.

11. Yerushalmi and the Midrash as brought above.

210 | On Your Walls, O Jerusalem

Hadrian told the Kuthite to bring him the body if that were the case. The Kuthite went to find the body and found it with a snake wrapped around it. It was clear to all that Beitar and bar Koziba had been given over by God to their enemies. If not, no one would have been able to conquer them.

It was again the bitter and dark day of Tisha B'Av when Beitar fell. 80,000 legions of gentile soldiers[12] fought in that last battle. They massacred everyone. It was even worse than the fall of Yerushalayim. Not one single soul was left alive in Beitar out of the millions of citizens that lived there.[13] According to the *Gemara*,[14] the number of adults that were slaughtered reached 4,000,000![15]

In addition, there were 64,000,000 schoolchildren in Beitar. This number is derived from the following calculations. In Beitar there were 400 synagogues. Each had 400 teachers who had four hundred students.[16] And this number only includes the boys and not the girls!

---

12. If we assume that each legion had only one hundred men in it, we get to an astounding number of 8,000,000 soldiers.

13. Avos D'Rabbi Nosson 38. The Yerushalmi says that Rabbi Shimon ben Gamliel was from the young students of Beitar and was the only one who survived.

14. Gittin 57.

15. In the Yerushalmi it says that 800,000,000 people were killed in Beitar (also Eichah Rabba 2:4).

16. The Yerushalmi says that there were only 500 schools, each having at least 500 students. In Eichah Rabba 3:80 we find that every school had at least 300 students. With these numbers, we get to "only" 250,000 *tinokos shel bais rabban*. The Yerushalmi doesn't mention how many children learned in the higher level schools. Therefore, the numbers could be much, much higher. It would be hard to assume that in a city of 800,000,000, there were only a quarter million schoolchildren.

The Fall of Beitar | 211

These children were so sure of themselves that they declared that if the enemy would enter the city, they would stab them with their pens and, though their sheer numbers, overcome them. But Hashem decreed, and the children were killed. Each one was wrapped in his books and burned!

Hundreds of millions were killed by sword. Their blood created a mighty stream that flowed all the way to the Mediterranean Sea, a *mil* away from Beitar![17] The blood also ran into the two streams that flowed from the place called Bekat Yadim. Our sages estimated that a third of the water that ran in those streams was blood of the Jews of Beitar. The gentile farmers who used that water to irrigate their fields didn't need fertilizer for seven years, because of the blood![18]

Another description of the destruction that we find in *Chazal* says that a horse walking in the streets of Beitar would be covered up to his nose in blood. The blood flowed so strongly that it reached a depth of four *mil* in the sea. The strength of the gush of the blood was powerful enough to move rocks that weighed forty *seah*!

300 containers of *tefillin* were found in Beitar full of the *tefillin shel rosh* that the men of Beitar used to wear. Each of those containers contained 300 *seah* of *tefillin*![19] 300 brains from babies' heads that were smashed were found on one rock in Beitar![20]

---

17. The Yerushalmi says the distance was forty *mil*.
18. Gittin 57.
19. Tanna Devei Eliyahu 30. The *Gemara* says there were three containers of forty *seah* and forty containers of three *seah*. One group had the *tefillin shel rosh* and the other had the *tefillin shel yad*.
20. Yerushalmi as above. The *Gemara* (Gittin 58.) says there were four *kabin* according to one opinion and nine *kabin* according to another. That may be the source for the number 300 brains.

The murdered people in Beitar also didn't merit to be buried.[21] Hadrian had a very large vineyard, eighteen *mil* by eighteen *mil*. He used their bodies as a fence. He hoped to accomplish two things. One, he would fertilize his field with the blood that dripped out of their stabbed bodies. Second, when their flesh dried up, the bones that were left would make a good fence.[22]

It was only years later when Hadrian was replaced that the new ruler ordered the people to be buried. The blessing of *Hatov V'Hameitiv* was established then to give thanks for two things, that they were finally brought to burial and that their flesh did not rot until then.

Hadrian hated the Jews so much that he wasn't satisfied just killing the community of Beitar; he decided that he wanted to kill every Jew, wherever they were.

Chazal tell us about one of his killing sprees. He sent out messengers throughout the Land of Israel, telling the people to gather in the Valley of Beis Rimon. They announced that the Jews would be given a chance to request anything they wanted from Hadrian and that he promised to fulfill their wishes. "Until now, you've asked the emperor to allow your brethren to return from exile. He was upset about that and wouldn't grant your request. But if you ask him now that you yourselves will not be exiled, he will listen," the messengers announced.

Many Jews in their naivete gathered there, falling into Hadrian's trap. Hadrian commanded his officers, "Before me I have a piece of cake and a thigh of a chicken. Before I finish eating them, make sure that there is not even one Jew left alive in that valley!" His officers followed his command exactly. Within a few minutes, there was a

---

21. Gittin 58., Eichah Rabba 3:80
22. Anaf Yosef

The Fall of Beitar | 213

massive river of blood flowing from the Valley of Beis Rimon into the Kiprus River.[23]

Others, who understood that Hadrian was setting a trap, didn't come to the valley. They were forced, though, to hide out in caves. The starvation there became so severe that they even ate the corpses of their fellow Jews that were scattered among the mountains.

Chazal describe that every day the Jews in the caves would send someone to search the mountains for dead bodies for everyone to eat. One day, the scout went out and found his own father's body. He couldn't bring himself to eat his own father and hid him in a cave, marking where he was. He returned empty-handed to his friends.

The starving group didn't give up. They sent another person to find a body. The new scout followed the putrid smell of the father's rotting body that his son had hidden. He brought back that body, and the group ate it. After the meal, the son found out, based on the place and sign, that it was his father they had eaten. He cried, "Woe that I have eaten my father's flesh!" Yechezekel's[24] words had come true, "Fathers will eat their sons in your midst, and sons will eat their fathers. I will smite you and scatter your remains in all directions."

The people went through a period too horrendous to imagine. Hadrian had a indescribably great hatred for the Jews. *Chazal*[25] tell us that a Jew passed Hadrian and greeted him, and Hadrian asked him what nation he was from. When he found out the man was a Jew, he was killed on the spot for having the audacity to address his majesty! Another Jew walked by. Having learned from what just happened, he didn't greet Hadrian. Hadrian asked what nation he was from. When

---

23. Radal says this was an island, not a river.
24. Yechezkel 5:10
25. Eichah Rabba 3:20

he found out he was a Jew, he killed him for having the audacity not to greet his majesty!

His officers didn't understand what he was doing. They asked him, "So what do you expect a Jew to do? You kill him for greeting you and then kill him for not greeting you!"

Hadrian's answer was, "My esteemed officers, don't teach me how to kill the enemy!" He had no interest in hiding his deep loathing of the Jewish people.

Another story[26] tells of a man[27] who sent Hadrian a letter accusing him of hating the Jews. The letter read, "If you hated anyone who was circumcised, you would also hate the Ishmaelites. If you were against anyone who kept the Sabbath, you would also be against the Kuthites. But you only hold these two things against the Jews! That means you have a blind hatred for them, based on nothing. And God will pay you back!"

Hadrian was livid. He sent for the wise author of the letter to be brought before him, promising him a gift. The man appeared before the emperor. Hadrian sentenced him to death. Before executing him, he asked him, "Tell me, why did you do it? Didn't you understand you would be severely punished?"

The man answered, "I certainly did. That's why I wrote it, and that's why I appeared before you when summoned. I am suffering in three terrible ways. I have nothing to eat. My wife has nothing to eat. And my children have nothing to eat. I prefer death over this sort of life!"

---

26. Koheles Rabba 2:21

27. Some of the commentaries say his name was Eimiknatron. Others say that was a nickname for the exiled Jews, so calling him Eimiknatron was just saying that one of the Jews sent it.

Hadrian hated the Jews so much that he decided to let him live in his terrible suffering. It gave him even more pleasure than killing him. There was no rationale for this deep-seated detestation other than "It is a known rule that Esav hates Yaakov."[28]

The Destruction of Alexandria

The blood of the Jews was free for all in those days. Not only did Hadrian murder and torture at whim, but so did many others. As an example, Trachinus, the king of Egypt, killed a great many of the Jews of Alexandria.

Before we discuss the destruction of the community of Alexandria, we need to describe what the community was like in its glory. *Chazal*[29] tell us that whoever didn't see the main synagogue of Alexandria has not experienced the honor of Israel.

The main synagogue of Alexandria sat 1,200,000 people. On the eastern wall, there were seventy one gold chairs in honor of the seventy one members of the Sanhedrin. Each of these chairs was made of at least 210 *kikar* of gold, an amazing amount which teaches us about the incredible wealth of the community.

In the center of the *shul*, there was a fancy wooden *bima* where the *chazzan* stood. He had cloth flags that he would wave when they reached the end of a section or when it was time to answer Amen. The

---

28. Sifri B'haaloscha 11
29. Succah 51: says that Alexander Mukdon killed the people of Alexandria. The Hagaaos Hagra says it was Trachinus. The Tzemach David says there is no contradiction between the two. It could be that Alexander Mukdon was the army general that killed the people.

synagogue was just too large for everyone to hear what the *chazzan* was saying.

The *shul* had designated seating areas that were divided according to the trades of the people who sat there. There was a section for the goldsmiths and one for the silversmiths, another for the blacksmiths and one for the weavers. This gave everyone a place to sit as well as making it easier for newcomers to make a living. When someone joined the community, he would sit in the appropriate section. If anyone needed that sort of craftsman, he would know where to go, and the people there would have work.

The whole community was completely wiped out. Not one person survived. This was the punishment for the sin of returning to Egypt in order to live there.[30]

This is how the destruction is described by *Chazal* and the Midrash. The wife of the son of Trachinus gave birth on Tisha B'Av. The Jews didn't know what to do. If they mourned over the Temple, it would seem like they weren't happy about the birth of the newest member of the royal family. On the other hand, it wasn't appropriate to join the national celebration. In the end, they decided to mourn, as the Torah commands.

Trachinus's son didn't live long. He died during Chanuka. Again the Jews were in a quandary how to react. If they lit candles, as the holiday required, it would seem like they were rejoicing over the prince's death. This time, too, they decided to continue with their religious celebrations and lit candles.

---

30. The Otzar Midrashim and others say the people of Alexandria were descendants of the first exiles of Yerushalayim, of those who remained with Gedalia ben Achikam. After he was assassinated, they went to Egypt, against the directions of God through Yirmiyahu.

The Fall of Beitar | 217

The king himself was in a distant country fighting Barbarian tribes. Some people who hated the Jews told the queen that the Jews were rebelling. The queen sent a letter to the king, "Before you conquer distant lands, you should come and take care of the Jews who are rebelling and happy about our troubles."

The king immediately set out to return to his country. The trip normally took ten days, but a very strong wind pushed the boat to make it in five days.

The king hurried to the Alexandria synagogue. They were reading the verse in the Torah,[31] "Hashem will bring a nation from the ends of the world, as the eagle glides."

The Jews translated the verse for the Egyptian king. He told the people, "I am the eagle. I was to travel a distance of ten days, and it only took five days!" He immediately told his soldiers to surround the synagogue which was full of community members, and kill all the men. After the men were killed, they killed the women also when they refused to sin. The blood flowed from Alexandria to the River[32] Kiprus.[33]

These are the types of horrible stories about which it says, "On these I cry!"[34] But through our crying we can merit the salavation, as the *Gemara* says, "Those who mourn the destruction of the Temple are guaranteed to see its happiness in the future.[35]

---

31. Devarim 28:49
32. As mentioned above, the Radal says it was not a river, but an island.
33. The Anaf Yosef says it is difficult to determine the exact location of Kiprus, as we find a similar description of the blood flowing out of the valley of Beis Rimon.
34. Eichah 1:16
35. Taanis 30:

17

The Ten Martyrs

In the period of the Second Temple[1] and the decades following the destruction, there were ten great leaders of the Jewish people put to death. In this section, we will discuss the reasons for their deaths according to *Chazal*.[2]

The Midrash explains that after the destruction of the Second Temple there were those people who said, "What is missing now that the Temple is gone? We still have great scholars to guide us how to keep the Torah and its laws."

---

1. We find many different opinions about what period the *asara harugei malchus* were killed in. In the *kinah* Eleh Ezkera as well as in the Midrash Eleh Ezkera, it sounds like the ten were caught and killed at the same time. The Tzemach David in the name of the Seder Hakabbalah of the Raavad says that two of the ten martyrs (Rabbi Shimon ben Gamliel and Rabbi Yishmael ben Elisha, as well as Rabbi Chanina *Sgan Hakohanim* according to the Sefer Yuchsin,) were killed at the time of the *churban* itself. The rest were killed later, at least fifty two years after the *churban* or longer.

2. We are not going to list the exact sources. What is discussed above is based on the Midrash Eleh Ezkera from the Otzar Hamidrashim (Eisenstein) page 440 and on. Where there is a contradiction between what it says there and what it says in *Chazal*, the difference will be noted in the footnotes.

The Ten Martyrs | 219

Hashem, therefore, put it in the emperor's heart to learn the Torah of the Jews.[3] From there he was brought to killing the scholars.

The emperor began learning the Torah from Beraishis, but he soon came to the section of Mishpatim. There it discusses a person who kidnaps someone and sells him and that he is punished by death.[4]

This was just what the Jew-hating emperor had to hear. First, he ordered his palace filled with shoes, around the walls. Then he called in ten Jewish sages. He sat them on gold chairs and said, "I have a question of law, and I ask you to give me an honest answer. What is the ruling about someone who kidnaps one of his brothers and sells him?"

The sages answered him, "Death."

"If so, then you deserve to die!" the emperor answered the surprised sages. The emperor told them that he read about the sale of Yosef in the Torah, and that, according to them, Yosef's brothers deserved the death penalty.

The emperor continued, "If Yosef's brothers would still be alive, I would bring them to justice before you and kill them based on your verdict.[5] However, since they are no longer alive and you are equal to

---

3. In one of the versions of the Midrash Eleh Ezkera it names the emperor as Luliano. Another names him as Turnus Rufus. In the Seder Hakabbalah of the Raavad, it says that Adrianus was the one who killed the ten martyrs as a result of his anger about the rebellion of bar Koziba and Beitar. As we mentioned before, the Raavad's opinion is that only two (or three, according to the Sefer Yuchsin,) of the ten were killed at the time of the *churban*. His mention of who killed them refers to the ones who were killed later. The ones who were killed at the time of the destruction were killed by Titus himself.

4. Shemos 21:17

5. This is what the emperor said. We have to know, though, that all the brothers did was done according to *halacha*, according to their judgment.

them,⁶ you must bear their sin." He acted as if the injustice done to Yosef would leave him no rest.

Actually, the emperor had already given a hint as to why he was gathering the sages by filling his hall with shoes. He was referring to the shoes that Yosef was sold for.

The verse⁷ clearly says that Yosef was sold for twenty silver pieces to the Yishmaelim. Yosef was one of the most handsome men in the world. It doesn't seem right that someone so good looking would be sold for such a low price.

Hashem even joined in the oath they took not to reveal what had happened to their father. We have no understanding about what the brothers did and we cannot judge why they acted as they did. The sin that was found in them and that resulted in the ten martyrs' deaths is not at all within our ability to understand.

6. From the words of the Midrash Eleh Ezkera it seems clear that the ten martyrs stood before the emperor at one time and that they are the people listed above. The Tzemach David in the name of the Seder Hakabbalah says it is impossible that that happened because Rabbi Shimon ben Gamliel and Rabbi Yishmael *Kohein Gadol* (and Rabbi Chanina *Sgan Hakohanim*, according to the Sefer Yuchsin,) lived in the generation of the destruction of the Temple or right afterwards. Rabbi Akiva and the others lived in a generation that hadn't seen the Temple. The Tzemach David doesn't mention the Midrash Eleh Ezkera, but when referring to the *kinah* Eleh Ezkera says that it is a mistake to present it as if they were all killed at one time.

It could be that the judgment of the emperor about killing all ten took place during the destruction in front of ten sages of that generation, even though they weren't the ten that were to be killed or that, in fact, different people were killed instead of them in later generations. If we say that, though, it is hard to understand how it fits in with Rabbi Yishmael going to heaven and hearing that the decree was on those ten sages and how they were equal to the brothers.

7. Beraishis 31:25

When he was sold, though, he wasn't looking as handsome and robust as he normally did. The brothers had thrown him naked into a pit filled with snakes and scorpions. Yosef was so afraid that his face changed. Hashem stopped the animals from hurting him, but when he was brought out of the pit, he didn't look like himself.

Hashem was not going to let him be taken by the Yishmaelim with no clothing. Yosef was wearing an amulet. Hashem told the angel Gavriel to make clothing come out of the amulet. These clothing were worn by Yosef all through his travels and during his stay in Egypt, even when he became part of the Egyptian royalty.

When his brothers saw these clothes, they asked the Yishmaelim for the clothing back, saying that they had sold him naked and the clothing was not included in the sale. After a debate, the Yishmaelim gave Yosef's brothers four pairs of shoes as payment for the clothing.[8]

It was these shoes that the emperor was reminding the sages about, telling them that they deserved to be put to death because of the sale.

The sages, hearing what the emperor said, asked for three days, claiming they wanted to find a way to excuse themselves from the judgment. They told the emperor that after three days, if they could not find some merit for themselves, he could do with them as he saw fit.

They were not really looking for a way to remove their guilt in the emperor's eyes. They knew the whole thing was just an excuse to kill them. They also could have saved themselves from death using God's holy names.

They wanted to use the time to find out if God had decreed that they should die, and, therefore, accept upon themselves the decree with

---

8. We must stress again that we have absolutely no understanding what this interchange was about between the brothers and the Yishmaelim. It is obvious that a bit of profit was not the motivating factor of the *shevatim*!

love. They sent Rabbi Yishmael *Kohein Gadol*,[9] Rabbi Yishmael ben Elisha, to the heavens to check the decree.

Rabbi Yishmael prepared himself and immersed in the *mikvah*. He then wrapped himself in *tallis* and *tefillin* and said the *shem hameforash*. Immediately, a wind brought him to the heavens. Since we can't understand what it means, we will skip the description of what was said there. Rabbi Yishmael did hear from the angels clearly that there was a decree in heaven that they should be killed in place of Yosef's brothers. From that generation until this one, there had never been one time that ten righteous people equal to the brothers[10] lived in one generation.[11]

---

9. In one of the versions in the Midrash Eleh Ezkera it mentions that Rabbi Nechunya ben Hakanah was the one who sent Rabbi Yishmael ben Elisha to go up to the heavens.

10. See the Midrash where it says that Samael (the angel of Rome) spoke against the Jews every day until this decree was announced. He was even willing to accept upon himself an awesome punishment, as long as the ten martyrs would be killed. See there also regarding the great punishment that was given to Rome (the nation that Samael represents) at that time. "Six months of the plague of leprosy, tumors, parasites, spots, chlorosis, and bad boils on the wicked Rome. Sulfur and fire on the people and the animals and the silver and gold and all they own until one man will say to his friend, 'Go to Rome. You can find everything there for a pittance.' But his friend will answer him, 'I have no interest, for I have no pleasure from them.'"

11. It is obvious that the prophets were just as great as these *tannaim*. It seems, though, that there were not ten *tzaddikim* in any other generation of the caliber that there was here.

The Ten Martyrs

Rabbi Yishmael came down and told the other sages what he had heard. It was a sadness mixed with joy. They were sad about the decree, but happy that they were considered equal to Yosef's brothers.[12]

They then divided into five pairs:[13] Rabbi Yishmael ben Elisha *Kohein Gadol* and Rabbi Shimon ben Gamliel,[14] Rabbi Akiva and

---

12. They were also happy that, because of their deaths, Rome was going to get a terrible punishment as mentioned above.

13. There are only seven of the people listed above that everyone agrees were part of the ten martyrs. They are: Rabbi Shimon ben Gamliel, Rabbi Yishmael ben Elisha *Kohein Gadol*, Rabbi Akiva, Rabbi Yehuda ben Bava, Rabbi Chanina ben Tradyon, Rabbi Yehsaivav Yeshvav Hasofer, and Rabbi Chutzpis Hameturgeman. About Rabbi Elazar ben Shamua, Rabbi Yehuda ben Dama and Rabbi Chanina ben Chachinai there are different Midrashim, as will be explained further on.

14. As mentioned before, in the Seder Hakabbalah it is brought that Rabbi Shimon ben Gamliel and Rabbi Yishmael *Kohein Gadol* (as well as Rabbi Chanina *Sgan Hakohanim* according to the Sefer Yuchsin) were killed during the period of the destruction of the Temple and the rest were killed in a later period. It seems, though, from the Tanna Devei Eliyahu (30) that when Rabbi Shimon ben Gamliel and Rabbi Yishmael *Kohein Gadol* were led to their deaths, Rabbi Shimon cried that they were being killed as being deserving death from *beis din*. Rabbi Yishmael *Kohein Gadol* comforted him that perhaps they were being killed because one of their judgments hadn't reached the level of complete truth. Or perhaps they hadn't interrogated the witnesses enough and, therefore, they were able to give false testimony. Or maybe they were involved in eating or bathing when a widow or orphan came to ask for sustenance and their assistants pushed them off and caused them pain. Any of these things would be enough to make them deserving of death. It seems like from the words of the Tanna Devei Eliyahu that even though Rabbi Shimon ben Gamliel and Rabbi Yishmael ben Elisha were being led to their deaths alone, it is not like what is described in the Midrash Eleh Ezkera, and is according to the Raavad in the Seder Hakabbalah.

Rabbi Chanina ben Tradyon, Rabbi Elazar ben Shamua and Rabbi Yeshvav Hasofer, Rabbi Chanina ben Chachinai and Rabbi Yehuda ben Bava, Rabbi Chutzpis Hameturgeman and Rabbi Yehuda ben Dama.[15]

Even in the face of tortuous death, these great men didn't lose their equanimity. They used the time they had left to study *maseches* Pesachim, a tractate in the Talmud. The officer who came to get them was astounded! Even though both the emperor and his officers saw the incredible piety and greatness of these men, the decree stood.

The emperor[16] called the first pair that he was to kill, Rabbi Shimon ben Gamliel and Rabbi Yishmael *Kohein Gadol*. He asked them to decide who should be killed first.

Rabbi Shimon said, "I am a *nasi* the son of a *nasi* and from King David's royal lineage. I have the right to be killed first so that I should not see Rabbi Yishmael killed."

Rabbi Yishmael countered, "I am a *Kohein Gadol* the son of a *Kohein Gadol*. I deserve to be killed first and not witness the death of Rabbi Shimon."

---

15. In this chapter we will also talk about the death of Rabbi Elazar ben Dama. As we mentioned in the beginning of the chapter, there are only seven people that everyone agrees were the martyrs. There is a difference of opinion about the other three. Other names that are mentioned are: Rabbi Yossi, Rabbi Yehuda Hanechtum, who was cut into pieces (Midrash Tehillim Mizmor 9, Eichah Rabba 2:4), Rabbi Tarfon and ben Azai (Eichah Rabba 2:4), Rabbi Chanina *Sgan Hakohanim*, Rabbi Elazar ben Charsom (Eichah Rabba 2:4), and more.

16. According to what is brought in the Seder Hakabbalah that Rabbi Shimon ben Gamliel and Rabbi Yishmael *Kohein Gadol* (and Rabbi Chanina *Sgan Hakohanim* according to the Sefer Yuchsin) were killed during the time of the destruction, the one who killed them was Titus (Tzemach David).

The Ten Martyrs | 225

Since they didn't decide amongst themselves, the emperor cast lots and Rabbi Shimon's name was drawn. Immediately, he was beheaded.

It was now Rabbi Yishmael's turn. Before he could be executed, Rabbi Yishmael asked for a break to eulogize his great friend. His request was granted. Rabbi Yishmael picked up Rabbi Shimon's decapitated head and laid it in his lap. He put his eyes on his eyes, his nose on his nose and his mouth on his mouth, and cried bitterly.

"Is this the Torah and is this its reward?! The mouth that explained the Torah in seventy languages, how is it now licking the dust? The mouth that fought mightily the battles of the Torah of our holy and pure nation, the mouth that gave out pearls, who put you in the dust? How were you punished with this horrible death?" So eulogized Rabbi Yishmael.

The emperor didn't understand. "What happened, old man? Why are you crying about your friend? You should cry about yourself; you are about to die just like he did!" the emperor commented with contempt.

Rabbi Yishmael answered him, "You are making a mistake, emperor. I am not crying about myself, but rather about my friend who was greater in Torah and wiser."

When the emperor's daughter heard Rabbi Yishmael's bitter cries,[17] she looked out the window where she saw Rabbi Yishmael, who

---

17. In the Midrash Eleh Ezkera it says that Rabbi Shimon ben Gamliel and Rabbi Yishmael ben Elisha *Kohein Gadol* were killed at the same time. That is also what is brought in the Seder Hakabbalah of the Raavad. The Tzemach David brings in the name of the Sefer Yuchsin that Rabbi Shimon ben Gamliel was killed in the time of the *churban*, but Rabbi Yishamel ben Elisha lived after the *churban*. That means there were years between the two executions. It could be that since the emperor's daughter asked that Rabbi Yishmael's death be delayed and his skin removed, his

was one of the seven most handsome men in the world. She asked that the execution be delayed until she requested something of her father.[18]

Her father said, "Ask for whatever you want, but not that one of these ten men should be left alive."

The daughter's face fell. She had wanted him to leave Rabbi Yishmael alive so that she could enjoy his beauty. She didn't give up, though. Instead, she asked that his face be peeled off while he was alive so that she could keep it to enjoy his loveliness.

The emperor agreed to this sickening request, and it was done. Amazingly, Rabbi Yishmael didn't utter a sound the whole time they were peeling off his skin. But when they reached the place of his *tefillin shel rosh*, he began to scream in a bitter voice about the *mitzvah* he was losing!

Addressing the emperor's question as to why he was quiet the whole time and just now began to scream, he answered the following. "I am not crying about my soul, only about the place where God's lofty name was on the *tefillin*."

Even in the face of such greatness, the emperor found place to mock. "You still believe in your God's name? If He's so great, let Him come save you from me!"

Rabbi Yishmael let out two cries. One shook the entire world. It even awakened the angels to beg God for mercy. Hashem quieted them by saying, "Let this righteous man suffer, so that his merit will last for future generations."

---

death was pushed off for a number of years until after the destruction of the Temple. It may be that it wasn't simple to remove his face in one piece in a way that would preserve its beauty.

18. In the Tanna Devei Eliyahu Rabba (30) it says that Rabbi Yishmael was killed by sword while he was eulogizing Rabbi Shimon ben Gamliel. It seems to be these are two different opinions.

The Ten Martyrs | 227

The second scream Rabbi Yishmael let out shook the Throne of Glory, until Hashem wanted to return the world to a state of nothingness. Had Rabbi Yishmael let out the third scream he was about to, Hashem would have returned the world to the state of nothingness that existed before it was created.

Therefore, the angel Gavriel[19] came down and said to Rabbi Yishmael, "If you scream one more time, the world will return to its state of nothingness." From then on, he was quiet until his soul left him.[20]

The Romans still have Rabbi Yishmael's skin preserved in Rome,[21] embalmed in *afarsimon*,[22] so that it would look the same. There is a holiday involving Rabbi Yishmael's image that is celebrated every seventy years.[23]

Every seventy years, the Romans take a healthy person and put him on the shoulders of a handicapped person. This was to symbolize Rome, the one complete in his body, who was still ruling over Yaakov that limped. They would dress the healthy man in the special clothes of Adam Harishon that Esav used to wear. They would put on his head Rabbi Yishmael's image. They would also hang on him *paz*, a very expensive and rare stone, weighing four *zuz*.

---

19. In a different version in the Midrash Eleh Ezkera it says that a heavenly voice announced that if one more sound was heard from Rabbi Yishmael, the world would revert to nothingness.

20. See the Midrash there which describes the order of eulogies that were given for Rabbi Yishmael in the heavens.

21. This was said in the time of the Talmud. The source for this is in the *Gemara* (Avodah Zara 11:) as explained above.

22. Rashi Avodah Zara 11:

23. Avodah Zara 11:

228 | On Your Walls, O Jerusalem

They would announce, "The end of the exile that Yaakov prophesized about is a lie! Esav's brother, Yaakov, is a liar. He stole the blessings deceitfully. But behold, we see with our eyes that Esav is the ruler. Whoever looks at this scene will see it. Whoever doesn't, won't, because it won't happen again for another seventy years! Look what happened to Yaakov, the swindler and liar! The blessings didn't come true for him, but for us, the children of Esav!"

That is what they would say. But then they would add, "Woe to this whole man when the handicapped man under him gets up!" They were saying, "Woe to the children of Esav when *Bnai Yisrael* rise out of the dust and are redeemed!"

It was now[24] Rabbi Akiva's turn to be killed.[25] Something caused a delay, though. The emperor was informed that the king of Arabia had started a war in order to conquer his land. He had to leave immediately to go to battle. He left Rabbi Akiva in jail. When he came back, he hurried to deal with Rabbi Akiva's execution.[26]

---

24. Tzemach Tzedek brings the opinion of the Sefer Yuchsin that Rabbi Chanina *Sgan Hakohanim* was amongst the *harugei malchus*. According to this opinion, he was killed at this point (before Rabbi Yishmael *Kohein Gadol* or after him), certainly before Rabbi Akiva who lived two generations later.
25. From the Midrash Eleh Ezkera it seems that this was close to the execution of Rabbi Shimon ben Gamliel and Rabbi Yishmael *Kohein Gadol*, but as we said before, the Raavad explains that Rabbi Akiva was killed at least fifty two years after the *churban*, while the first two sages were killed during the destruction itself.
26. *Chazal* (Berachos 61:) describe the events that led up to Rabbi Akiva's death.
When the wicked Romans forbade the learning of Torah, Papus ben Yehuda, a Roman collaborator, met Rabbi Akiva gathering a group in

The Ten Martyrs | 229

Before we describe his death, we need to take a minute to understand who he was. The *Gemara*[27] tells us that when Moshe

---

public and giving his *shiurim* without fear of the government. Papus asked him, "Akiva, aren't you afraid of the government?"
Rabbi Akiva answered him calmly with a parable: "There was a fox walking on the shore. He saw fish swimming back and forth. The fox asked them, 'What are you running away from?'
The fish answered, 'From the nets of the fishermen who are trying to catch us.'
The fox offered them a 'solution,' 'Why don't you come up on the shore and we'll live together as our ancestors always did.'
The fish answered him, 'You're called the wisest of all animals? You're nothing but a fool. Even if we are scared in our natural habitat, the water, our situation would be much worse on dry land where we would surely die!'"
Rabbi Akiva explained the parable to Papus. "Our situation is similar to the fish. Even though we have to run away from the nations who try to kill us, if we leave the Torah, our life source, we will surely die!"
Papus left.
At a later time, Rabbi Akiva was caught teaching Torah and sentenced to death. Papus was in jail with him for something stolen that was found on him. Papus said to him, "You are fortunate that you were caught for the Torah. Woe unto me that I was caught for other things!"
The above story from the *Gemara* doesn't fit with the Midrash's opinion that the ten martyrs were killed in one period because the emperor wanted to judge them for what was supposed to be done to Yosef's brothers. The *Gemara* says that he was killed for teaching Torah in public against the law at the time. On the other hand, the Raavad's opinion that Rabbi Akiva and his contemporaries were killed by Adrianus because of the rebellion of bar Koziba fits perfectly with the opinion of the *Gemara*, because at that time there was a law forbidding the learning of Torah.
See the Midrash on Mishlei (9). There it sounds like the law forbidding Torah study was decreed after the deaths of Rabbi Shimon ben Gamliel and Rabbi Yishmael *Kohein Gadol*, and shortly after this Rabbi Akiva

Rabbainu went up to the heavens to get the Torah, he saw Hashem sitting and attaching crowns to the letters. Moshe asked, "What is the meaning of these crowns? What do they teach? What secrets do they hint at?"

Hashem didn't explain what they meant but said, "In a number of generations there will be a man named Akiva ben Yosef. He is going to explain these crowns. From the top of one small yud he will learn many, many laws!"

"I want to see Rabbi Akiva," Moshe requested. Hashem told Moshe to follow Him to go see Rabbi Akiva learning. When Moshe came into the lesson Rabbi Akiva was giving, he was only able to get up to the eighth row. He couldn't understand the *pilpul* of Rabbi Akiva. The people in the rows in front of him were able to understand what Rabbi Akiva was saying well.

Moshe lost heart. He wasn't calm until he heard Rabbi Akiva say to his students, "This is the law given to Moshe from Sinai." Moshe heard that Rabbi Akiva was teaching the same Torah that he was to give the Jewish people. The way of learning called *pilpul* that Rabbi Akiva was using wasn't necessary for Moshe's generation, but the Torah was the same.

When Moshe saw Rabbi Akiva's greatness, he asked Hashem in his humility, "Master of the World, if You have someone like Rabbi Akiva, why don't You give the Torah through him?"

Hashem answered, "Quiet! This is what I thought to do!"

---

was killed. It doesn't have to mean that he was killed immediately after, it could be that Rabbi Akiva was just the next in line of the sages to be killed.

27. Menachos 29:

The Ten Martyrs | 231

When Moshe heard that answer, he dropped the topic. He did have one more request, though. "After I have seen Rabbi Akiva's incredible greatness, I would like to see what happens to him in the end, what his reward is."

Hashem showed him a terrible scene. He saw Rabbi Akiva's flesh being weighed as in a butcher shop, as if he was an animal killed for food.

"Is it possible?! This is Torah and this is its reward?!" Moshe said.

Hashem again answered, "Quiet! This is what I thought to do!"

This is what the *Gemara* tells us about Rabbi Akiva, that Moshe thought Rabbi Akiva should give the Torah. Hashem didn't disagree, He just said that He thought differently without explaining why.

This Rabbi Akiva was put to death in a tortuous way.[28] His flesh was combed with metal combs, a slow death that could take hours.

What did Rabbi Akiva do while this was happening to him? He remained totally calm, as if what was happening had nothing to do with him, and he said the Shema.[29] After all, the time for saying Shema had arrived.

His students, appalled by what was happening, couldn't hold back from asking, "Our teacher, do you have to go so far?"

---

28. Berachos 61:

29. This is what it says in the *Gemara*. In the Midrash Eleh Ezkera it says that every time they combed his skin, Rabbi Akiva would justify the suffering he was experiencing by saying, "Hashem is righteous. The Rock's actions are perfect as all of His ways are just. A trustworthy God that has no fault. Righteous and straight He is." He did so until he died.
A heavenly voice announced, "Fortunate are you, Rabbi Akiva, that you were righteous and straight and that your soul left you on 'righteous and straight.'"

Rabbi Akiva answered them something astounding. "My whole life, when I read the Shema in the morning and the evening, I thought of the verse[30] I was saying, 'And you should love Hashem with all your heart and all your soul and all your strength.' I was upset that I couldn't fulfill loving Hashem with all my soul properly, meaning *mesirus nefesh*, giving up my life. I've been waiting for this moment my entire life! Now that I have the chance to accept the yoke of heaven with love and happiness despite the horrible torture, I won't give it up!"

Even the emperor himself[31] was astounded by Rabbi Akiva's tranquility.[32] He asked Rabbi Akiva, "What are you mumbling?"

When Rabbi Akiva answered him that he was saying the Shema, the emperor asked further, "Why are you smiling? Aren't you suffering horribly and want to rebel against the pain? Perhaps you are a sorcerer and you don't feel anything."

"Heaven forbid! I am not a sorcerer. The pain is excruciating, but it hasn't crossed my mind to rebel against the pain. Every day of my life I have declared that I will serve my God with my whole heart, my whole soul and all my strength.

"The first part, with all my heart, I have fulfilled completely. With all my strength, the last part, I have fulfilled by giving all my possessions for the service of Hashem. The middle part, with all my soul, I never had the chance to do correctly.

"Now I have the chance! Since you are killing me in such a horrific manner because I am a Jew who clings to his Creator and loves Him, I can stand and say that what I have proclaimed my whole life I am now doing!"

---

30. Devarim 6:5
31. The Midrash says this was Turnus Rufus.
32. Midrash Mishlei 9

When Rabbi Akiva reached the word "*echad*" in "*Shema Yisrael Hashem Elokeinu Hashem Echad*," he drew out the last word until he died. A heavenly voice announced, "Fortunate are you, Rabbi Akiva, whose soul left him on the word *echad*! Fortunate are you, Rabbi Akiva, that you are invited to the World to Come!"

After his death, the emperor wasn't ready to leave him alone. He would not allow him to be buried[33] and commanded the jail warden to personally watch the body in prison.

Hashem had decreed that Rabbi Akiva should die in a gruesome way, but did not decree that his body should be desecrated after his death.[34] He therefore sent Eliyahu Hanavi to see to his burial.

That night, Eliyahu Hanavi went to Rabbi Yehoshua Hagresi, Rabbi Akiva's student and attendant. Eliyahu Hanavi greeted him and then told him that he was a *Kohain* and that he wanted to inform Rabbi Yehoshua that Rabbi Akiva's body was laying in the jail.[35] He told him that he needed to bring him to burial.[36]

---

33. Midrash Mishlei 9

34. We mentioned above that Moshe Rabbainu saw Rabbi Akiva's flesh being weighed by a butcher, which implies that he wasn't buried. It could be these are contradictory opinions or that some of Rabbi Akiva's body was buried and some was weighed by a butcher.

35. Here too we find a difference between the Midrash Eleh Ezkera and the *Gemara*. In the *Gemara* it mentions what his students said to him, meaning that they were present. In the Midrash it seems that Rabbi Yehoshua Hagresi didn't know of Rabbi Akiva's death.

36. It seems from this Midrash that Rabbi Yehoshua Hagresi didn't recognize Eliyahu Hanavi, but just thought he was a *Kohein* who came to inform him of his teacher's death. They then went together to take him out of the jail. In the Midrash Eleh Ezkera it says that Eliyahu Hanavi alone took Rabbi Akiva out of the jail. He then met Rabbi Yehoshua Hagresi who recognized him as Eliyahu Hanavi immediately.

234 | On Your Walls, O Jerusalem

Eliyahu Hanavi and Rabbi Yehoshua Hagresi went to the jail. Miraculously, they found the doors open and all the guards sleeping. Eliyahu Hanavi took out Rabbi Akiva's holy body on his shoulders.[37]

When they exited the jail,[38] there were groups and groups of angels eulogizing Rabbi Akiva, saying, "He executed the justice of Hashem." Their path was brightly lit.

Eliyahu Hanavi and Rabbi Yehoshua Hagresi walked all night[39] until they came to a place called Antipters shel Kotzrim.[40] There they went up three steps and down three steps.[41] Suddenly, a cave opened before them. Inside it was a chair, a bench, a bed, a table and a lamp. They laid Rabbi Akiva's holy body on the bed and turned to leave the cave.[42] As they left, the lamp lit and the door of the cave closed behind them.

He was surprised that Eliyahu Hanavi was allowed to carry the body, as he was a *Kohein*. Eliyahu Hanavi answered that the righteous don't bring impurity.

37. The Midrash says that Rabbi Yehoshua Hagresi asked Eliyahu how he was allowed to touch a body of someone who had died since he was a *Kohein*. Eliyahu answered that it was permissible since *tzaddikim* do not cause impurity.

38. The second version of the Midrash Eleh Ezkera

39. The Midrash Eleh Ezkera says it was a distance of five *parsa*.

40. In the second version of the Midrash Eleh Ezkera it is called Papilion shel Kisrin.

41. The second version of the Midrash Eleh Ezkera says that they went down three steps and up six.

42. The second version of the Midrash Eleh Ezkera says that the angels cried for three days and three nights over Rabbi Akiva until Rabbi Yehoshua Hagresi and Eliyahu Hanavi reached the cave. It was only after three days and nights that Rabbi Akiva was buried in the cave. The day after his burial, Eliyahu Hanavi took Rabbi Akiva to the *yeshiva shel*

When Eliyahu Hanavi saw this, he exclaimed, "Fortunate are the righteous, fortunate are those who toil in Torah, and fortunate are those who fear Hashem. For them is hidden and preserved a place in Gan Eden! Fortunate are you, Rabbi Akiva, that you found a good dwelling place when you passed away!"

Rabbi Chanina ben Tradyon was the next[43] to be put to death. He had a special pleasantness about him. He was pleasant to Hashem, pleasant to the creations and he never uttered a curse against his fellow man.

Chazal tell us the story of his death. It took place at a time when it was forbidden to learn Torah. Rabbi Chanina gathered large groups of people publicly in the marketplace of Rome, holding a Torah scroll.[44]

When he was caught[45] by the emperor in the end, the emperor asked him, "Why did you learn Torah?"[46]

Rabbi Chanina answered him fearlessly, "I did the command of my God."

The emperor ordered him wrapped in his Torah and burned.

---

maala to teach the souls of the righteous about the crowns on the letters of the Torah.

43. There is debate about the order of the executions.

44. We have to look more deeply into this. According to the Midrash, the decree on Rabbi Chanina ben Tradyon was given with the other ten martyrs and not because of an incident that happened. Here, the Midrash says he was killed because of an incident that happened. This fits in better with the *Gemara* that we mentioned above about Rabbi Akiva.

45. The *Gemara* (Avodah Zara 17: - 18.) describes that this took place when the emperor and his entourage returned from the funeral of Rabbi Yossi ben Kisma, who was respected even by the government officials.

46. Avodah Zara 17: - 18.

236 | On Your Walls, O Jerusalem

Right away, the emperor felt the beginning of divine retribution for what he had ordered.[47] Suddenly, with no warning or apparent cause, all the members of his household were killed, including his wife, mother and concubines. Destructive demons came down from heaven and destroyed his family.

These people were not brought to burial, as an additional part of the punishment. Whenever someone came to bury one of them, the earth would swallow the body up. The body would be spit out again when the person gave up trying to bury it.

Seeing Hashem's power, the emperor's advisors told him to leave Rabbi Chanina alone. The emperor declared, "Even if all of Rome is destroyed and I and my house will die, Rabbi Chanina will be put to death!"

In short order, Rabbi Chanina was wrapped in the Torah. He was surrounded with branches, which were set on fire. In order to increase his suffering by prolonging his death, his heart was covered with wet sponges. This was to make sure his heart wouldn't burn right away and he would stay alive.

When his daughter witnessed what was happening to her father, she cried, "Woe that I have seen this happening to you!"

Rabbi Chanina calmly answered his daughter, "If only I would have been burnt, it truly would be hard for me. Since the Torah is being burnt with me, I am sure that He who is going to avenge the insult to the Torah will avenge my insult as well."[48]

---

47. This paragraph is from the Batei Midrash *chelek* 1, Pirkei Halichos Rabbasi 7. See there the incident that is described with Emperor Lupinus.
48. In a different version in the Midrash Eleh Ezkera it says that Rabbi Chanina told his students that he was crying because the Torah was being burnt with him. He didn't see reason to cry over his own death, but he did cry over the disgrace of the Torah!

Rabbi Chanina's students who were present at the time asked Rabbi Chanina what he saw.[49] He answered, "I see the letters of the Torah flying in the air. Only the parchment is burning!"

"Rabbi," they continued, "why don't you open your mouth so the fire will enter and you will die faster?"

He answered calmly, "I prefer that my Creator who gave me my life will take it away without my taking part in causing my death."

The executioner asked Rabbi Chanina then, "Rabbi, if I take the wet sponges off your heart to hasten your death, will I merit a portion in the World to Come?"

When Rabbi Chanina answered that he would,[50] the executioner asked Rabbi Chanina to promise. Rabbi Chanina promised.

The executioner took off the sponges and stoked the flames. Rabbi Chanina died. Immediately after, the executioner jumped into the fire and burned to death.

A heavenly voice announced, "Rabbi Chanina and his executioner are invited to the World to Come!" From here our rabbis learn, "Someone can acquire a share in the World to Come in one hour!"

---

49. Tosafos in Avodah Zara 17: - 18. on the words beginning *ma ata roeh* explains that the students assumed that their teacher was witnessing scenes from the heavens, or they heard the letters flying and didn't understand what they were hearing.

50. This needs to be studied further. Rabbi Chanina could have opened his mouth so the fire would enter and kill him faster. He didn't, because he preferred that Hashem would decide when he would die. Why, therefore, did he promise the World to Come to the executioner for hastening his death? It could be that Rabbi Chanina didn't initiate the idea, but when the executioner asked if he would get the World to Come for lessening the suffering of a *tzaddik*, he answered the correct answer which was that he would. The executioner was the one who used that information to do something.

238 | On Your Walls, O Jerusalem

The emperor got his just desserts too. That day he died. No one knew that he had died. Rabbi Chanina sat on his throne, in the guise of the emperor, while the emperor was burned the way Rabbi Chanina was. This went on for six full months.[51]

About Rabbi Yehuda ben Bava it is said that from the time he was eighteen until he was eighty,[52] he never slept more than "the sleep of a horse,"[53] meaning no more than sixty breaths. He also never tasted sin. He never erred in a *halachic* ruling, saying that something that was impure was pure or that something pure was impure. There was no one in the *bais midrash* that he didn't enlighten with his words of Torah. All of this was in addition to the life of ascetics he led. He fasted for twenty six years. He was also humble; he would call his students "my master" and would learn with them day and night.

Rabbi Yehuda ben Bava was taken out to be killed on *erev Shabbos*,[54] after the ninth hour of the day.

When he was taken from his students,[55] he was fasting. They suggested that he eat something so that he wouldn't die in his hunger.

---

51. It also says in the Midrash Eleh Ezkera, in another version, that all ten of the martyrs sat on the emperor's throne while they were being killed and the emperor suffered instead of them. This obviously doesn't fit in with the simple reading of the words of *Chazal* in the Midrash and in the *Gemara*.
52. Another version says seventy.
53. Another version says that he slept less than the sleep of a horse.
54. Another version says that he was taken on the fifth day of the week, when he was seventy years old. This fits in with the Midrash that discusses how little he slept until he was seventy years old.
55. The *Gemara* (Sanhedrin 14.) gives a different description of the death of Rabbi Yehuda ben Bava. At that time, the government had decreed

The Ten Martyrs | 239

Rabbi Yehuda refused, saying, "If until today, when I didn't know that I would be dying soon, I fasted, certainly I should fast if I know I am going to leave this world soon."

Rabbi Yehuda had one final request. He asked that his death be delayed until the onset of Shabbos so that he would merit one final *mitzvah* of sanctifying the Shabbos.

"You still trust your God?" his enemies asked. When Rabbi Yehuda answered that he did, they asked, "Do you still think that your God has power?"

---

that it was forbidden to appoint judges and doing so was punishable by death for the one giving *semicha* and the one getting *semicha*. The city it was done in would be destroyed and the area uprooted.

Rabbi Yehuda stood between two mountains that were between two towns so that no city could be held responsible. He stood between the areas of Usha and Shafaram, so that neither area could be found guilty. There he gave *semicha* to five sages: Rabbi Meir, Rabbi Yehuda, Rabbi Shimon, Rabbi Yossi, Rabbi Elazar ben Shamua, and, some add, Rabbi Nechemia. The group saw the Romans coming. It was clear that if the students would be caught with their teacher, they would be killed. Rabbi Yehuda ben Bava told his students to hurry and save themselves, as he was not strong enough to run and escape. With no other option, they ran away, knowing that nothing would be gained by their being killed with their teacher.

Rabbi Yehuda ben Bava was caught, and 300 swords pierced his body, leaving him like a sieve.

Again, the *Gemara* shows that the ten were not condemned to death at once, but each caught on their own. As is explained in the Seder Hakabbalah, Adrianus was the one who decreed that Torah couldn't be learned, and this led to the deaths of these sages.

The Midrash Eleh Ezkera follows its opinion that there is no reason to find an excuse for why Rabbi Yehuda ben Bava was killed, as he was condemned to death with the rest of the ten martyrs.

Rabbi Yehuda again answered that he did and added the words of the verse, "Hashem is great and deeply praised; there is no fathoming His greatness."

"If your God is so great, why doesn't He save you and your associates from the government?" the Romans asked, trying to prove that he was wrong.

"We are dying because Hashem decided that we should be killed. We are being given into the hands of the emperor so that God can punish him later!"

They told the emperor what Rabbi Yehuda had said. The emperor called Rabbi Yehuda and asked him if it was true. "Did you say that God will pay me back for your blood and your friends' blood?"

Rabbi Yehuda emphatically stated that he would. The emperor couldn't stand Rabbi Yehuda's calmness. "These Jews are so strong! Even when they are about to die, their impudence is up to the sky!"

Rabbi Yehuda answered him, "Woe unto you, emperor… wicked man, the son of a wicked man! Hashem saw the destruction of His house and wasn't zealous to fight His enemies right away. Do you think He is going to rush to punish you for killing me? No! Hashem doesn't rush, but the day will come when He will take revenge."

Obviously, Rabbi Yehuda's words fueled the emperor's anger. His students asked him, "Rabbi, wouldn't it be better to subjugate yourself to the emperor and flatter him?"

Rabbi Yehuda answered his students, "My dear students, anyone who flatters a wicked man falls into his hands in the end. If I would flatter the emperor, it wouldn't better my situation. The most it would do is strengthen his hands."

Rabbi Yehuda took advantage of his audience with the emperor to make his request. He asked that since Shabbos was so close, that he be allowed to sanctify it before his death.

The Ten Martyrs | 241

The emperor agreed. In the meantime, Shabbos started. Rabbi Yehuda began to recite Kiddush. He said the words of "*Vayechulu*" sweetly and aloud. When he came to the end of the words, "that Elokim created to do," the Romans didn't let him continue and killed him while the word "Elokim" was on his lips.

A heavenly voice announced, "Fortunate are you, Rabbi Yehuda, that you resembled an angel in your lifetime and your soul expired on the word 'Elokim.' Fortunate are you, Rabbi Yehuda ben Bava, that your body is pure and your soul left in purity!"

The emperor took Rabbi Yehuda's body and had it chopped into pieces and thrown to the dogs.

Rabbi Yehsaivav Yeshvav Hasofer was put to death next. He was also arrested while he was fasting and also refused to eat. "If Rabbi Yehuda ben Bava was killed while he was fasting, it is right that I, too, should not eat," he explained to his students.

His students asked him, "Rabbi, what will become of the Torah after you die?"

He answered, "The Torah will be forgotten from Israel! The wicked nation brazenly found a way to take away our gems from us. I wish that I would be an atonement for the people, but I see that there is no street in Rome that does not have someone killed by the sword lying in it. This wicked nation is going to spill innocent Jewish blood!" Rabbi Yeshvav Hasofer Yehsaivav saw through the divine spirit that rested on him that terrible things were to happen to the Jewish people.

"What will be with us? What should we do to strengthen ourselves so that we will be able to survive this period?" they asked.

He answered, "Every man should strengthen his friend. Love peace and judgment. Maybe there is hope!" He was saying that if everyone strengthens each other, there is a chance that together they will survive this dreadful period in history.

At this point, the emperor turned to Rabbi Yeshvav HasoferYehsaivav. "How old are you?" he asked.

"I am ninety years old." He then added mockingly, "Know, emperor, that before I came out of my mother's womb, it was decreed that I and my associates be given over to your hands so that later He can avenge our blood from you."

"And when will He avenge your blood? Is there any other world besides the world I rule over?" the emperor asked.

"Yes," Rabbi YehsaivavYeshvav Hasofer answered him. "There is another world. Woe unto the emperor and his disgrace when he is punished in that world!"

The emperor was infuriated by his words. He ordered Rabbi Yeshvav Hasofer to Yehsa be put to death immediately, while he mocked Hashem. "Kill him fast! Let's see what his God's power is! Let's see what He can do to me in the World to Come!"

It was on the second day of the week that Rabbi YehsaivavYeshvav Hasofer was killed, when he was ninety years old. The emperor ordered him killed[56] while he said the words of Shema, "And Hashem said to Moshe."

A heavenly voice declared, "Fortunate is Rabbi Yeshvav HasoferYehsaivav that he knew all of Moshe's Torah!"

He was also thrown to the dogs after his death.

---

56. The version in the Midrash Eleh Ezkera says that Rabbi Yeshvav HasoferYehsaivav was killed by fire, and he therefore could not have been thrown to the dogs. It could be he was burnt until his soul left him, but not until he turned completely to ash. It could be his charred body was thrown to the dogs.

The Ten Martyrs | 243

The next of the *harugei malchus* was Rabbi Chutzpis Hameturgeman. *Chazal* say he was equal to Rabbi Yonasan ben Uziel. He could explain the *Chumash* Vayikra in 180 ways. He knew how to make the pure impure and the impure pure, bringing proofs both ways. He had a command of seventy languages and knew how to speak them all well. He was also physically very handsome. He looked like an angel. He was 130 years old when he was arrested with his students to be taken to be killed. Actually, he was 130 years old less one day. When the officers of Rome saw his beautiful face and its special glow and heard his age, they asked the emperor to spare him.

The emperor refused. He entered into a philosophical debate with Rabbi Chutzpis after Rabbi Chutzpis asked him to let him live for one more day so that he could reach the age of 130.

"Why do you care if you live one day more or less?" the emperor asked Rabbi Chutzpis.

Rabbi Chutzpis answered that the one day didn't mean much to him, but that he wanted the *mitzvos* he could do in that day, amongst them saying the Shema twice so that he could accept God's kingship on himself.

The emperor called out, "A stiff-necked people! A stubborn people! For how long will you continue to trust and believe in your God? The reality shows that He can't save you from my ands! My fathers burned His Temple and threw the bodies of His servants around Yerushalayim without burial!

"Perhaps your God was once mighty, like when He smote Pharaoh and Sancheriv. But today, He is weak. If not, He would have punished those who destroyed His Temple!"

Rabbi Chutzpis began to cry and tore his clothes. He couldn't bear to hear the horrible blasphemy! "Woe unto you! What will you do when Hashem sends to Rome all the punishment it deserves?!"

244 | On Your Walls, O Jerusalem

The emperor angrily ordered Rabbi Chutzpis stoned to death, and then commanded he should be hanged in disgrace. When his advisors and officers pleaded that they should be allowed to bury Rabbi Chutzpis in honor of his old age, he was allowed to be buried and was greatly eulogized.

We have now finished discussing the seven *harugei malchus* that there is no debate about. We will elaborate now on some other *tannaim* that are mentioned as part of the *asara harugei malchus*.

The first is Rabbi Yehuda ben Dama.[57] He was arrested on *erev* Shavuos. He asked that his death be postponed until the holiday started and he would be able to thank Hashem for giving us the Torah!

The emperor began a conversation similar to that which he had held with the others. "Do you still trust your God?" the emperor asked. Rabbi Yehuda answered that he did, to which the emperor said, "And what reward are you getting for your Torah?"

Rabbi Yehuda answered in the words of King David, "How great is the good that is put away for those who fear You."

Deriding the rabbi's words, the emperor said, "The Jews are such fools that they believe there is a world after this one!"

"It's the opposite," answered Rabbi Yehuda. "There are no bigger fools than you, the gentiles, who don't believe in the Living God! Woe unto you and woe unto your disgrace when in the future you will see the Jewish nation sitting with God in the light of the living while you are sitting humiliated in the lowest levels of hell!"

---

57. A different version in the Midrash Eleh Ezkera says this was Rabbi Elazar ben Dama who was killed because he kept the commandment of *tefillin* when it was forbidden by the Romans.

The emperor commanded that he be killed by tying his hair to the tail of a horse and having him dragged that way through the streets of Rome. After he was killed, he was cut into pieces and left unburied.

Hashem wanted him buried, so he sent Eliyahu Hanavi to gather the pieces and bury him in a cave near a river near Rome.

For thirty days, an inhuman cry emanated from the cave. The emperor wasn't moved. "Even if the whole world returns to nothingness, I will not go back on my plan to kill the ten sages," the emperor told his people who advised him that it wasn't wise to start up with God after they heard the cries coming out of the cave.

Having no choice, the people were quiet, all except one old man. He said, "My master the emperor, I have to tell you that you are making a mistake in your approach. You made a great mistake when you sent your hand against the nation of God without mercy! Your end will be bitter!"

The emperor ordered the old man strangled to death. When word of the decree reached the old man, he circumcised himself and joined the Jewish nation. He wanted to merit to join them in the future after he died. After he was strangled to death, his body disappeared!

Seeing this, the emperor became very fearful. He realized there was a God in heaven. In his great wickedness, though, he didn't change his ways and continued with his plans to kill the ten sages.

According to some opinions, Rabbi Chanina ben Chachinai was one of the *asara harugei malchus*. *Chazal* tell us about him that from when he was twelve years old until he was killed at the age of ninety five, he fasted every day!

His students also suggested that he eat before he was executed. He answered as the others had, "If until today, when I didn't know that my death was near, I fasted, all the more so I should fast when I know I am about to die."

Rabbi Chanina, like Rabbi Yehuda ben Bava, was able to sanctify the Shabbos, getting up to the words of "*Vayechulu*." He was killed while he said "*vayekadesh oso*."

A heavenly voice announced, "Fortunate are you, Rabbi Chanina ben Chachinai that you were holy and your soul expired in holiness on the words "*vayekadesh!*"

Rabbi Elazar ben Shamua[58] was also amongst the ten sages that were martyred, according to some opinions. He was 105 years old when he was killed. Out of those 105 years, he fasted for eighty.

The sages praise him by saying that for his entire life, since he was small, no one ever heard him speak unimportant things. He also never fought with anyone, not in words and not in action. He was very humble and unassuming.[59]

He was put to death on Yom Kippur. His students asked him as he was being led to his death what he saw. He answered, "I see the bier of Rabbi Yehuda being carried in the air and next to him I see the bier

---

58. The Tzemach David proves through calculations that Rabbi Elazar ben Shamua lived many years after Rabbi Akiva and his contemporaries were killed, and he was certainly not killed with them.

59. In another version of the Midrash Eleh Ezkera it says that a discussion ensued between Rabbi Elazar ben Shamua and the emperor, similar to the one that Rabbi Yehuda ben Bava had. The end of his life also took place when he was sanctifying the Shabbos, just like Rabbi Yehuda ben Bava. Since the situation was described above, it is not repeated at length here. It could also be that there is a debate if this happened to Rabbi Yehuda ben Bava or to Rabbi Elazar ben Shamua.

The Ten Martyrs | 247

of Rabbi Akiva. They are speaking in learning and arguing about a point of Jewish law."

"Who is deciding between them what the *halacha* is?" the students asked. Rabbi Elazar ben Shamua answered that Rabbi Yishmael ben Elisha was.

"And who won the debate?" the students continued to question.

"Rabbi Akiva won, and that's because he especially exerted himself in Torah, working hard with all his might."

Rabbi Elazar ben Shamua revealed more of the secrets of the heavens. "My children, I see that the souls of all the righteous men are purifying themselves in the waters of the Shiloach so that they can enter the *yeshiva shel maala* and hear Rabbi Akiva's discourse on the topics of the day. I see the angels bringing gold chairs for each *tzaddik* to sit on in purity." When he finished his words, the emperor ordered him killed immediately, the word "purity" being the final word he uttered.

A heavenly voice announced, "Fortunate are you, Rabbi Elazar ben Shamua, that you were pure and your soul left you in purity!"

18

The Light in the Darkness

Before we end, there is another topic that we need to cover, one that can bring us consolation.

Here are three stories that show us that in the worst of times, when it seems like there is no hope, sparks of the redemption shine.

Rabban Gamliel, Rabbi Elazar ben Azaria, Rabbi Yehoshua and Rabbi Akiva were walking somewhere about 120 *mil* from Rome when they heard joyous music.[1]

They tried to figure out where the music was coming from. It was coming from Rome - happy, celebrating, carefree Rome.

The sages started to cry bitterly. "These gentiles, these evil idol worshipping gentiles, these enemies that destroyed the Holy Temple, are jovial and celebrating. But us, our Temple is in ruins!"

Rabbi Akiva, on the other hand, smiled. They asked him how he could hear the celebrations of the gentiles who had destroyed the *Mikdash* and not cry.

He asked them why they were crying. When they told him, he said that was why he was happy. "Their joy is what is making me happy!

---

1. Makkos 24, Eichah Rabba 5:18

From them we can learn how great Hashem's goodness is. If the wicked ones who go against God's will have so much good, imagine what His beloved sons, who work hard to fufill His will, imagine what goodness they will get!"

A similar incident[2] happened when the group of sages saw a fox come out of where the Holy of Holies had been. They cried inconsolably at the sight of a fox roaming about the holiest place in the world as if it was an ownerless field. The place where even David Hamelech couldn't step foot, where only the *Kohein Gadol* entered once a year dressed in pure white, where the *Kohein Gadol* would emerge resplendent when he exited, that place was overrun by animals!

Rabbi Akiva smiled. The sages asked him how he was able to be happy at such a sight. He asked them what they were sad about. When they told him, he answered, "That is exactly why I rejoice. There were two prophecies given about Yerushalayim. One was by Uria, stating that Yerushalayim would become an ownerless field. The other was by Zecharia who prophesized about the glorious future of Yerushalayim when it would be rebuilt.

"We find that these two prophecies are connected, two sides of one whole. It says in the Navi,[3] 'I will bring reliable witnesses for Me, Uria the *Kohein* and Zecharia ben Yivarcheihu.' The verse is hard to understand. There was never any relationship between Uria, who lived during the days of the First Temple, and Zecharia, who lived during the days of the Second Temple. The explanation is clear, though. The verse is telling you that the prophecies of Zecharia are contingent upon the prophecies of Uria coming true.

---

2. Makkos 24, Eichah Rabba 5:18
3. Yeshaya 8:2

"Until the harsh prophecies came true, I was worried that maybe the joyous ones would not come true. When I saw the words of Uria come true, I was sure the words of Zecharia will also come true! Therefore, I was happy!"

The sages accepted his words and answered, "Akiva, you have consoled us! Akiva, you have consoled us!"

Even in the darkness, Rabbi Akiva was able to find the light.

Not only is there darkness in the light, but the redemption of Israel grows out of the destruction!

There is a story[4] told of a Jew from a far away land[5] who was plowing his field using his cow. All of a sudden, the cow let out a deep moo for no apparent reason. The Jew went on, not giving it much thought.

At that time, a local Arab who knew the meaning of cows' noises passed by. He asked the Jew what nation he came from. When the Jew told him his roots, the Arab answered him by saying, "Let your cow go, put down your plow and stop working. The Temple of the Jews in the Land of Israel was destroyed."

While they were speaking, the cow let out another loud moo. The Jew didn't make anything of it, but again the Arab told him its meaning. "You can return to plowing. The cow has announced that the savior of the Jews has been born." The Arab even told him the child's name and his father's name and the city he lived in.

---

4. Eichah Rabba 1:51, Yerushalmi Berachos 17:
5. A similar story with a few changes is brought in the Midrash Zuta.

The Light in the Darkness | 251

The Jew was very curious to find out more. He sold his cow and plow and instead bought children's clothing to sell.[6] He then made his way to the Land of Israel, selling children's clothing along the way.

He went from country to country that way until he reached the Land of Israel. He came to sell his wares in the city that the Arab had named as the home of the savior of Israel. The women of the town all came to look at his goods, except one woman who stood at the side. This woman, it turned out, was the mother of the child he was looking for.

"Why aren't you buying clothes for your baby?" he asked her.

She answered him in pain, "Please, don't remind me about that child! He brought bad luck with him when he was born! On the day he was born, the Temple was destroyed!"

"Don't speak that way!" the man said. "I am sure that just as his birth brought the destruction, through his hands the Temple will be rebuilt!" He tried to console the mother with his words. He then added, "Take some of my clothing for your son. When I come back at a later date, I will ask you for payment."

The woman accepted the offer and took some of the clothing. The merchant left the city satisfied. He had found the child and now had his address and an excuse to check on the child's development in the future.

After a period, the man decided it was time to check on the boy's progress. He went to the city and visited the woman's house.

"How is the child?" he asked the mother when she answered the door.

---

6. Some say he sold children's clothing, or more exactly, diapers. Some say he sold toys.

She replied in a pained voice, "Have you come to pour salt on an open wound? I've already told you that child has brought bad luck. From the day you last visited the city and gave me the clothes, I haven't seen him. Strong winds came and carried my child away. I have no idea where he is."

The merchant now understood that the Arab had been correct. The redeemer of Israel was born the day the Temple was destroyed. When his identity became known, Hashem had to take him away and hide him until he was ready to redeem the people.

He consoled the mother, saying, "That is what I told you! Your child was born the day the Temple was destroyed and he will build it again to last forever! God's will caused the winds to carry him away until the right time arrives!"

From the destruction sprouts the redemption. May we all be amongst the mourners of Zion who merit to see it rebuilt and to see the consolation of Zion forever!

Glossary

Akaida: Historical event when Yitchzak was prepared to be sacrificed by his father

Aleph Bais: The Hebrew alphabet

Amah, Amos: Cubit(s)

Aron Hakodesh: The holy ark in the Temple

Asara Harugei Malchus: Ten Martyrs

Avos: Forefathers; refers to Avraham, Yitzchak and Yaakov

Azara: Temple courtyard

Bais Hamikdash, Mikdash: The Holy Temple

Bais Midrash: Torah house of study

Beis din: Rabbinical court of law

Bnai Yisrael, Klal Yisrael: The Jewish people

Chatzer: Courtyard

Chazal: The sages of the Talmud

Chazzan: Cantor

Chilul Hashem: Desecration of God's Name

Churban: Destruction of the Holy Temple

Daas Torah: The opinion of the sages or the religious leaders of the generation

Drashos: Speeches

Eilim: Rams

Eretz Yisrael: Land of Israel

Erev: Eve of

Gadol Hador, Gedolei Hador: Greatest rabbinical leader(s) of the generation

Galus: Exile

Gemara: Talmud

Goyim: Gentiles

Hakadosh Baruch Hu: God

Halacha, halachik: Jewish law, having to do with Jewish law

Har Habayis: Temple Mount

Harav hagaon: The great rabbi

Hashem: God

Hashgacha: Providence

Heichal: Sanctuary

Kadshim: Foods that need to be eaten in the sanctity of Yerushalayim

Kal v'chomer: Fortiori argument

Kareis: Divine excision

Kav, Kabin: Measure of volume equal to the volume of twenty four eggs

Kehillos: Communities

Kehuna: Priesthood

Kikar: Measure of weight equal to 3000 selaim

Kinah: lamentation

Kodesh: anterior chamber of the Mikdash, the Holy

Kodesh Kedoshim: Innermost chamber of the Mikdash, the Holy of Holies

Kohein Gadol, Kehuna Gedola: The High Priest/Priesthood

Kohein, Kohanim: Priest(s) who served in the Temple

Korban Pesach: Pascal sacrifice

Korbanos: Sacrifices

Kzayis: Olive sized amount

Levi, Leviim: Member(s) of the tribe who served the priests as they served in the Temple

Levona sacrifice: Frankincense sacrifice

Litrin: Measurement equal to the volume of six eggs, a pound.

Maasros: Tithes

Masechta, Masechtos: Orders of the Talmud

Mashiach: the Messiah

Mefarshim: Commentaries

Mikrah: The five books of the Pentateuch

Mikvah: Ritual bath

Mil: 2,000 amos (between 3,000 and 4,000 feet)

Mincha sacrifice: Flour offering brought in the afternoon

Mishna: Organized teachings of the tannaim

Mitzvah, Mitzvos: Commandment(s) of the Torah

Mizbeiach: Altar

Nasi: Prince, head of the Sanhedrin

Navi, Neviim, Nevuah: Prophet(s), prophecy

Nedava: Voluntary sacrifice

Olah: Totally burnt offering

Oy: Woe!

Parsa: Measure of length equal to 8,000 amos

Pasuk, Pesukim: Verse(s)
Perek: Chapter
Pilpul: Dialectics
Rasha: Wicked man
Ruach Hakodesh: The Divine Spirit
Sanhedrin: High court of the Jewish people
Seah: Measurement of volume
Sefer Torah: Torah scroll
Sefer: book
Sela, selaim: Silver coin(s)
Semicha: Rabbinical ordination
Shabbos: Sabbath
Shamayim: Heaven
Shechina: God's Presence
Shelamim: Peace offering
Shem Hameforash: God's ineffable holy name
Shevatim: Tribes
Shiurim: Torah discourses Righteous man/men
Tzitzis: Fringes worn on corners of garment
Urim v'tumim: Holy parchment in the Kohein Gadol's breastplate
Yerushalayim: Jerusalem

Shmitta: Sabbatical year for the land
Shul: Synagogue
Tallis: Prayer shawl
Talmidei Chachamim: Torah scholars
Tanna, Tannaim: Sage of Mishnaic period
Tefach, tefachim: Handbreadth(s)
Tefillin (shel rosh, shel yad): Phylacteries (of the head, of the arm)
Teshuva: Repentance
Tinokos shel bais rabban: Pure schoolchildren
Tuma: Ritual impurity
Tumas meis: Ritual impurity caused by contact with a dead body
Tzaddik, tzaddikim:

Yeshiva shel Maalah: Heavenly house of study
Yeshiva, yeshivos: House(s) of study
Yichus: Lineage
Zuz: Monetary unit or coin

לעילוי נשמת

סבנו, האי גברא רבה, ידיו רב לו בתורה ובמעש"ט
הר"ר **יעקב יצחק** בהר"ר משה הכהן **קליין** זצ"ל
נלב"ע ה' טבת ה'תשנ"א

וזוגתו סבתנו הצנועה והצדקנית
מרת **מירל** ע"ה בת הר"ר שלום זצ"ל
נין הרב ר' שמעלקא מסעליש זי"ע בעל ה'צרור החיים'
נלב"ע א' באדר ה'תשמ"ג

ת.נ.צ.ב.ה.

לעילוי נשמת

סבתנו אצילת הנפש, אשת חיל עטרת בעלה
מרת **ציפורה אסתר וייס** ע"ה
בת הגאון הצדיק רבי רפאל בלזם זצ"ל
בעל ה'נחלי אפרסמון'
נלב"ע ג' ניסן ה'תשס"ג

ת.נ.צ.ב.ה.

לעילוי נשמת
אבי מורי ישר הדרך, רודף צדקה וחסד
עמירם בן ישעיהו **למברסקי** ז"ל
נלב"ע י"ב סיון ה'תשס"א
ת.נ.צ.ב.ה.

לעילוי נשמת
האי גברא רודף צדקה וחסד, אהוב על הבריות
אשר נזדכך ביסורים קשים וגדולים
הרב **רפאל אשר** זצ"ל בהר"ר צבי **טאוסקי** שליט"א
נלב"ע י"ב אייר ה'תשס"ב
ת.נ.צ.ב.ה.

לעילוי נשמת
האי גברא רבה תמים במעשיו, עמוד התפילה,
שייף עייל ושייף נפיק ולא מחזיק טיבותא לנפשיה
הרה"ח **משה טוביה** זצ"ל בהר"ר ראובן חיים הכהן **פישר** שליט"א
נלב"ע כ"ו שבט ה'תשס"ז
ת.נ.צ.ב.ה.